WELCOME TO THE
FIFTH DIMENSION

WELCOME TO THE
FIFTH DIMENSION

The Quintessence of Being,
the Ascended Masters' Ultimate Secret

Diane LeBlanc

North Atlantic Books
Berkeley, California

Published by   Translated by Cécile Mennesson and Misha Baumann
North Atlantic Books   Cover art by Pierre A. Morin
Berkeley, California   Cover and book design by Suzanne Albertson
                                      Interior illustrations by Martine Dussart and Gilles Bélair

Printed in the United States of America

Welcome to the Fifth Dimension: The Quintessence of Being, the Ascended Masters' Ultimate Secret is sponsored and published by the Society for the Study of Native Arts and Sciences (dba North Atlantic Books), an educational nonprofit based in Berkeley, California, that collaborates with partners to develop cross-cultural perspectives, nurture holistic views of art, science, the humanities, and healing, and seed personal and global transformation by publishing work on the relationship of body, spirit, and nature.

North Atlantic Books' publications are available through most bookstores. For further information, visit our website at www.northatlanticbooks.com or call 800-733-3000.

Library of Congress Cataloging-in-Publication Data

LeBlanc, Diane.
    [Bienvenue dans la 5e dimension. English]
    Welcome to the fifth dimension : the quintessence of being, the ascended masters' ultimate secret / Diane LeBlanc.
        p. cm.
    Summary: "A comprehensive, accessible, and grounded guide to living in a continual state of Grace through the practice of Quintessence, a self-coaching approach that brings together many leading New Age disciplines"—Provided by publisher.
    Includes bibliographical references.
    ISBN 978-1-55643-840-0
    1. Alternative medicine. 2. New Age persons. 3. Spiritual life. I. Title.
    R733.L423 2009
    610—dc22
                                                              2009036823

5 6 7 8 9 10 VERSA 19 18 17 16

Printed on recycled paper

This book is dedicated to creators of the new world
working together in all the dimensions
celestial as well as terrestrial.

ACKNOWLEDGMENTS

I would deeply like to thank Cécile Mennesson and Misha Baumann, without whom this book would probably still be a dream. They not only introduced me to North Atlantic Books but managed to translate the whole book in a very short time, working long hours in order to deliver the final manuscript before the deadline, even though Cécile's pregnancy was in its final stage.

I tip my hat to Christopher Church, who did a marvelous job editing my friends' translation work, and express my appreciation to Hisae Matsuda and the North Atlantic team for their wonderful collaboration throughout this whole process. Let me also honor the talent of the illustrators, Martine Dussart, Pierre A. Morin, and Gilles Bélair, who made the content of the book so pleasant to look at.

Likewise, I would like to express my gratitude to my French editor, Claude Rousseau-André, who believed in this book even before it was written. Indeed, he made the decision to publish it based only on documentation from my seminar, which was a set of forty slides (the tables and charts in this book). He supported me through the writing and editing phase, as he strongly believed that the content was worthwhile. God bless him: time proved him right.

My acknowledgements extend to all those wonderful writers and researchers who explained so clearly ideas such as defense mechanisms (James Redfield), the steps of mourning (Elisabeth Kübler-Ross), and many other concepts from so many other authors. All of it was capital to my own research into myself, and in the end it helped me come up with this simple self-coaching approach.

I would never have published such a method without experimenting, testing, and validating my assumptions. For that, I want to thank the thousands of clients, seminar attendees, and all those people whose paths have crossed mine over the last twenty years, for they are a significant part of what you hold in your hands.

Last but not least, I would like to thank the people I share my day-to-day life with: my four kids, Charles-Antoine, Marlène, Émile, and Médéric, who taught me about the soul families just by truly being themselves. Their presence also helped me become a better person, and I will eternally be thankful for that.

And, of course, many thanks (and kisses) to my husband and coach, Serge, who supported me through this wonderful but sometimes painful journey. Our life together has been a very efficient laboratory, a place where we have experimented on all the concepts depicted in this book, the integration of which has changed me forever.

I hope this book will do the same for you, and for readers around the world.

From my heart to yours, sincerely,
Diane LeBlanc

CONTENTS

Contents

PART TWO

The Human Experience 85

CHAPTER 6
The Five Dimensions of the Human Brain 87

CHAPTER 7
Becoming Attuned to the Messages
of Our Bodies 107

CHAPTER 8
Vibrating in Love 123

Contents

CHAPTER 15
The Five Phases of Ascension 295

Preface

Who Is Bianca Gaia—in the Heart of Diane LeBlanc?

Truth seeker, before talking about Gaia, I would like to tell you a bit more about myself so that you may understand that you and I are one: no more, no less.

The Indigo Child in Me

I was born in Sherbrooke, Quebec, in April 1964. As far as I can remember, I have always enjoyed a privileged relationship with the hereafter. As a child I used to speak to my guides, who would answer me with love and compassion.

I was what we call today an indigo child. From a young age I felt God's presence in me, in every one of my cells, like a burning fire of love. The image I had of Him did not resemble that of a wise old man with a white beard sitting on a cloud, as depicted by the religion of my time. I perceived Him rather like a luminous wave present in all living things, distinct from me but at the same time merged with all that is, outside as well as inside.

Even though I knew who I was, I felt a bit like an angel with its wings clipped, trapped in a body too small for me. That is probably why, as the years went by, my body gained in fullness, in length as well as in width. I believe that I didn't really want to incarnate. I was born with one foot on the other side of the veil: perceiving people's auras, the entities that accompanied them, and the wounds they denied in themselves.

My Terrestrial Family

Fortunately for me, my soul had chosen parents full of wisdom. Very early, they rejected these "abnormal" and "dysfunctional" aspects in me, the eldest of their three children. Probably feeling unconsciously that I had some difficulty in channeling this energy of light in serenity and balance, and that it would harm me both on emotional and relational levels, they quickly turned me away from the hallucinations of a sensitive child.

Of course, I resisted as much as I could—to the point of blowing up light bulbs when my emotions were too strong. I thought my parents didn't love me, didn't understand me, and that I would be better off in heaven rather than here on Earth. Every night before going to sleep, I would ask Jesus to come and get me and take me away up there with Him. I found life too difficult in this rigid and cold world.

Although I held a grudge for a long time against those close to me for not having welcomed me as I was, today I recognize the gift they gave me, and I thank them from the bottom of my heart. I now know that without them I couldn't have adapted to my three-dimensional environment to become grounded in the material world. Forced to place some distance and cut contact with the invisible world for more than ten years, I was allowed to choose my life rather than suffer it like a bad spell.

Back to the Source

It is only toward the end of the eighties that I reconnected with this luminous part of my being. In fact, I didn't have any other option than to turn to the invisible world to ask for a miracle when my first-born son, afflicted by a degenerative and insidious pulmonary illness, was condemned as incurable by the doctors. Charles-Antoine was a blessing in my life, for he allowed me to open up to the new medicine: the medicine of the soul, which allows each of us to expand from within the healing energy in its purest essence.

Having completed academic studies in theology and social service, faced with the powerlessness of conventional medicine to save my son, I turned to all the alternative resources available. I studied and integrated into my life naturopathy, homeopathy, massage therapy, meditation, creative visualization, and various energetic harmonization methods (magnetism, Reiki, therapeutic touch, the Lecher antenna, luminescence, etc.), all with more than extraordinary results: today, Charles-Antoine, like my three other children, Marlène, Émile, and Médéric, enjoys flourishing good health.

Messengers of Light

These holistic approaches have allowed me to bring consciousness into my life a bit more each day, understanding that we are spiritual beings having a human experience and not human beings having spiritual experiences. And it is now what I teach to those all around me. With the help of my guides, of my soul family, and of the ascended masters, I have accepted the role of a light messenger radiating the love of God in everything I say, everything I do, and especially everything I *am*.

My path has led me to regard the entities of the higher dimensions as brothers and sisters, united in a similar evolution, in communion with the source of all that lives. Our ultimate goal is not only to elevate our cellular vibrations to join with theirs, but also to incarnate more each day our divine essence to fully and totally experience our cocreating selves.

The choice we have made before incarnating on Earth is to experiment with our divinity in matter; but we are not limited to this physical envelope. Our subtle bodies go through all the extratemporal dimensions, and we can easily access all the information of the universe by connecting to it through the heart and becoming one with all that is.

Uniting in Love

The part of me that knows who I am, my multidimensional essence, revealed itself to me in 1995 under the name Bianca. For years I worked in channeling, communicating with various light entities such as Sananda, Melchizedek, Saint-Germain, Kwan Yin, and of course Gaia, our good old planet Earth. The first teaching I received, coming from our planetary consciousness, was accompanied by a merging energetic experience like nothing I had ever lived before.

"I am you, and you are me," she told me. "We are one in the universal divine essence, issued from the same spark of life. All the teachings, all the information that you receive, you already have them within you, present in all of your cells. You just need to remember who you are, in communion with all that lives. That is why, from now on, there won't be any distinction between you and me, and you will have to transmit those messages to the world under the name Bianca Gaia."

Saying Yes to Who I Am

Imagine the difficulty I had, then, to integrate this new state of reality: it is easy being a medium, to channel beautiful light energies, but when it comes to taking responsibility for and integrating your own divinity, affirming it loud and clear in front of everyone, it is a completely different story.

"Every living being on the planet can do the same, though," Gaia continued. "Somebody has to stand up and proclaim the truth: as a child of God, you are God. Just like you carry your parents' last name and their name is also yours, without distinction, you live on this Earth, so you are therefore part of my family, and we have access to the same vibrations, in love and peace. We will ascend together, indivisible. You just have to say 'yes' to who you are."

Since that time, every day, I make sure to remind myself at all times that I am a multidimensional being, unlimited and living in bliss. I have united with Gaia, and from now on I accept that all the information useful to the integration of my divine quintessence can be revealed to my heart. The fifth dimension is no longer a goal to reach, but a state of grace to be maintained at every second of my life in this world.

May this path be yours too: Gaia awaits you, in the secret part of your heart.

—From my soul to your soul, united in light, Bianca

Introduction

Do you believe it is possible to choose joy, simplicity, and ease at every instant, no longer to work hard on yourself? What if, in order to access the higher dimensions, rather than continuously working at eliminating your darkness, healing your inner wounds, or attempting to kill your ego, you only had to recognize the wonderful being that you already are? Could your shortcomings and your weaknesses be no more than some luminous aspects of yourself wanting to be recognized, accepted, and integrated so as to become one with all the dimensions of your being? Everything is already here within you; all you have to do is say "yes."

Yet, as you know, this is only possible once you have managed to align all of your subtle bodies and transcend the duality between your personality and your divine self. To do so, it is as important to affirm your luminous potential as it is to welcome your shadows, the unloved aspects within you. Fortunately, you can rely on the special connection uniting you with your soul family, guides, and guardian angels who walk with you. They can help you accomplish your incarnation mission and guide you through the challenges you have to deal with on a daily basis. Their goal, just like yours, is to unite more each day with the God present within you.

Inspired by a workshop available for several years in Canada and Europe, *Welcome to the Fifth Dimension* offers three simple steps to help you recognize and integrate your multiple dimensions, both existential and divine. Through the following chapters, you will be invited to regain your cocreating power, but mostly to fully experience the infinite state of grace that takes over once you reconnect with your divine quintessence.

Of course, most of the notions contained in these pages will probably be familiar to you, for they resume, elucidate, and simplify the major current spiritual schools of thought, with the aim of making them more accessible or even more coherent for any truth seeker, untrained as well as experienced.

You will see that all the chapters are structured approximately the same way. They all begin with a metaphor or a message channeled by Bianca Gaia. Then, the subject of the chapter is developed around an illustration or a chart, briefly summing up the teaching received. The chapter is accompanied by practical exercises and concrete examples to support a better understanding of the concepts that are elaborated on. All the chapters end with an eloquent conclusion favoring the integration of the content in all the dimensions of your being—or by guided meditation aiming to encrypt those teachings within your cellular memory.

Titled "The Multidimensionality of Being," the first part of this practical guide toward ascension speaks of the five dimensions of the self, which are most important in regaining balance and cultivating your daily happiness, as well as their corresponding five energy fields. Next, we will proceed to the identification and activation of your ruling chakra in order to reconnect you to the soul family you have chosen to belong to in this life. We will then introduce the five major soul families described by Bianca Gaia in channeling, and lastly, we will give you an insight into the ideal way of maintaining a serene balance on a daily basis.

However, we know that at times it might be hard to remain in harmony when certain events affect us. Therefore, in the second part of the book, we will discuss the ups and downs of the human experience. We will discover how to cope with the numerous challenges we face throughout our lives. We will come to understand that everything is played out within the five dimensions of the human brain.

In the chapter titled "Becoming Attuned to the Messages of Our Bodies," we will see how a health problem evolves according to the degree of tension and pressure that we are subjected to. Then, the chapter "Vibrating in Love" will help us make the link between the multidimensionality of the being and the way our bodies react to certain energetic blockages. Later on, in "The Five Ways of Acquiring Energy," we will uncover a simplified approach to defense mechanisms—as formulated by James Redfield in *The Celestine Prophecy*—and we will explore some helpful concrete tools to transcend those defensive positions. Lastly, we will clarify the differences that exist between "Ensuring Survival, or Living Fully."

Even after years of spiritual progression and realization, it is not easy to undo completely our primary mechanisms. Yet we know that it is not possible to ascend before having succeeded in integrating all the aspects of ourselves. So, in order to help us see and love ourselves as we are, we will consider the following enigma: is a coin worth less on the head side or on the tail? This simple question casts light on the difficulty we may have in going forward and recognizing who we really are. We often feel that the aspects of ourselves that we dislike and that seem imperfect in our eyes sully or minimize the impact of our luminous part, which already is and has always been in harmony inside us.

In the third step of this personalized progression, we will take on the latter reality: by becoming aware that all the aspects present within us are only two sides of the same coin, we allow ourselves to accept ourselves fully. It is by welcoming without judging the "Five Steps to Acceptance" that we access the ultimate phase of our terrestrial evolution: the divine quintessence.

In the following chapters, the issues of the pyramid of duality will be explained in detail, revealing clearly how to allow the various aspects of our personalities to integrate our true inner light. Some simple methods will follow in "Uniting All the Aspects of the Self," and in the chapter "The Divine Cocreating Expression" there is an overview of our real capacities to bring out our spiritual gifts and extrasensory faculties from within, such as in "The Children of the New Earth." The book will conclude with an exploration of the "The Five Phases of Ascension" as an integrating process of our cocreating selves in all the dimensions of our being.

A multitude of recommendations, exercises, and testimonies will be offered to you in order to support this approach toward your full realization in individual as well as collective terms. Isn't this what makes this New Age so wonderful: the fact that the ascension process is no longer a matter of individual but of planetary evolution? We are living in a grand, historical, extraordinary moment, and we are privileged to be able to take part consciously in this ultimate transformation.

Therefore, in the name of all our stellar, angelic, terrestrial, and intraterrestrial brothers and sisters, in my own name and in Gaia's, I would like to thank you for your openness, your courage, and your endless perseverance. Thanks to you, everything has already come into place for present and future generations to savor eternal joy, the fifth state of being that opens the gates to heaven on Earth. Welcome to the fifth dimension!

PART ONE

The Multidimensionality of Being

CHAPTER 1

The Being's Five Dimensions

Uniting All the Dimensions of Oneself

Message from September 7, 2004

Dear children of light: your cellular memory knows that all the dimensions are neither places nor time-spaces but rather, properly speaking, states of being. Everything else is just an illusion. The pseudoreality surrounding you, this world in which you have chosen to "densify": all is nothing but experimentation and life experience in order to learn to master your creating self.

You have long lost contact with the divine part within you. You have experimented with the materialization of your physical body (first dimension: the state of body), then the taming of your emotional body (second dimension: the state of soul), and the development of your mental body, called intelligence (third dimension: the state of mind). The fourth dimension, also called the state of awakening, is simply opening up to your relational body: the intrinsic consciousness of being a part of everything that surrounds you and of being connected to the universal creative source, regardless of what you call it—God, energy, or simply life.

Once you have tasted the awakening of consciousness, all your life's experience is transformed. You can no longer consider reality as being outside of yourself. All the people you meet, all the symptoms you feel, everything then appears as a mirror of your self, the revelation of your deeper being.

Since the beginning of time, your thoughts create, your emotions create, and your life choices create: they create this unreal world in which you had yourself locked up. The veil is definitely being lifted between the unconscious—which is subject to every event without understanding the meaning of it—and the higher consciousness, which henceforth knows that everything is a reflection of the creating self, whether it is subjected to your own inner duality or not.

The Multidimensionality of Being

Consequently you are already a multidimensional being. You are connected to all that lives, and as a result you have access to all the past experiences, all the knowledge accumulated through the centuries, and all the healing available in the universe. You only have to ask, to reclaim your cocreating power—and say yes to your full potential, to the divine being that you are.

The past no longer exists. As soon as you open up to universal consciousness, you are no longer subject to unhappy experiences or traumas from the past. You only have to activate your cellular memory to get in touch with your inner wisdom, the part of you that knows it is already healed, in absolute love for the divine being that dwells within you. You only have to forgive yourself for your passing blindness: not for your errors or failures, but only for the temporary forgetfulness of who you really are.

It's too simple, you say? Try it out. Reactivate this thought of light: "I am who I am, in communion with the universal source," and watch miracles unfold before your eyes here and now. Encrypt this absolute truth in each of your cells simply by visualizing a beautiful violet ray (the violet flame), which not only purifies and eliminates your old programming but cauterizes all your old wounds to give way to unlimited happiness and joy. This state of consciousness, "I am," is the ultimate secret of ascension. You simply have to seal this message of love in all your living cells in order for joy and the perpetual state of grace, also called the fifth dimension, to arise in you.

So, you no longer have to "work hard," continue to walk forward, or evolve further: everything is already here, written in your cellular memory, and just a single thought of serene love can fully reactivate it. This love is contagious. It spreads around the whole Earth not like a deadly virus but like an eternal one.

The planetary rising of consciousness depends on that final "yes" to the fusion of your entire being with your divine essence. Don't resist anymore; there is no effort required. Just remember who you are and renew your "yes" at every instant, every second of eternity in your soul and in universal consciousness. That's it; you've finally arrived: goodbye duality! Welcome to your own place. Welcome home.

—Bianca Gaia

Accessing Universal Wisdom

Imagine that you possess within you, in your own DNA, the entire genetic bundle of your ancestors, going back all the way to Adam and Eve. What if, rather than considering the burden of a heavy or karmic transgenerational heritage, you focused instead on the positive aspects: the knowledge, the strengths, and the skills bequeathed by your predecessors?

If you believe in reincarnation, you might also add to your list of positive experiences all those from your past lives, unscripted in your cellular memory. Once again, allow yourself to retain only the best. Choose to benefit from all the solutions that you've already found previously or those you've already had access to during this life or your numerous previous ones.

The same goes for what connects you to your life environment, the places you live, the community you belong to, and the area or country in which you reside. Your social and cultural heritage is also a well of endless unconscious resources, if you reconnect to the energies surrounding you.

At last you know you are accompanied, guided, and supported in the invisible world by all your brothers and sisters of light: angels, archangels, departed souls, ascended masters, and intraterrestrial and extraterrestrial entities. God himself only wishes you well, and you can invoke Him at all times to receive the assistance you need, at any place or time.

This is only a glimpse of the vibratory resources available inside as well as outside of you. Therefore there is no reason for you to fight or to try to save humanity as a whole. Just like you, each and every individual has access to their own being's multidimensionality. Just like you, all they have to do is reactivate their cellular memory, individual as well as collective, for all the answers to resurface within them, and for the right tools to intuitively introduce themselves, in order to solve any of their problems in a practical, simple, easy, and joyous way.

Have you heard of the theory of the hundredth monkey? First reported in 1979 by the anthropologist Lyall Watson in his book *Lifetide,* the story involved a scientific study conducted over nearly thirty years on various Pacific islands located quite far from one other. The study consisted of observing the behavior of Japanese macaques grouped in scattered colonies. In 1952, wanting to check how the monkeys would react to new food, scientists offered them sweet potatoes. At first skeptical, the monkeys ended up getting a taste for them, and soon they were all joyfully eating sweet potatoes as if they had always eaten them. Where the tale becomes fascinating is when one of the primates being observed, an eighteen-month-old female named Imo, started rinsing her potatoes in a stream prior to eating them. All the young monkeys in her group rapidly got into washing their potatoes too, while the eldest continued to eat them covered with dust. Yet after a few years, despite the fact that there was no possibility of contact between the groups on the various islands, scientists observed that all the subsequent generations of monkeys of that species would also go to the nearest stream to rinse their sweet potatoes.

According to Ken Keyes Jr., who popularized this story in the eighties, it is as if an invisible link connects the animals. And so, from the moment a certain number of monkeys—a "critical mass" of individuals—had been initiated into this new knowledge, it rapidly spread to the whole tribe through waves of their collective unconscious or via a vibratory or energetic contribution through the devas of the simian race. If macaques can benefit from such a connection among themselves, imagine all the vibratory power that connects us to each other as humans, and all the knowledge stored in our universal and global consciousness.

So why work so hard? You know that everything has already been accomplished within you for centuries and millennia. All the wisdom of humanity and of the higher dimensions is available to you if you choose to open yourself up to receive all of its benefits. You only have to adopt my catchphrase: "simple, easy, yet joyful." Indeed, why complicate our lives and let ourselves be touched by outside incidents when it is so easy to delegate all the work to our friends present in the hereafter who want nothing but to help us? They only aspire to show us the way, leading to the completeness of our being and absolute happiness at every instant of our lives.

In fact, the fifth dimension isn't a time-space location, an "out of time" place, or a remote planet. It is possible, here and now, to reach this fifth dimension in our physical bodies, because this simply equates to an alignment within ourselves. But if we do not know what we ought to align, it is difficult to establish whether or not we are in harmony.

The Being's Five Dimensions

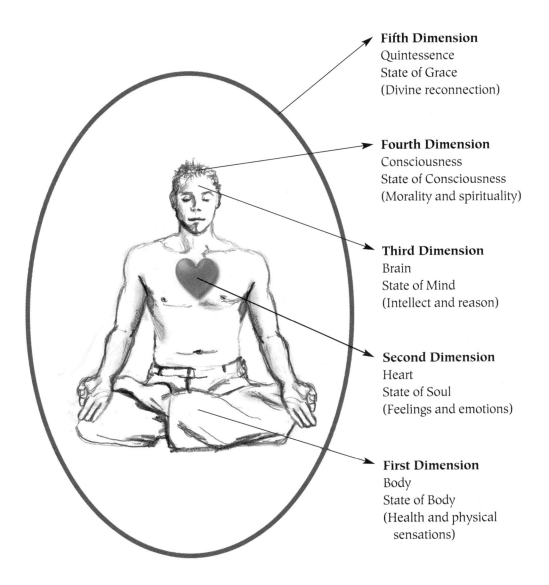

Fifth Dimension
Quintessence
State of Grace
(Divine reconnection)

Fourth Dimension
Consciousness
State of Consciousness
(Morality and spirituality)

Third Dimension
Brain
State of Mind
(Intellect and reason)

Second Dimension
Heart
State of Soul
(Feelings and emotions)

First Dimension
Body
State of Body
(Health and physical
   sensations)

You will notice that the following illustration, as well as most of those presented in this book, is oriented from the bottom to the top. This has a simple purpose: not only is the visual progression easier to follow, it also allows for nourishment not only of the mental body but of the entire being. By starting from the bottom, we are forced to interiorize ourselves, to go back inside ourselves to rediscover who we truly are.

The five dimensions of the being are identified as body, heart, brain, consciousness, and quintessence:

First Dimension: The State of Body

Here we address the primary functions of the individual: the state of our health, physical sensations, and responses to our essential needs to ensure our survival. This includes everything that is connected to the physical body, to the material and tangible dimension of the being.

Second Dimension: The State of Soul

The soul can be defined in many ways but usually refers to a person's emotions and feelings. In popular language, the soul is symbolized by the heart, the emotional center of the being.

Third Dimension: The State of Mind

As for the spirit, it is generally connected to the mental abilities of the individual: the intellect as well as the capacity to reason. These are the cerebral cortex's own analytical faculties, the part of the human brain able to think and make considered decisions.

Fourth Dimension: The State of Consciousness

The notion of consciousness in human beings seems to be the most controversial one. Does it simply relate to the morality of each individual, to their respect for laws and social conventions, or is it defined by humanitarian and altruistic virtues that characterize certain people regarded as "spiritual," for instance Mother Teresa?

What if, knowing that we are all part of everything that surrounds us, this could be the invisible link that connects us to one another? Consciousness might well be this ability we have to perceive reality beyond all the illusions of this world we live in, and our willingness to act according to the universal laws that govern the universe. This would explain why it is frequently associated with the awakening state and spirituality, like the perfect path that leads to illumination.

Fifth Dimension: The State of Grace

At some point or another in your existence, you have certainly experienced the state of grace. It is a moment of pure magic in which one feels overwhelmed by some indescribable joy, as if floating on a cloud of absolute happiness. It may have been the day you got married, the first time you held your newborn in your arms, or when you obtained the promotion you'd been dreaming of at work. You can surely recall the delicious shiver that went through you, the sudden state of delight that pumped in your heart. In that moment you experience such well-being that you felt filled with unconditional love toward every living thing. For a short instant it seems as if all parts of you align themselves to center on the completeness you feel, and you remain connected only to the present moment.

Could it be that such a state of beatitude takes place when the human self and the divine self fuse together in a subtle spiritual hug? This divine reconnection happens when all the parts of our selves, the four lesser dimensions discussed above, align and harmonize themselves to give us access to the fifth dimension, our divine quintessence.

The reason we do not remain in the state of completeness, why the energy goes back down, is because we tend to forget how to get there. We have forgotten, neglected, or refused to listen to one part or another of ourselves, and subsequently we feel off-center, out of alignment.

The purpose of this book, therefore, is to allow you to know how to align and balance all the parts of your being. As you read on, you will notice how each dimension is connected to the subtle bodies, the spheres of life, and human experiences; in short, that everything is interconnected. The number 5 is also truly magical, for when we succeed in aligning the four parts of experience, both spiritual and human, the fifth dimension comes into place, a bit like the capstone of a pyramid.

Aligning All the Dimensions Present within Oneself

What if there was a field of action or a way of interacting with our reality specific to each dimension of the human being, in accordance with the partial understanding each of them gets in its own universe?

This could look like four blind people attempting to ascertain what an elephant is through touch: "It's a long hose," the one feeling the trunk will say. "No, it's more like a solid column," the one whose arms are wrapped around a leg will contradict. "You've got it all wrong: it's a big fan," the third one will shout, flapping the creature's ear. "No, no, it's a wall, all wrinkled and warm," the last one will say while feeling along the animal's flank.

Who is right and who is wrong? Each of the dimensions of our deep being holds only a portion of the truth that we interpret through information accumulated through the years, contributing by deduction to maintaining some comfortable and reassuring illusions of the whole. It is on the basis of this limited information that all our decisions are made and all our actions are taken:

1. The physical body, occupied with ensuring survival, applies itself to getting all the resources available in response to its primary needs, taking care of itself first—taking its place, finding means to achieve its ends, and taking the best part for itself. In short, the body acquires what it needs to maintain good vital energy.
2. The emotional dimension of our being aims to supply our secondary needs: safety, human warmth, and self-esteem. It is busy giving itself an appropriate environment, a cozy nest or cocoon—armor to protect itself from the outside and to feel secure inside. In nature it would be called a den, a safe place to rest after hunting. The emotional dimension is also directly connected to the expression of our creativity, when we dedicate ourselves to some form of artistic work or to a cause or project.
3. The intellectual dimension, particular to human beings, is related to the state of our spirit, the thoughts we are preoccupied with, and our need to analyze and understand the universe within us as well as around us.

Human beings are the only ones on the planet who ask existential questions: Who am I, and where do I come from?

4. The spiritual dimension of human beings remains quite ambiguous in itself. Scientifically, it has been established that the human brain is subdivided into just three parts (see Chapter 6, "The Five Dimensions of the Human Brain"). How can the existence of a fourth one, which can be called consciousness (human, social, global, and universal), be proved? This dimension is easily perceptible on an energetic level and is explained at length in philosophical and theological writings. Its function remains undeniable: it distinguishes good from evil, and it often puts the interests of the community before those of the individual. It is the altruistic part of every one of us: our parents (in the wide sense) have educated us to give and to serve others, risking inevitable guilt should we disobey.

5. As for the fifth dimension, it appears as a celestial calling, situated above all the human vicissitudes. It is the state of grace, the recognition of the divine being that I am, unifying all the previous dimensions into a perfect harmonic balance, respectful of the unique aspects of each of them, without judgment and constraint, out of time and three-dimensional space, beyond all duality, in ultimate peace and serenity.

This leads us to consider how to favor this balance and to allow each of these dimensions to combine in perfect cohesion. If it is difficult at times to reconcile the first three aspects of oneself (body, heart, and reason), imagine what happens when we add the pinch of salt that is consciousness.

Yet could it be that the keys to paradise and the bridge to the new world can be found in the harmony we obtain? And that once the first four dimensions of the being are aligned, we are automatically launched into the fifth dimension, the quintessence we all ardently aspire to? What if it was enough to learn to respect ourselves, to be more attentive to our inner voices, and to have the courage to ask for help from the universal wisdom present in our selves and in every luminous being surrounding us?

Exercise: *Your Soul's Song*

This exercise enables you to become aware of the multidimensional being living within you. You simply have to allow yourself to be guided by your inner sage, who holds all the solutions you aspire to at every instant. For your natural wisdom to reveal itself totally, it is important to read the following indications in the right order, completing each step before going on to the next one.

Get a pen and a blank piece of paper. Take a few moments to settle comfortably, and internalize yourself by taking three deep breaths.

Firstly, let a song rise from within, the first one that comes to mind. It could be a song you are particularly fond of, that you recently heard on the radio, or one dating back to your childhood, when you still used to sing in the shower.

Give yourself a few moments to sing along with this song, either out loud or internally. Try to remember the chorus and the various verses. Do you remember the words? If so, write down a few words or sentences from memory.

Then write down what touches you in this song, what feelings and emotions it triggers in you, while remaining aware of the melody within you.

For the second step of the exercise, think of a situation that has recently affected you: an event that has distressed you, a problem preoccupying you, an interpersonal conflict affecting you, a worry that is eating you up, or something similar.

Now describe the nature of your preoccupation: what was the triggering element? Who are the individuals concerned? How does it make you live, or how has it made you live? Where do you stand with it all today?

When you have thought the matter through, breathe deeply again to enter into communication with your being's multidimensionality, the part of you that has all the solutions and answers you need here and now.

Your cellular memory knows that you have already evolved in similar circumstances in the past or in one of your past lives and that you have most certainly managed to overcome this challenge. This is why your subconscious has already anticipated your request and has offered you one or many leads *to reflect on, to help you regain peace within yourself. What are they? They are expressed through the **words of the song** that has been inspired in you by your divine essence.*

Take some time to read again those lines you wrote at the beginning, in light of this dynamic affirmation: "My being's multidimensionality sheds light on the most beneficial solutions for all and on the positive attitudes at the heart of this situation that would be in my interest to adopt, which means a lot to me."

Remain open and available, in heart and spirit, so that it is easy for you to establish links between the themes of the song you have chosen and the situation you have described. If you need help to decipher the hidden meaning of the text or to clarify the symbols evoked in the song, it is suggested you ask the opinion of a person close to you who, not being directly implicated, will probably see through it clearly and let their intuition guide them.

Finally, if you want to, write down the conclusions you have drawn from this experience and keep them at hand to inspire you if another challenge of the same type appears in your life again.

You can resume this exercise at will, any time you need to resolve a situation or solve a specific problem. You always have access to the multiple dimensions of your being; you simply have to put yourself in a favorable disposition.

Similarly, when you have a song running through your mind for a while, stop for a moment at the words and ask yourself what it is trying to tell you. This is more significant if the song in question hasn't just played on the radio, as it could well be that your unconscious is trying to give you a message concerning what you are currently going through.

Consciously Choosing to Be Happy at All Times

Why are people unhappy? It is simply because of their way of conceiving the reality that surrounds them. They have a tendency to think upside down: most individuals tell themselves, "When I have money, I will have my dream house built, and *then* I will be happy"; "When I retire, I will be able to do what I please, and *then* I will finally be free to be myself"; or "When I have some time available, I will be able to travel, and *then* I will feel good."

Having, Doing, Being

"When I manage to have what I need, I will be able to *do,* and only then will I be able to be happy." What if you could chose to develop an attitude totally contrary to your habits?

Being, Doing, Having

"I am happy, so I will do what it takes to remain that way, by developing fulfilling solutions *(doing)* and by attracting to me *(having)* the best solutions to allow me to obtain the desired results in all things." Or in simpler terms, "I am happy, so I will make the right choices that will keep me in that state."

"It is therefore by consciously (the spiritual dimension, consciousness) aligning my thoughts (the intellectual dimension, the mind), my emotions (the emotional dimension, the heart), and my actions (the physical dimension, the body) that I obtain alignment of all the aspects present in me to enjoy a perpetually luminous existence."

In simpler terms, "The happier I am, the more I harbor joy in all my being, and the more I radiate happiness. I then become like a powerful magnet, attracting to me anything I desire, anything that fills me and allows me to radiate even more."

Isn't this what everyone has aspired to from time immemorial? "What if it was enough for me to simply make the decision to be happy and to put everything in place, do whatever is in my power to remain in that state, and in this way create for myself and manifest this wonderful life *(having)* that I have always dreamed of?"

Integration: *Positive Affirmation*

Congratulations! You have chosen to say yes to the manifestation of your full creating power in divine love toward yourself and all living things. From now on, all your cells are being activated to affirm "I am" loud and clear.

You no longer have to make any effort, to fight, or to work hard, for all is already accomplished by your inner divinity, radiating more each day. This ultimate recognition of the self is the key to open the door of the fifth dimension, allowing you to bathe in a perpetual state of grace: the joy of your quintessence.

The multidimensional being that you are has access to all the wisdom of creation. Everything your cellular memory has recorded throughout the ages is available to you from now on. You simply have to ask for it with confidence.

You are invited to get a symbolic object to carry with you at all times (a bracelet or a stone, for example) that will be an expression of this luminous decision. It will remind you that from now on your being's multidimensionality, your divine essence, acts through you; you just have to let it be.

This way, the next time you encounter a difficulty or experience a problem or troubling event, simply ask yourself the following question: "Could it be that I have already been through this challenge in this life or in a previous one, and that I came out of it fine?" Most certainly the answer is yes. You then only have to ask all your living cells to access here and now the perfect solution, which will appear without delay, even beyond your expectations.

CHAPTER 2

The Five Energy Fields

Incarnating Well to Ascend Better

Message from August 31, 2005

For several years you may have noticed that everything in and around you seems to be going very fast. The energy appears increasingly favorable to new departures, new life decisions, new relationships, and useful insights.

Many among you have considered changing careers or partners, moving, or getting involved in very promising projects. Many, trusting in access to abundance, have entrusted a part of their savings to investors promising them substantial returns, which are proving slow to manifest.

Others have left stable well-paying jobs to embark on their genuine life mission and are now finding themselves in precarious financial situations. But, you might say, you really believed in it with all your heart. So why is life being so harsh?

You say you are trying to transcend the duality in you, but the three-dimensional life conditions are getting more and more difficult to handle. You are filled with faith, and you have recognized within you the ascension symptoms described by this century's prophets, but it is increasingly hard for you to remain centered on a daily basis.

Could it be because you perceive the ascension not as a permanent state of being but more as a liberation or a way to escape this life of contradictions that seem to imprison you? If you spend your time wondering why you are still here on Earth, if you can't wait to get on the other side of the veil or are no longer able to enjoy the present moment, perhaps it isn't because your vibration level is too high but rather because you are still resisting to incarnate fully.

Could you be one of those people who still believe that the grass is greener on the other side? Or, like the apprentice in Paolo Coelho's The Alchemist, *one of those who goes to the ends of the Earth in search of a treasure that is to be found in their own garden? Understand that the new Earth and the new world do not exist anywhere but within you. No matter what you do, where you go, or who you come across, if happiness isn't present in your heart first, you won't find it anywhere outside of you, whether in this dimension or in any other.*

Beware of those false prophets who are taking you away from your divine essence by promising you a better future provided by someone other than yourself. Don't expect divine interventions to happen around the world, amazing phenomenon to occur in your favor, or miracles to come and sort out everything in your life, as if by enchantment.

If your brothers and sisters of light—angelic, stellar, intraterrestrial, and extraterrestrial—are here to help and support you in your path to recognizing who you really are, they can in no way sort out the faith of humanity in your place. Everything outside of you is essentially the reflection of what is going on inside you—don't ever forget that! You alone have the power to become cocreator with God and to take part actively in planetary changes. You alone can make all the difference.

Right now, everything you attempt to do—to accomplish, to succeed in, or to control in the long term—seems to be delayed or to elude you. Every new day brings its share of surprises and unexpected things, some pleasant and some disturbing. All the points of reference that were giving you a sense of safety are being removed from your life. All your old ways of doing, the recipes that used to bring you success, have stopped working.

You manage to accomplish miracles for others, to serve the source with serenity and patience, but in your own life, you no longer see any concrete results. Only small satisfactions, little daily delights, allow you to preserve some kind of happiness. You are even amazed to notice how you manage to remain positive and peaceful over long periods despite all the pitfalls.

Can you see your higher self in action through all this? It is inviting you to ask yourself the greatest of existential questions: does your happiness rely on outside results, or is it a permanent state of grace, continuously maintained inside of you?

You know that in the ascension process it is impossible to leave even a tiny portion of yourself behind. It is therefore essential for every cell of your being to become one with your divine essence. No part of you can be left behind or surrounded by darkness, fear, ignorance, or lack of awareness. Here and now is the auspicious moment to spring-clean your old programming, chaotic emotions, and contradictory thoughts.

Do you feel vulnerable or fragile at times? Isn't it the perfect opportunity to look at those wounds still left in your soul, to make peace with those parts of you that you have forgotten or neglected all your life? To forgive yourself for all your mistakes and all your lack of love? Sure, you have incarnated, but at what cost? Could a part of you still be longing for unconditional love and acknowledgement of its own value, both human and spiritual?

Ask yourself daily about your level of trust in God, the source of all living things. Have you managed ultimately to let go regarding your present, past, and future? You know the ego feeds on the control it believes it has over the reality surrounding it, and that the mental body values its power to act on the outside world. If you are at times disappointed, it is a sign that you still have expectations.

Yet expectations and desires remain the prerogative of the mental body and indicate that the ego still has a grip on you. The only way to outsmart it, to disarm it, is to fully enjoy the now in perfect harmony with all the parts of you, leaving none out.

Various personalities coexist inside of you, according to what you are and what you have been. What place do you have in your life for your inner child, the artist in you, the inventor, the builder, the environmentalist, and so on? Is there a proper balance in your life between giving and receiving? Do you take as good care of your body and your personalities as you do of others? How do you express your creativity and your ability to manifest on a daily basis?

Here are all the questions you need answer in order to live in total acceptance of your being. Before totally uniting with your quintessence, you need to fully incarnate, unconditionally accepting who you really are, but also accepting everything that is. It is necessary for all forms of duality to merge and unite in divine love at every instant. Everything is perfect. Everything is necessary. Everything is an invitation to let this unconditional love reach you, more deeply, in all of your cells.

Many of you see the ascension as a perfect integration of your divine light, a big fire of love that will set all of your being ablaze. So, if some parts of you aren't ready, having not yet been purified, integrated, or united in unconditional love, they are like green wood: they cannot burn rapidly. If you don't want the process to keep on *being so long and laborious, thank your soul for the challenges, problems, and obstacles it sends in your life right now. These are golden opportunities to bring into the light the weaknesses left in you and to establish unconditional peace in all of your being once and for all.*

You don't need to work hard on yourself, to dig and dwell on your old stories. Honoring the difficulties is allowing the purifying energy to act on you at every instant, making space for the parts of you that still aspire to be considered, healed, and loved unconditionally—gradually, as they occur. You just have to commit yourself not to neglect your needs any longer, nor to tell yourself stories or embellish the deficiencies or dissatisfactions of the ego, but instead to accept yourself in all simplicity.

The only way to escape the traps of the mental body is to live fully, incarnated in the now, knowing that no matter what happens around you, divine love awaits you in the silence of your heart. There, no waves, no swirls persist; there is only total peace, perpetual plenitude, and the infinite state of grace preceding the ascension.

The fifth dimension is here, awaiting you within yourself and in every one of your cells, because you are the fuel that feeds the divine fire. Your presence to yourself is the spark that allows the celestial flame to set ablaze your entire being. Taste it at every moment with every single breath. Then, like a forest fire that spreads wildly, you will transmit this bright light all around you in a contagious way, through your own radiance, devoid of illusions and duality.

You are the new Earth. You are the fifth dimension. You create tomorrow's world. It will be made in the image of your fusion with divine and planetary energies. The fruits of your incarnation will be proportionate to your happiness, fully integrated and therefore unlimited. And so be it.

—Bianca Gaia

Incarnation and Amplification of the Subtle Bodies

What if our only mission on Earth was to accumulate as much energy as possible, then to spread it to others—to humanity and to the entire planet? Imagine for a moment that rather than sacrificing yourself for others, giving them your attention and caring for them in order to be happy, you could change the world through the simple emanation of your own radiance?

The reality is simple: the more fully you incarnate, the more you ground yourself, the more your energy field extends and radiates brightly. This is how the prophets and awakened ones of this world (Jesus, Buddha, Saint Francis of Assisi, Saint-Germain, and others) have been able to accomplish miracles, heal crowds, or raise the vibrations of a multitude of people: through their simple luminous and loving presence.

However, it is as though most people on Earth only partially remember the life contract they have committed to. Some apply themselves to accumulating as much energy as possible for themselves (possessions, wealth, power, etc.), while the rest of the world strives to spread the best of themselves, neglecting even their own needs or risking their own survival, investing themselves in a cause, a humanitarian project, or a noble objective in order to be at mankind's service, to make society fairer and more just.

Take a moment to visualize a receptacle inside you holding all your energy reserves, as if you had a glass of water representing all the vital energy at your disposal to be healthy, to maintain your quality of life, and to enjoy well-being. Every time you give part of your energy to others, it is like giving them water from your own glass. No wonder you feel exhausted or drained: even though your inner glass of water isn't even half full, you hurry to share some drops or even the majority of this precious vital energy with the people around you. It's enough to make you feel dehydrated, dispossessed, or powerless at times when it comes to facing your own personal obligations; having given so much to others, there is nothing left for you.

What if you applied yourself to taking good care of you instead? Isn't there a saying that charity begins at home? It is the same advice you hear on an airplane, when the crew tells you that in case of a loss of cabin pressure, you should first put on your own oxygen mask before helping your kids—the lack of oxygen could cause you to faint before you can do it. The life of your child, just as much as your own, is put at risk by not putting yourself first.

This is not being selfish; it is being realistic. If you fully dedicate yourself to others every day, you won't have enough energy left to maintain a balance. That's why the number-one priority is you.

Every time you look after yourself, take care of your own needs, relax a bit, and treat yourself well, you store more energy. You fill up your inner glass of water. Instead of emptying it as you go, if you grant yourself a multitude of daily little joys and pleasures, you store treasures of positive energy, and your glass will be constantly full. If you put yourself first in all areas of your life, it could even overflow. Thus you could have an extra glass of water at your disposal, which everyone around you could benefit from without ever draining you.

It is the same principle as teaching others to fish rather than giving them a fish. Every time you take care of yourself, respect your own needs, and remain in balance, you teach others by example to do the same for themselves. Just like you, every person around you possesses within themselves all those extraordinary limitless resources; why prevent them from reaching those resources by finding solutions in their stead or feeling sorry for them?

One of the most beautiful gifts you can give humanity is to radiate a luminous, balanced, and harmonious energy. By maintaining a good vibratory balance you nourish, align, and amplify all of your energetic bodies and become radiant, like a luminous sun that warms and brightens everything around it.

The following chart allows you to find out (if you haven't done so yet!) which primary subtle bodies your energetic field is composed of, and the area of action to which each of them relates, to make it easier for you to understand how to nourish them healthily to align them properly.

The measure of your light cocoon will then allow you to determine the shape of your energetic field and what it reveals about your general way of approaching life and reacting to the fluctuations of your inner states.

To close this chapter, a grounding exercise presented as a guided meditation is provided to enhance your global reharmonization and to amplify your energetic potential—in other words, to refill your "glass of water").

First Field: Etheric

Once again, the explanation starts from the bottom of the illustration. Very close to the body, very close to the skin, we find the first subtle body, called the etheric field. It is the most easily perceived dimension in energy because it is the densest. It represents the physical dimension inside us and thus the electricity that we emit.

The Five Energy Fields

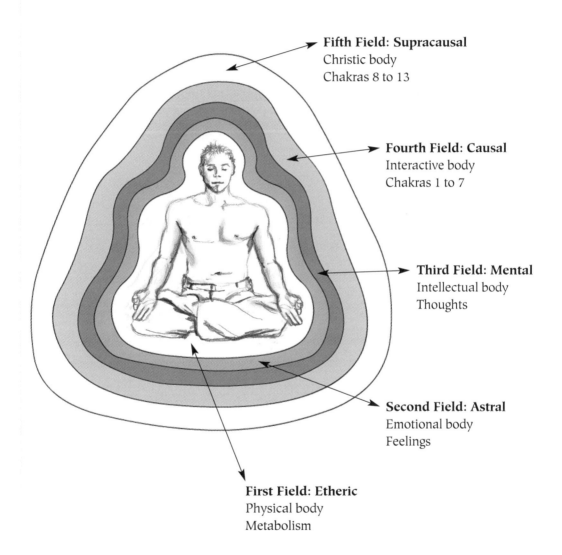

Fifth Field: Supracausal
Christic body
Chakras 8 to 13

Fourth Field: Causal
Interactive body
Chakras 1 to 7

Third Field: Mental
Intellectual body
Thoughts

Second Field: Astral
Emotional body
Feelings

First Field: Etheric
Physical body
Metabolism

At the extrasensory-perception level, when we are in a crowd, for instance attending a conference, this subtle body will show itself as a halo, a small whitish glow around the lecturer. With a bit of practice we can perceive different colors in it. Because the etheric field is connected to the physical body, it is where we can perceive trouble and illnesses in someone's metabolism. Often intense unease is signaled by a bright red dot in the aura, while a dark-gray shade reveals a severe illness already settled in the body for some time.

Second Field: Astral

The second energetic sphere surrounding the human body is connected to the emotional dimension of the person, their feelings, and their moods. It fluctuates according to mood, feelings, and the way events are experienced by each individual.

When a person experiences a very intense emotion, either positive or negative, their subtle body reacts very quickly. Therefore, when we fall in love, for instance, the radiance of the astral body could widen to embrace the next dimension (the mental field). On the contrary, if you receive some bad news that puts you in a state of shock, this subtle layer shrinks until it is as thin as a sheet of paper. If you experience anger, resentment, or frustration, it could even take on a nasty navy, greenish, or brownish shade, and you will immediately feel some discomfort around the heart or the solar plexus.

Third Field: Mental

The mental body comes in third position. This subtle layer may vary just as much as the first two. It is the field of thoughts, connected to the intellectual dimension of the being. It is influenced by the ideas we nourish, the preoccupations that absorb us, and the worries that wear us down.

This energetic field can also invade the two previous layers, for when we nourish negative thoughts toward ourselves it brings us down and ends up being an impediment to our fulfillment as well as to the radiance of the other fields. This is why the mental body has a darker shade in the illustration, to demonstrate that our states of mind have the biggest impact on our energetic balance and determine our harmony on all planes.

Fourth Field: Causal

Also called the karmic field, the causal field contains all that we have accumulated through our past and present experiences, and everything that has left some conscious or unconscious imprint on our subtle bodies.

It is not as easy to perceive the fluctuations of this field as it is for the others, as it is related to our first seven chakras and not to our three-dimensional reality—that is, to our seven inner energy centers (see the next chapter, "Activating the Ruling Chakra").

The Five Geometric Shapes of the Light Cocoon

GEOMETRIC FORM	CHARACTERISTICS
△	Energetic field wider near the ground and narrowing toward the upper body; physical dimension is predominant
◇	Energetic field wider at the heart level, narrowing at both ends; emotional dimension is predominant
▽	Energetic field wider at the head level, narrowing toward the lower body; intellectual dimension is predominant
□	Energetic field wider at the head, heart, and feet levels, with an absence of natural curves; moral dimension is predominant
✶	Ovoid-shaped radiant energetic field harmonious from head to toe, with shining iridescent rays; ascension vehicle

Fifth Field: Supracausal

This is our most luminous field. The supracausal is our Christic envelope, our divine essence. It is linked to the chakras situated outside of us, those connecting us to heaven.

This part of us normally never fluctuates. It's a bit like here on Earth: no matter what happens, above the clouds, the sun keeps shining. Apart from cases of very severe trauma, this field usually remains harmonious and emits a powerful luminous radiance.

Exercise: *The Various Shapes of the Light Cocoon*

When we measure a person's energy field, it is easy to identify which geometric shape it seems to have. It will certainly be similar to one of the five shapes described in the chart above.

To measure the dimensions of each individual's energetic field, we may use a pendulum, a Lecher antenna, or other tools of this type, but the simplest and cheapest way is a homemade dowsing wand made from a Bic-type pen from which the ink tube has been removed. Into the tip of this hollow cylinder we insert a metal coat hanger that has been cut in half and folded in an L shape, so that the pointer can be balanced on the top of the cylinder.

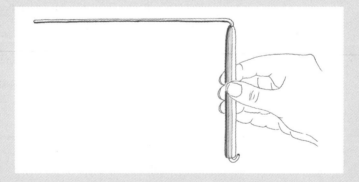

The measure is taken three times: at knee level, at heart level, and finally at head level. Both the person who measures and the person being measured

---

stand twelve to fifteen feet apart. The person holding the pointer then points toward the three points of measurement one by one, first aligning the tip of the metal rod toward the knees, then the heart, and finally the head. The person holding the wand slowly moves toward the other person until the pointer changes direction or turns in all directions, which indicates that a person's energy field has been reached. To distinguish the outlines of the light cocoon, we simply note the approximate distance between the pointer and the person being measured for each of the three measurements.

Does the Shape of the Light Cocoon Define the Way We Approach Life?

Through the results we obtain, it is possible to identify one of the five geometric shapes described in the previous chart: the triangle, the diamond, the inverted triangle, the square, or the iridescent oval.

For each of the first three shapes of the energy field, there is a predominance of one of the three first dimensions of the being: a preponderance of the physical aspect for the triangle, a predisposition to emotions (the heart) for the diamond, and a marked preference for the intellectual aspect of things (the mind or mental body) for the inverted triangle. The fourth shape, which could at first seem quite balanced, is the square. It shows strong energy at all levels, but it does not have any natural curves, which reveals that the individual's ability to receive is closed to a certain degree.

Finally, in some very rare cases, we find another rather uneven shape that presents a stronger energy at both the lower part of the body (the knees) and the upper part (the head) but which is marginally narrower at the heart level. This shape, which looks more or less like an hourglass, is not mentioned in the chart because it is actually an inverted triangle profile in which the physical dimension has become predominant because of the nature of the person's work, usually manual labor, and not through the quality of grounding.

Generally speaking, measurements of the fields as described above give a strong indication of how a person reacts to the events of his or her life. For instance, people with inverted triangle shapes refer to their intellect or mental aspects to define their existential field of experimentation. The diamond shapes will tend to find solace at the level of emotions or feelings. If their mood is good and they are calm, everything is fine; but if their emotions are strong, it becomes harder for them to approach life positively. As for the triangles, they are often Earth's guardians. They are connected to the planet and have given themselves the task of maintaining and protecting it. The squares represent the majority of people for whom the spiritual dimension is predominant. Their energy is often very strong and dynamic, and they are connected to the people around them and have great abilities to listen to others and to help, enlighten, and counsel them. But as mentioned above, their great difficulty is receiving.

None of these forms of expression are preferable or less appropriate to the others in energetic terms. If, for instance, the energetic field is triangle-shaped, this simply means that the person draws their energy from their groundedness, their down-to-earth side. Similarly, the diamond-shaped cocoon doesn't necessarily mean that those individuals are more in balance, because their emotions always dictate their behavior. In the case of an inverted triangle, their way of understanding and of seeing life takes over. Their reference system is then associated with their thoughts. People with square-shaped auras have a tendency to make themselves responsible for others and feed from the validation gained from it.

The dominant shape of our light cocoon simply indicates our primary way of fetching energy to evolve better. The experiences we have been through since childhood have forged these energetic traits that are generally present in our lives. This personality trait has often been encouraged by the people with whom we have evolved: our relatives, friends, bosses, and colleagues, all those with whom we have had privileged relationships and who have sensibly influenced our personality or even shaped it at times into what it is today.

No matter where the preponderance of your energy lies, it is always possible to change the shape of your auric field. You simply have to take three deep breaths while standing with your knees slightly bent for all your fields to align and naturally take the shape of a beautiful light cocoon. Try it: when you breathe deeply, you reconnect to the sky and you ground yourself into the Earth so that harmony gently settles inside you. You then return to a state of centeredness, the ultimate shape: the iridescent ovoid, which all of us aspire to get back to, maintain, and perfectly master, because it is our ascension vehicle, also called Merkaba, achieved through a constant and perfect balance of all the dimensions of the self.

Why and How to Ground Yourself

When it comes to grounding, many people become perplexed. Why ground ourselves while we are in full upward transmutation? How can the movement go both toward the top and toward the bottom? Isn't there a contradiction in terms? Yet most of the texts from Bianca Gaia help us to understand that ascension is not about leaving the Earth to elevate ourselves to heaven but rather to incarnate our divine essence in the unlimited cocreative plenitude. This is why the ascension process is only possible when we fully assume our divinity *and* our humanity, in communion with the entire planet. We channel higher celestial vibrations through all of our being, including our physical bodies. For it to manage to store those powerful energies, it is important that we are well rooted.

A striking example to understand this phenomenon is the rose. The most beautiful part of the plant is neither its leaves nor its thorns but its flower, once it blossoms and emanates its exquisite perfume. However, if we cut the stem as soon as a bud appears, there is little chance of it coming into bloom. It is necessary to wait for the right time and to give the rose and the plant the right balance of sunlight, water, fertilizer, and care. But most importantly, we have to make sure it is well rooted in the ground, and we must not attempt to transplant it when it is blooming. Do you see the metaphor?

In my view, the ascension is the blossoming of our divine being. We have implanted ourselves on this Earth in a physical body to grow and evolve. We have adorned ourselves with leaves (our talents and successes) and thorns (our personality and challenges), but first of all we must be properly rooted in order to be able truly to flower—that is to say, to radiate our celestial light.

So wouldn't the right way to ground ourselves lie in incarnating fully, feeling how connected we are to all that lives and understanding how we are fueled by the energy of the entire planet? Just like plants, we know that we can be influenced by what happens outside of us. For them it is the temperature and the environment, and for us it is situations, people, and the surrounding climate. We decide what we do with the information we receive. We choose to interpret events to our advantage or disadvantage.

Grounding draws from the Earth all the necessary energy to remain strong and firm to cope with the tempests that can rage around us, whether we are involved or not. Grounding means to recenter ourselves every time events push us around, taking the time to remove all that could disturb us as we go along, through our privileged connection to the Earth—our anchor or energetic lightning rod, if you prefer.

To do so, imagine solid roots growing out of your feet from every one of your toes and sinking deeply into the ground under you. These will act the same as a plant's roots, allowing you to remain firmly anchored in your physical body while also acquiring the planetary "sap," the vitality and energetic resources to nourish and consolidate your entire being.

Would you like to know if you are well grounded right now? Imagine that somebody pushes you. If you lose your balance, it means you are not physically well anchored.

Now visualize the position of a basketball player waiting for a pass, or of a martial arts expert. The weight of their bodies is centered around the lower abdomen, their legs are spread as wide as their shoulders, their knees are slightly bent, and their pelvises are a little swung, in a partially sitting position, so that the spine is nicely aligned perpendicular to the floor. The body remains in a stable position, perfectly balanced. Try to push someone around when they have this posture; it is nearly impossible to make them fall, or even to budge them, while conversely it is very easy to destabilize someone standing straight with just their two feet on the ground as contact points.

It is not necessary to start practicing yoga or judo to ground yourself properly. The anchoring position described above can be adopted any time you are stationary: waiting in a line, washing the dishes, talking on the phone. Try it. This posture could feel a bit uncomfortable at first, and your legs might shake or weaken after a few minutes. To help the energy in your legs flow better, you can even flex the knees a bit more, always keeping the pelvis well aligned with the spine until you start feeling some tingling along your thighs and your calves shake slightly. This is a good sign: it means your blood circulation is increasing. You can then swing your weight lightly from one leg to the other to reestablish the flow of blood. Take two or three deep breaths, making sure you inflate the abdomen as well as the lungs, and you will feel better everywhere within.

Once properly aligned and anchored, your entire body, physical as well as subtle, becomes a powerful energy channel. It then receives all the beneficial purifying waves available on the terrestrial and celestial planes. It harmonizes all your being to constantly recharge your battery and even allows you to give or transmit this energy without ever running out. This is what "radiating" means: to emanate this powerful transmutation energy from every pore of your skin for your higher benefit, and the benefit of the entire planet, which receives those luminous purifying waves through you, through the quality of your energetic grounding.

Can you see now the importance of being properly incarnated? Your physical body works as a vehicle for your divine essence and can only store a level of energy that is bearable in relation to its capacities for channeling and anchoring. The more grounded you are, the more freely the energy will flow within you.

Everything is a question of balance. Imagine a table with only two legs, or one with three legs. Which one is more stable? Because human beings only walk on two legs, in order to balance ourselves it is beneficial for us to equip ourselves with energetic roots, or to create a third leg for ourselves by visualizing an energetic extension of the spine going down into the ground.

What matters is to feel the energy of love, light, and healing penetrate the entire body and firmly anchor in our cells, then to root into the depths of the Earth. Thus we become one with the entire planet, favoring the circulation of purifying energy and concretely incarnating the vibrations of the ascension that we all aspire to.

To help you ground yourself, this simple visualization exercise will allow you to connect to Mother Earth.

Meditation: *"I Am a Tree"*

Comfortably settled in a position that allows me to breathe freely and align my spine properly, I imagine that I am a tall and majestic tree. My body stands as straight and solid as the trunk of a tree, which nothing can disturb.

Powerful roots grow underneath my feet from each of my toes. I imagine that those roots, firmly set into the ground, go deeply into the Earth and fork out into several branches. These spread out far around me to anchor me and draw from the Earth the energies I need to regenerate my whole being. My roots now unite with Mother Earth, who nourishes me with a revitalizing, serene, and beneficial sap.

Moving up along my legs through my veins and arteries, this vivifying sap circulates all around my metabolism. It cleanses and purifies each of my organs, liberating all the existing toxins and blockages. The healing energy flows through all the parts of my body, from the bottom to the top, intensifying in my chest and around my heart. I welcome this soft heat that surrounds, comforts, and appeases me with tranquility.

My arms, like the tree branches, open up to let my feelings and emotions flourish as leaves tossed by the wind. In my head I let thoughts of joy, gratitude, and bliss flower toward this new life that flows into me. My mind empties of any negative thoughts to simply welcome this magical sap that now gives birth to bubbles of love toward me and the universe that lives within.

I feel the sunlight caressing my skin, illuminating my entire being, which now vibrates at the rhythm of the seasons. I myself am light, with my hair like thousands of antennae, seeds harnessing the energy of the cosmos. Internally I know these seeds will give birth at every moment to the fruits of an unlimited inestimable happiness, continually for the rest of my life.

I breathe deeply, feeling fulfilled and overflowing with energy. Very slowly, I get back in contact with the reality that surrounds me, knowing that, from now on, my energetic roots allow me to remain well grounded and to radiate love toward all that lives.

CHAPTER 3

Activating the Ruling Chakra

The Importance of Remaining Centered

Message from April 27, 2005

The years leading to 2012 will sort out those who say "yes" to their full unlimited potential from those who will remain caught up in their fears and resistance. It isn't about judging or condemning anyone. This is an invitation or a challenge to the whole of humanity to awaken to its inner divinity. Although all of us are called on, it is important to respect the will of those who choose not to answer the call.

In the East, various spiritual traditions have been preparing people for the great planetary shift for millennia. In the West, however, more materialistic cultures are dumbfounded by these inner and outer disruptions, known in India as krya or "purification." We need to find a new language and familiar symbols to explain the new realities we are now confronted with.

Let's look at an example that will allow you to better understand the size of the challenge at hand. Take a healthy person who runs one or two miles every day to stay in shape. At times, he or she might resist going out because of the rain or cold. That doesn't matter too much; missing a day won't weaken his muscles. Yet after three or four days, getting back to the track becomes harder. The following day, his body will get cramps. This is normal. It doesn't make him a bad athlete, only an amateur.

Now imagine a runner training for the Olympics, aiming for victory and for the most important prize of her life. Neither rain nor snow will slow her rhythm. She will give herself fully every day, not only to running but to her overall training to make her body a perfect tool that won't let her down when it comes to the crucial moment. She can't afford to train only her legs and increase the capacity of her heart and respiratory system; she must reinforce every single muscle and tendon in her body as well.

In addition to running a few hours a day, she will spend just as much time at the gym working out. She will watch her diet and look after her body. She is perfectly aware that the state of the track on competition day, the weather, and her opponents will not determine the results. She knows that everything depends on her, her will power, her diligence, her perseverance, and more than anything, her ability to remain centered and focused on her objective.

Do you believe she is less subject to temptation than you are? Every day, there are numerous opportunities to distract her from her focus and many reasons to slack off: a pulled muscle, a bad day, a failure at an intermediate-level race. It would be so easy to lose hope and quit. Outer challenges are sometimes even easier to overcome than the discouragement that happens when you don't feel good enough, fast enough, or able enough, the many pretexts that drain motivation, disperse energy, and bring down self-esteem.

Those moments of doubt, fear, and resistance hurt the most and can ruin everything. They make the difference between losing and winning, quitting and persevering. The distinction between the amateur and the professional athlete is played out inside between the simple disciple and the master-to-be, between the human and the divine self.

It is important to ask yourself today, right now, and at every moment of your life: to what degree are you invested in your spiritual approach? Who do you believe yourself to be in those crucial moments before the coming of the new Earth: an amateur sportsman or an athlete of absolute sovereignty?

If you aspire to live in a body of light, how do you treat your physical body, the tool of your energetic ascension? You know your physical body is the temple you have chosen to dedicate to your divine essence. How do you look after it? How do you respond to your essential needs and your personal objectives, by putting all your energy into them, or by allowing yourself to get distracted by things outside yourself?

If our runner is part of a team, she will still be on her own, facing herself at the crucial moment. Even if she has a specific trainer and follows all the recommendations to perfect her style and her performance, everything still plays out inside her. She alone can make all the difference.

Your physical and energetic bodies are sustained by seven main energy centers called chakras. Each chakra relates to a sphere of your existence that sustains and ensures its proper functioning. Whether it be your primary needs (health and hygiene), personal needs (security and achievement), emotional needs (acceptance and freedom), relationship needs (social belonging and affection), creative needs (expression and communication), cognitive needs (intellectual and intuitive matters), or spiritual needs (peace and illumination), in this order from the first to the seventh chakra, none can be denied, ignored, or forgotten.

Stop burying your head in the sand like an ostrich. If you believe you are ready to fully assume your divinity, definitely to enter the fifth dimension with all that you are, ask yourself if there are some areas in your life that still need to blossom and in which investing your time and energy could make all the difference. You are no longer a mere amateur. The time of planetary challenges is coming; will you be ready? Despite everything becoming agitated inside and outside of you, the main thing is to remain centered: not to get distracted, not to give your power away to others, and not to compromise, meaning no longer to give away a part of yourself to others in order to "make them happy."

Assert who you are loud and clear. Take time to tune in, to free yourself of fears and tensions, to respond to your essential needs, and to follow your intuition. Don't give in to the old dualities of good and bad, darkness and light. Be pure love in all that you are, in all that you say, in all that you do. This is the ultimate training. There isn't any place for judgment, limitations, and the negation of who you truly are.

It isn't about elevating yourself but about welcoming your divine lineage in all your cells, in all your chakras, in all your being. Become a professional athlete of love and bliss in all areas of your life. Give it all your might, all your energy, and all your time, and watch wonders unfold before your eyes.

—Bianca Gaia

The Seven Main Chakras and Their Related Spheres of Life

Now that you know the geometric shape of your light cocoon, and you have discovered that you are able to recenter yourself through a simple deep-breathing exercise, you are ready to discover which soul family you belong to in order to activate the ruling chakra that connects you to it.

Let's first define what a chakra is. A chakra is an energy center or "energetic chimney" present in our physical bodies. In the following illustration, the seven luminous circles of different colors at various places in the body are the seven main chakras.

First Chakra: The Root

At the bottom of the image we find the root chakra, located at the level of the perineum and displaying a red color. It is fueled by a healthy response to one's essential needs: taking care of one's body, health, and hygiene; eating well; getting quality sleep; taking time to get in shape or do some physical activity; and taking pleasure in giving oneself a certain level of comfort and material security. Everything that is connected to our survival, our incarnation, and our groundedness depends on this center. In other words, it is about taking the place that is our birthright.

Second Chakra: The Sacral

Next is the sacral chakra, also known as the center of sexual energy. It has a beautiful orange shade and is located about two inches below the navel. Because it is also in this area that the female reproductive organs are located, we often associate it with procreation and sexual pleasure. In fact, it is the seat of self-esteem and of personal and professional self-worth: our fulfillment of the daily routine, our feeling of accomplishment and success at work, the achievement of our objectives, the capacity to give birth and ensure our lineage, etc.

Third Chakra: The Solar Plexus

In bright yellow, the third chakra or solar plexus is located at the base of the sternum. It is the center of emotions and feelings. To maintain our sometimes precarious balance, it is important to learn to openly express our emotions in order to untangle our real feelings from what the intellect might tell itself, to deal with and even eliminate the fears and anxieties that assault us at times, to solve our interpersonal conflicts as they present themselves, to free and heal our wounds from the past, and especially to accept ourselves unconditionally as we are.

The Seven Centers of Vital Energy

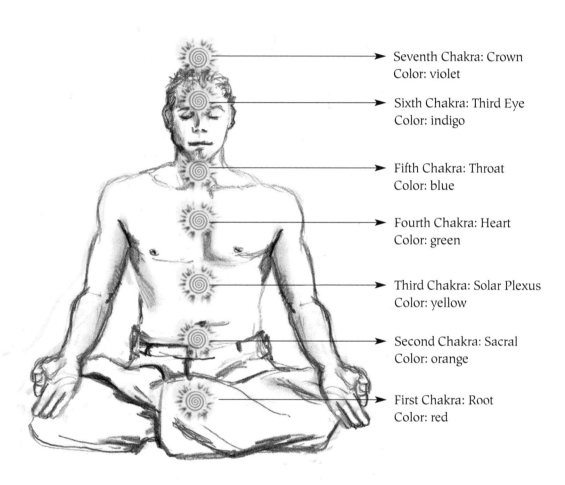

Seventh Chakra: Crown
Color: violet

Sixth Chakra: Third Eye
Color: indigo

Fifth Chakra: Throat
Color: blue

Fourth Chakra: Heart
Color: green

Third Chakra: Solar Plexus
Color: yellow

Second Chakra: Sacral
Color: orange

First Chakra: Root
Color: red

Fourth Chakra: The Heart

The fourth chakra is the heart, located at the level of the physical heart but in the middle of the chest, not on the left. It reveals itself to be a beautiful emerald green. Essentially it is fed by the quality of our interpersonal relationships: the flowering of our affection; our natural generosity; the connections we establish in love, with friends, and on the social level; our ability to express our feelings and to engage in durable and intimate relationships; and the unconditional love we feel toward ourselves and others.

Fifth Chakra: The Throat

The throat chakra, also called "laryngeal," is found at the level of the physical throat, and its color is sky blue. It relates to the expression of our inner truth: our ability to communicate and express ourselves verbally; exploration of our artistic creativity; the practice of leisure and personal growth activities; and respect for our identity, our originality, and our own authenticity.

Sixth Chakra: The Third Eye

The sixth chakra, or third eye, is located above the eyebrows in the middle of the forehead between the eyes and is colored indigo. It carries within itself the vibration of our level of evolution and personal growth. It refers to the moral, human, social, spiritual, and universal aspects of our consciousness: our social status, recognition of our skills and the need to share them with others, the thirst for new and universal knowledge, the opening of our intuition, and our natural and spiritual gifts.

Seventh Chakra: The Crown

Finally, the seventh chakra, the crown, is a kind of purple or violet pointed hat above the head. It is our privileged connection to heaven and to our upper chakras. It represents the spiritual aspect within us: our ability to appreciate and enjoy life; to maintain a good level of inner peace through relaxation, meditation, or prayer; consciousness of being part of a whole; and our facility to let ourselves be guided by God, energy, and our higher self.

Naturally, the colors indicated above are those of the chakras when they are totally open and in perfect harmony. Since I have been working with energy for over fifteen years, I have developed the ability to perceive the colors of auras and chakras. In color analysis, I always sense at least two colors for each of the seven main chakras. Independent of the complementary color of each chakra, it is possible for me to know how open or veiled the chakra is, what blockage prevents it from being fully open, and when this blockage settled in. This allows me to know what may have disturbed or withheld nourishment from any of the chakras. By measuring the percentage of openness of all the chakras, we can evaluate the state of a person's health.

For instance, let's take the case of Julie, evolving in a romantic relationship based on unconditional love in which she feels completely fulfilled. Her heart chakra would then display a shiny emerald green. On the other hand, if the same woman lives in a state of emotional dependency, we will see much more pink at that level. Similarly, an opaque dark olive green will indicate that Julie has been deeply hurt in her life and that her rancor and frustrations affect her capacity to love openly. The list of variations is nearly infinite, for any complementary color can be found in any chakra, making us unique and in constant evolution.

The Ruling Chakra, Gateway of Celestial Energy

For now, it is important to know that the chakras are in fact energetic gates. Some of these gates are directed toward the outside: the more luminous we are, the more in harmony we are, the more our chakras radiate. But it can happen that some energy centers located inside us are weaker and more fragile. Those doors are there to allow us to draw on divine energy so as to find our balance when we have been wounded or when we feel vulnerable in a destabilizing situation.

One of our chakras allows us to reconnect directly to our own soul family (this notion will be further explained in the next chapter, "The Five Great Soul Families"). It is our ruling chakra, the one that is normally the most open when we arrive on Earth. The ruling chakra should be the most radiant at the time of our birth because through it our soul family has given us the push we were missing to get the courage to come back down here.

Through our ruling chakra, we can feel the reassuring presence of those who love us the most, our soul family, the ones who constantly whisper in our ears, "Go on, you can do it. We are here, and we believe in you."

The soul family presents itself as an invisible aid, assisting every incarnated soul in the mission it has given itself. This mission isn't necessarily directly connected to the dimension of the being that is most present within us. Our energetic field is often influenced more by our life experiences and our wounds from the past. However, our ruling chakra remains our favored connection to our soul family, which allows us to rebalance and reinforce the parts of ourselves that feel fragile or that wonder whether they will succeed in accomplishing their individual as well as collective destiny.

The ruling chakra is therefore our direct line to heaven, our hotline or emergency number to dial when we feel powerless, taken aback, or in need of a radical solution here and now.

The most important thing for every one of us, then, is to identify where the phone jack is located within ourselves. Alas, this notion is not taught in schools. Even worse, most individuals on this Earth do not even know they possess this precious connection with the invisible world. Before further exploring the benefits of your ruling chakra, allow yourself to find out which of your energy centers is truly connected to the soul family you have chosen to guide you in this life.

There are various ways to identify your ruling chakra. You can use a pendulum or the dowsing-wand pointer described above and used to measure energy fields, but these methods are not fully reliable, as a chakra that is too open can often alter the readings. You can also use your intuition or simply try to feel the energy by going over your body with your hands, looking for which of the seven centers is really your ruling chakra. Finally, some people, including me and numerous energy healers, possess the ability to remotely sense your aura and can help you identify it.

However, if these suggested methods do not suit you, the most reliable method remains muscle testing, which is used in applied kinesiology. In order to use this technique, you need to get another person to act as the tester.

Exercise: *The Muscle Test*

Procedure: The tester and the person being tested stand next to each other. Ideally, the tester stands behind, so that the person being tested remains concentrated on their feelings and not on the other person.

So as not to influence the results, both people center themselves by taking three deep breaths and making sure they are well grounded.

The tester asks the other person to stretch one arm to the side while maintaining a certain tension and remaining flexible and not rigid. You can try both arms to figure out which one seems to give the best answer or is the most comfortable.

Ask the person being tested to concentrate their attention not on the questions that will be asked but rather on obtaining a precise and adequate result. Free both your minds by breathing deeply together. Visualize that you are both free of reticence and any thoughts that might influence the test results.

Now proceed to the subject's cellular memory, starting by asking the body if it is disposed to answer your questions. If this doesn't work, each participant may also place their thumb and middle finger on the back of their own neck, on the neuropsychological points of disconnection, in the two depressions located under the cervical vertebrae. Those two little bones are found at the base of the skull, and when pressed gently while bringing them closer to each other, will allow you to disconnect from your own unconscious tensions and at the same time cut the energetic connections you might have with the person being tested, which may or may not influence the coming results.

If the result remains negative, drop the exercise and start again at some other time.

For each question, if the muscular tension remains firm and stable, it means that the body is in resonance with the question asked, meaning that it maintains a good relationship to what you are affirming. If, on the contrary, the arm goes down or a kind of slackness is felt, it means the body is in dissonance or that it feels disturbed by the information you are sending it.

For instance, you might ask, "Are you allergic to eggs?" A maintained tension means the body is receptive to eggs. If the arm goes down or the tension weakens, it means the body is disturbed by eggs. In the same way, you might ask, "Do you have prostate cancer?" If the body doesn't suffer from this illness, the arm will remain strong, but if it is present in the body, even latently, the arm will weaken.

It is preferable to start with some questions you already know the answer to in order to familiarize yourself with the muscular resistance of the person being tested, such as, "Is your name John?" or "Is arsenic good for your health?"

Next, go through the chakras one by one, asking the cellular consciousness if this is the ruling chakra of the person being tested at the time of their incarnation in this life. When the tension is significantly maintained, it shows that we have identified the ruling chakra.

Note: If you want to be certain not to influence the subject with your own opinions or theirs with regard to the results obtained, ask the question silently, or alternately write down a few questions on pieces of paper that you fold, mix up, and use one by one by having the person being tested hold them in the hand of the arm used in the test.

Reconnecting with the Best in Ourselves

When we do not know which chakra is our ruling chakra, we have a tendency to connect either to heaven, by asking divine grace to come down on us, or directly to the ground, to let the energy of the planet rise up inside us. The problem is that if there is a leak anywhere, this energy will be lost.

If you are used to connecting to celestial energies through the crown chakra in the hope of recharging your batteries, but a leak exists in you, for example at the solar plexus level, you may have the feeling of being constantly tired and that you never succeed, because the energy does not feed the lower two chakras; it has gotten lost on the way.

It could therefore happen that your ruling chakra remains veiled during nearly all of your existence. Why would this be so? Let's take the example of Gerard, a noble and proud soul who undertook the mission of showing his terrestrial family the possibility of becoming the creator of one's own life by being an artist and remaining in the light of being while also fulfilled and radiant. This charming child found himself in an intellectual family that valued only mental aspects and hard work and for whom life could be summed up in one sentence: one needs to work hard to make a living. Gerard wanted to show them that it was possible to live differently and to make other choices, but he became broken, shattered, cut off from himself. While growing up, this wonderful soul had no choice but to protect himself as best as he could, no longer to be exposed to the wrath of his parents, who didn't want to admit any part of his personal utopian longings. An opaque veil formed over his ruling chakra, settling in a subtle but permanent way.

We may have more than one veiled chakra; sometimes even all of them are veiled. This is the situation, for instance, of autistic children, for whom all the chakras are blocked except the seventh or crown chakra. They settle for using their only remaining chakra to get out of their bodies and escape toward kinder dimensions. They are not able to inhabit their physical bodies, as it would be like living in a house without windows.

Some people may have one or several chakras veiled, but reconnecting to their soul family helps realign not only the ruling chakra but also opens and frees all the others.

What you must remember is that no matter what you have been through, suffered, or been subjected to, your ruling chakra has remained intact. It isn't damaged, destroyed, or unusable, but simply veiled. Reconnecting to your soul family means counting on it again to fight for you so that you no longer have to do it all by yourself.

When we appeal to our soul family, it quickly comes to meet us, bringing us all the energy we need to revitalize ourselves through our ruling chakra to accompany and support us in the development of our lives.

Some will easily connect with their soul families. Others, because of unfortunate experiences, may have cut themselves off from their inner Christic dimension. The connection is no longer established, and consequently their ruling chakra has become veiled. When this is the case, people are at lose ends, not knowing how to solve the problems they are faced with or how to sort out the endless torments that come to trouble them.

To reverse the tide, you can do the following exercise: imagine that your ruling chakra is like the large hose of a vacuum cleaner. Through that hose, you suck all the necessary energy to fill everything that needs to be fed, nourished, and reinforced inside you. This exercise will allow you to rebalance yourself while filling the voids that may exist in any dimension of your being.

The more connected you are to your soul family, the more solid and balanced your energy is. The more you neglect certain aspects of yourself, the more you will see deficiencies, darkness, and weaknesses settle inside you. You only have to ask for help for your soul family to rush to you. It is always there, not only behind you to inspire, enlighten, and guide you, but also in front of you to open the way for you and remove potential pitfalls.

Simply by sensitizing yourself to the presence of your ruling chakra and visualizing it feeding and regenerating your entire being, the door that has long been open outwardly instantly opens inwardly, finally allowing you to receive the beneficial and loving energy of your soul family.

This family is made up of your guardian angels and your guides, as well as all those on Earth who are on the same vibrations as you. It also includes some of the ascended masters who, in certain specific circumstances, will choose to work from a specific soul family. Pythagoras, for instance, was a great mathematical visionary connected to the universal source through his third eye, therefore at the level of thought. He has left traces of his genius throughout history, and his energy is still present among us, inspiring numerous scientists and researchers across the world.

Long before our incarnation, the choice of our soul family is made according to the areas in which we most need to be secured. Before incarnating, we already possess broad knowledge, skills, and wisdom that we aspire to transmit around us in the best way possible. But there is always a small amount of worry that we will fail at it, and as a result we associate with the soul family that will allow us to consolidate our inner flaws to allow us to go forward.

What we perceive of a human being is usually only what we see of them: the material aspect or physical body. Yet to think that we are limited to the physical realm alone would be the same as thinking that an iceberg is limited to what we see of it, the emerging tip. We are much more than our physical dimension. We also need to consider our emotional, intellectual, Christic, and other aspects present within us. Whenever you go forward, you are supported by your soul family, by the ninety percent of you that exists below the waterline; but you feel alone because you only see the ten percent that sticks out. When you reconnect to your soul family, you then allow yourself to visualize, even briefly, the ninety percent that you don't usually see but that is here nonetheless, supporting, accompanying, and pushing you forward.

Our ultimate goal remains to be aligned with all the soul families, reaching the hundred percent inside ourselves. People who have mastered all the parts of themselves will give and receive with all their being. We can then call them "realized beings." It is rare, however, to encounter them here, for the ascended masters rarely remain on the physical plane, although they sometimes come back to pay Earth a visit.

The reason most of us don't manage to maintain this perfect balance in ourselves is that there is still a part of us, even if it is a tiny part, that scares us and that we tend to hide from others as well as from ourselves. We either do everything to go unnoticed, or we surround ourselves with fat to protect ourselves. We either develop powerful mental abilities to prevent anyone from destabilizing us, or we choose to strike first before being attacked. No matter what method we use to escape from who we really are, the motive always remains the same: we are afraid of this dark side that could be our downfall.

Thus the shield we used to protect ourselves against the supposed hostile outer world only ends up imprisoning our own light. When we ask our soul family for help, we replace the shield that previously acted as our illusory protection with a true light cocoon. The masks we wore to feel recognized and socially accepted become useless. We find our true recognition of ourselves in the reconnection to who we really are: a full member of one of the five great soul families, all shining bright.

Meditation: *Activating the Ruling Chakra*

I comfortably settle in a position that allows me to breathe freely and deeply into my abdomen. I free my mind from all the thoughts that could distract me or scatter my luminous energy. Then I take the time to visualize all the muscles of my body relaxing, and all the recently accumulated tensions magically vanish.

I then take a strong breath in while visualizing the air entering my lungs, purifying and eliminating all the toxins stored in my body. With each new breath out, I expel all of the emotional residue that may have afflicted me or led me astray from my quest for daily happiness.

When I feel good, calm, and relaxed, so that I feel a certain lightness settling in all my being, I focus my attention on my ruling chakra, connecting me to my soul family at the time of my incarnation in this life.

I visualize this energy center as a door that now opens inwardly, to welcome inside of me a majestic beam of light displaying the color of my ruling chakra. Like a soft summer breeze, warm and caressing, the energy of light penetrates me, passing through this unique and privileged door, thus coming to nourish my ruling chakra, deeply purifying and revitalizing it.

My thirst for light and love turns my chakra into the hose of a vacuum cleaner, absorbing all the energy it can to reestablish the good functioning of this precious vital center.

The light energy spreads inside me and floods all of my being. Every cell, every organ, every part of my body is submerged in emotions of joy and bliss, resulting in an absolute well-being in all of my body and creating a harmonious plenitude in all the recesses of my soul.

During this moment of pure happiness and total felicity, I feel surrounded by friendly and reassuring presences that come to me to surround me with love and transfer to me their greetings filled with tenderness and love.

My soul family vividly celebrates this admirable reunion, so long awaited. I feel surrounded, cuddled, protected, draped in wonderful angel wings, loving and caressing, coming to me to cradle my soul and comfort my child's heart.

I know that I am part of this beautiful and broad family of luminous entities, that I am one of them and that all of them recognize me as such: a spiritual brother or sister united with them through the soul and animated by the same divine essence.

I also know that as of now, I will never be alone again. From now on, every time I feel in need, my guardian angels, my spirit guides, and my protectors—all the members of my real universal family—are awaiting me behind the door of my ruling chakra.

I simply have to open this portal of light a little for all the love they have for me to flow inside me and contribute to reinvigorating my whole being. The veil covering this chakra has disappeared for good, and I feel reconnected to my original family, those who will help me remember who I really am: a divine being, perfect, harmonious, and balanced here and now and for eternity.

CHAPTER 4

The Five Great Soul Families

A Soul's Journey in the Hereafter

Message from November 13, 2006

Celeste was an evolved soul. Therefore when she quit the Earth, leaving behind a body ravaged by illness, she was looking forward at last to meeting up with the people she had loved so much. Her loved ones welcomed her warmly and surrounded her with a touching effusion of tenderness. She was then taken to the Jade Temple in order to appear in front of the Sages' assembly.

Celeste was thrilled at the thought of finally meeting her guardian angels and guides, the brothers and sisters of light who had accompanied her on that not-so-easy most recent existence of hers. For a long while, she was invited by her soul family to make an assessment of her life as a conscious woman in a so-called "Western" society at the dawn of the second millennium, from which it was said a new world would emerge.

Reflections on a Lifetime

The lighthearted soul gave herself lots of time to think about her past evolution. She reviewed her failures as well as her achievements, the exploits she was proud of and those she was less proud of. She thought of all the people she had encountered on her life's long road: those who had "deserved" her attention and the others to whom she had refused her love, her help, or even a simple look.

There were some sad moments, and others filled with beatitude. Some experiences were more than beneficial to her, even if they had at first taken the shape of problems or difficulties, for Celeste had managed to draw the right lessons of life from them, and this had helped her until the end of her days. Other situations, on the other hand, were more conflicting, and because she couldn't figure out their meaning, they had a tendency to repeat themselves over the years. For instance, because Celeste had some difficulty in asserting herself and taking her due place, she regularly got snubbed by people who wouldn't hesitate to impose on her or even abuse her natural goodness.

Hating to raise her voice or vigorously to stand up for her rights, Celeste's personality was often confronted with power struggles between parents and children, teachers and pupils, and employers and employees. This soft and jolly woman had a tendency to shy away from oppressing situations and to run from restrictive obligations. In all circumstances she avoided confrontation, preferring to devote herself to others, even if it meant sacrificing herself or forgetting her own needs.

The consequence was that many of her dreams never came true. Many projects dear to her heart were put aside and forgotten. Celeste's generosity toward those close to her led her to nearly always take a backseat and faithfully to serve her entourage. When she wasn't lending money to her brother, who never gave her a penny back, her children were asking her to look after their own offspring, or the neighbors from the area would lead her into doing many hours of charity work per week.

Celeste never complained; quite the contrary, she was happy to serve and to feel appreciated. She couldn't see that she was deriving her sense of self-worth and her vital energy from being indispensable. The only times she regretted being that way were when she in turn needed help or support and then everyone around her was too busy to reciprocate.

Celeste's life had ended in a nursing home for elderly people, for the sick and weak but mostly for the left behind, the lonely and isolated. Yet in her great kindness, Celeste didn't hold a grudge against anyone. She understood that her loved ones were busy, caught up in the needs of this ever-moving capitalist society. There had been some moments of sadness and listlessness, but generally speaking the elderly woman wouldn't let herself drift into gloominess or nostalgia.

During those last years, stuck in a wheelchair, Celeste had had plenty of time to reflect on her evolution and had come to the conclusion that the only moment that matters is the present one. "We can't do anything to change the past, and whatever we might say, we can never control the future," she would tell herself. Throughout the years she had always reaped what she had sown. She had been treated the way she had treated herself: she was being neglected the way she had neglected herself through all those decades.

But Celeste wasn't bitter. She had had a good husband, healthy children, and a dozen grandchildren who had filled her with happiness. She had lived in relative comfort and had granted herself some little moments of gentleness to allow her creative side to blossom through leisure activities such as handicrafts and interior design. More so, reading had opened her mind to a world of infinite possibilities and had made her aware of who she was and what she could bring the world with her luminous presence alone.

Her final breath was filled not with fear but with peace and contentment. This explains why she obediently allowed herself to be guided by the angels through the light tunnel leading to this wonderful crystalline dimension, where the sun always shines and where all thoughts instantly manifest.

The Encounter with the Soul Families

Once her life's review was over, Celeste benefited from a well-deserved break. This allowed her to get used to her new existence as a light being. She enjoyed the absolute well-being of her energetic body, free of heaviness and both ageless and pain-free. At first she would often think of those left behind, but soon she only turned to those dear to her in her old life when they thought of her or invoked her in their prayers.

She had numerous pleasant encounters and quickly built some new and fulfilling friendships, for they were based on honesty and authenticity in all circumstances. At times her old personality would resurface; Celeste would then look for a way to be "useful." But because everyone could create at will whatever was needed, this generous soul continuously ended up back at herself.

Bit by bit, she observed several colors emanating from the people she would sometimes meet. Some rather white auras would suddenly display hues of orange, green, blue, or violet when people would gather. When she questioned her accompanying guide, Michra, about it, he explained that when souls are getting ready to incarnate again, they feel attracted to a specific soul family. This is what allows them to choose the most beneficial existence for them as well as for all the people they will meet on their way. He added that each soul family emits a different color according to the vibration that characterizes it.

Celeste was fascinated. At first she felt intrigued by a group of souls radiating a beautiful incandescent emerald green. "Green is the energy of the heart," she told herself. "It is normal that I feel at ease with this soul family, as I probably was one of them in my previous life." Among themselves, these luminous souls were exchanging some powerful vibrations of love that were transmitted to the whole environment, making the flowers blossom in the fields and helping the growth of the fruit trees. Their excess of energy even succeeded in going through the interdimensional veil to spread on Earth and illuminate the willing souls. At that moment the luminous rays would turn into a beautiful golden yellow color, and the light beings would be set ablaze like dozens of dazzling suns. Celeste felt amazed and fulfilled: she was really in fusion with the best in herself.

However, after attending the Artisans of Peace family ritual of creative love several times, Celeste felt the need to explore other light circles. She got close to the Visionaries, those beings whose upper bodies are constantly surrounded by a sky-blue or indigo halo. This soul family regrouped thinkers, scientists, inventors, and philosophers constantly in search of original ways to transform and better the terrestrial plane. The most innovative thoughts were nourished, cultivated, and improved by the group until reaching a considerable vibratory level, then to be transmitted mentally and perceived telepathically by the most powerful minds of humanity.

Although she was impressed by so many astute ideas and fabulous technological tools conceived by the blue beings, Celeste felt that her natural dynamism was much better expressed in doing rather than in thinking. So she went looking for another, more energizing group of souls.

Illuminated by the Violet Flame

Approaching a circle of luminous consciousnesses in the middle of which danced a violet flame, Celeste sensed a bubbly feeling coming over her. Who were those people? What were they doing around this fire, vibrating with so much intensity and mystery?

At the heart of this burning brazier, purple smoke formed images animated with a life of their own. They would display agitated human beings breaking up in all directions. Many scenes appeared one after another, coming from all four corners of the Earth. The blazing flames allowed her to see what was happening on Earth in real time.

Absorbed in their contemplation, the light beings were emanating an indescribable sense of peace and serenity. Celeste understood that they were applying themselves to transmit a liberation wave of deep healing to the whole of humanity. Through this prodigious transformation energy, some consciousnesses would awaken and briefly get a taste of divine illumination. Some complete metamorphoses would take place, and cellular transmutations would operate through the violet flame, which poured abundantly onto the open minds and souls with their thirst for light.

Celeste was speechless. Her heart jumped in her chest. She felt the calling of her soul like a commanding cry. An irresistible pull urged her to move even closer: This is what I want to be, *she thought.* I want to be part of this family of healers, therapists, and teachers with extraordinary and nearly magical powers.

"There isn't anything magical in the ritual of the Facilitators family," her friend Michra explained. "They simply make themselves available to the universal energy, which they channel through their own bodies, amplifying and concentrating it according to the needs of the people who ask them for help. Their only goal is to help terrestrial souls to open their consciousness and remember who they really are: light beings, divine and sovereign, just like us."

"How can I join the Facilitators family?" Celeste asked excitedly.

"You will need to cultivate the violet energy in yourself first, and then externalize it and master it with precision," he answered casually. "Then we will go to see the Sages' council to ask them for their blessing."

Celeste applied herself to grow the violet flame in all of her being, from the top of her head to beneath her feet. She then practiced spreading her energy outside the limits of her body, soon shining a violet light on everything around her that amused Michra and her other new friends. Soon Celeste was able to join the group and participate in the rituals of the light circle. She was expecting her guide to take her to meet the Sages, but he remained at a distance, his own energy field maintaining an orange, not violet, hue.

Celeste could feel that Michra was becoming more distant from her, but she was so excited by her supranatural powers and the connections she was making with the violet beings that she didn't really mind. She sincerely believed she was part of the Facilitators family and aspired with all her being to share the awakening light, not only in the higher dimensions but on Earth, in her own physical body, during a coming incarnation.

"Humanity needs to awaken," she would tell anyone who cared to listen. But as long as there are suffering and conflicts on Earth, people will only have access to a small part of their divine consciousness. The violet flame heals, alleviates, cures, and illuminates souls. Isn't that miraculous? Could there be any nobler mission in life? What a privilege to be part of the Facilitators family."

The Sages' Council

Most of the light beings were indulgent toward the violet newcomer with her out-going and sparkling tendencies. Some, however, felt the need to clarify their own situation: "The Artisans of Peace celebrate life in all its forms and watch over every-thing in nature, the fauna as well as the flora. They are the ones who give birth to respect and love in the hearts of human beings. The yellow and the green in their energy contribute to balancing human psychological and emotional dimensions. The Artisans inspire artists and introduce beauty, estheticism, and purity in this world of darkness and chaos. Isn't that work just as important?

Knowing that she had been part of the Artisans of Peace family during her pre-vious incarnation, Celeste had no other choice than to agree. She could understand the Visionaries' point of view as well when they pointed out to her that "had it not been for the knowledge accumulated through the centuries and for the inventions created to ease people's lives, such as electricity and running water, most civiliza-tions would have remained in a state of barbarian savagery. Humanity's evolution goes through information, communications, and cutting-edge technology. See how quickly the brain of the Homo sapiens has developed since they learned to use their five senses and their intelligence! In fact, even the sixth sense, intuition and extrasen-sorial perception, comes from a gland located in the frontal lobe—the pituitary. We can't neglect the contributions of our soul family to planetary evolution and the transformation process."

It sometimes happened that the blue being who had just spoken got carried away verbally. He would have loved to rally the entire celestial population to his cause. A fervent speaker, he always succeeded in attracting the crowds and convincing sev-eral souls to join his group. Celeste admired the ardor and the passion of this man but remained imperturbable with regard to her choices: she would be a Facilitator or nothing.

As for Michra, he remained resolutely silent, but this time his aura displayed scarlet red, as if all of his being were boiling inside. Celeste approached him cautiously, wondering if he was also going to lecture her or make a scene. Her guide simply led her toward the Jade Temple without saying a word.

In the council's large room, the seats were fully packed. There were some Facilitators, Visionaries, and Artisans of Peace, as well as some typically orange and red beings who were no doubt part of Michra's family. Holding court in the middle of the majestic compound were the Sages, the timeless souls glowing in multiple colors and dressed in bright gold clothing. They fixed their gaze, filled with goodness and serenity, on Celeste.

A masculine soul started to speak and announced in an eloquent and solemn tone, "The newcomer is ready to be heard by the members of the council and to announce her demands regarding her next incarnation in the third dimension."

Celeste, intimidated by the large crowd surrounding her, whispered, "I would like to go back to Earth as a representative of the Facilitators family, to transmit the violet transmutation flame to human beings, thereby to allow them to awaken to their own inner divinity. If the council so pleases."

The spokesperson of the Sages stood up again and signaled for Michra to approach. "Why does this young soul claim to be of a family other than your own when we personally entrusted her to you?" he asked the humble guide.

"She never wished to get close to my people, nor to our circle of light," said Michra.

"And why is that?" the Sage asked Celeste, who by now was shaking like a leaf. (Had she sinned? Would she be punished?) "Why is that so?" the council's representative insisted in a steady voice.

"I . . . I don't know," Celeste stammered.

The Incarnation Contract

The Sage, unwavering, continued, "Could it be because the Builders family represents everything you have spent your past existence running away from, o truth seeker? Don't the red and orange represent the colors of the incarnation, of *self-affirmation and carnal pleasure, so intolerable to your virtuous eyes? Are you afraid of falling into the lower depths of the human vicissitudes if you get closer to those scarlet souls?"*

Celeste, stunned, simply shook her head.

"Know, profane soul, that without this devoted and assiduous soul family, there would be nothing left on this planet so dear to you. They are the souls who have kept humanity alive through procreating and repopulating the Earth despite the surrounding dangers and the various climatic changes. They have encouraged humans to explore new continents and have largely contributed to making con-structive connections between the various populations of the world. Without their dynamism, their strength, and their constant courage, the structure of your fellow human beings' bodies would have weakened over the years, and so your state of health, putting the existence of the race itself at risk."

"I never mentioned any of that to her," Michra interrupted tactfully. "She knows nothing about our circles of fire, the intense moments when we apply ourselves to inspire determination and perseverance in the ruling souls of every collectivity, for them to maintain calm and order among the masses and in every home. She hasn't been initiated to our sacred rituals created to support the pacifiers in their approach to planetary reconciliation, nor the founders in their enterprise to construct the new world. She hasn't even tasted the power of manifestation and materialization of matter from the original substances of the source. Celeste chose the violet flame rather than the red sun, and I humbly preferred to respect her choice."

Everyone could read the sadness and the disappointment in Michra's eyes. Celeste felt bad for never having attempted to know more about the one who had accom-panied her without complaint in all of her mystical explorations. She opened her mouth to apologize, but was interrupted by the Sage speaking to her directly:

"Dear child of light, you haven't understood that you primarily need to be in balance within yourself to truly help others. We can only give what we truly pos-sess. You have opened your heart, your soul, and your consciousness, but what about the rest of you? You will need to learn to recognize and appreciate yourself as you are—not just for what you do—to truly be able to transmit the Facilitators' awakening flame. You need to build your inner strength, your audacity, your

tenacity, and your endurance if you want to bring the light in the dark ages of this chaotic civilization of yours.

"This is why I invite you to make an incarnation contract with the Builders family before associating with the Facilitators. While the latter will pour out the violet flame of transmutation on you, the former will first give you the resistance and the constancy you need to ground this energy in your every cell. You will be invited to teach respect and tolerance to parents who unfortunately will have succumbed to the need to appease their fears by the use of force, control, and even physical violence.

"From the start, at the heart of the human family that will welcome you, you will be confronted with the need to assert yourself vigorously and will have to impose your will in order for your moral as well as physical integrity to be respected. Several times, you will be tempted to drop everything, and you might even want to permanently quit this ungrateful universe where one person's pain is another's pleasure. But if you remain firm and don't let yourself be sullied by the venal brutality of some of your peers, if you know how to find light even in the most obscure recesses of their personalities, then you will be able to awaken their consciousness to the divine energy in themselves. This is when you will effectively become a Facilitator: a healer and a reformer of consciousness.

"By maintaining the balance and harmony within you, in all the dimensions of your being, you will unify your soul, your mind, and your consciousness at the heart of the frontiers of your three-dimensional body. You will then manifest your sovereign plenitude in matter, graciously unfolding your unlimited supernatural gifts, and will fully incarnate your cocreative divine quintessence so as to participate actively in the united effort of the five great soul families to create a better world, the terrestrial and celestial paradise we all aspire to."

The Return

As the Sage talked, Celeste was seeing her future life unfold before her eyes. She knew it was an optimistic vision of the materialization potential stored in her entire being. She also knew that she could count on the energetic support of her new soul family, the Builders, to nourish her quest and recharge her batteries every time she needed it. She was hoping to remember consciously the circles of light where all the souls of the same family were working at regenerating the subtle bodies of their terrestrial brothers and sisters and at accompanying their "ambassadors" in their incarnation contracts as well as in their personal and planetary life missions.

It was therefore with full knowledge of the facts that Celeste returned to Earth, supported first by the energy of the Builders, and then by that of the Facilitators. She later developed her artistic talents through writing, naturally letting herself be inspired by the Artisans of Peace family, and became an outstanding communicator, thus joining the cause of the Visionaries. All those around her, however, could only see in her the serenity and the natural grace of the Sages family.

—*Bianca Gaia*

Recognizing Yourself in One or More Soul Families

Did you recognize yourself in Celeste's story? Surely some elements of the story line have allowed you to identify which soul family you belong to or have previously belonged to, either in your present existence or in a past life.

Very often we have a tendency to do what Celeste did and choose to recognize in ourselves the aspects that are valued and accepted by our circle. We put our strengths forward, acting in the areas most familiar to us but at times neglecting some of our dimensions, even though they are well and truly present in us, not to mention essential to our blossoming and overall balance.

We have learned to adopt winning attitudes, to shape our personality according to what those close to us expect from us. During this time, the unique and exceptional being that lies sleeping within us never sees the light of day where at last it could shine brightly, and who knows, perhaps even change the face of the world.

Could it be that the parts of you that appear as "darkness" are in fact some original qualities only aspiring to be welcomed, accepted, and integrated within you?

From which soul family would you like to receive a particular helping hand in order to develop certain abilities that you have apparently been lacking until now? Are these qualities and talents truly missing from your personality, or have they been temporarily put on hold so as not to displease the environment you belong to?

The Five Great Soul Families

RULING CHAKRA	SOUL FAMILY	INCARNATION CONTRACT
Root/Red Sacral/Orange	**Builders** △	Those who lead the way, break free of the past, and help create and build the new world
Solar Plexus/ Yellow Heart/Green	**Artisans** ◇	Those who celebrate life by investing themselves with passion in everything; they believe in charity, causes, artistic creation, etc.
Throat/Blue Third Eye/ Indigo	**Visionaries** ▽	Those who help human evolution through knowledge, communications, and scientific discoveries
Crown/Violet	**Facilitators** ▢	Those who bring in the light and help raise human consciousness through healing, teaching, coaching, and spiritual guidance
All Chakras	**Sages**	Those who radiate love, joy, and light no matter where they are or what they are doing; they are simply showing us how to be who we truly are

Do you remember what job you dreamed of doing back in childhood? What your aspirations were for the future at the end of your teenage years? What about those ambitions and personal projects that you keep postponing, unable to dedicate even a minimal amount of time in a week to do something good for yourself and to face yourself?

Can you establish a connection between your ruling chakra, the one you identified in the previous chapter, and the related soul family as it is described in the following chart? Moreover, could this soul family coincidentally represent the part of you that most needs to be consolidated or to emerge in the full light of day?

First and Second Chakras: The Builders Family

If the ruling chakra you have identified as yours turns out to be either the first (root or red) or the second (sacral or orange), you are part of the great Builders family: the ones who lead the way, break free of the past, and help build the new world. They have chosen to incarnate in a human family with a great need to be "shaken." From an early age, they will attempt to demonstrate to their fathers, mothers, brothers, sisters, and even cousins that it is possible to open up to choices other than the restrictive, demeaning, or destructive ones inherited from generation to generation.

Generally speaking, just like Celeste in "A Soul's Journey in the Hereafter," those who choose to associate themselves with the Builders family in order to complete their incarnation contract need to learn to affirm themselves, stand up for themselves, and play a leading role in family, social, territorial, and planetary changes. It is in order to develop their courage, their determination, and their pioneer spirit that they deliberately choose to come to the world in a terrestrial family with rather heavy transgenerational baggage. From an early age, they put everything in place to attempt to neutralize the malfunctioning of this familial lineage so as to help themselves break from the past and rebuild on renewed foundations.

Their biggest strength is to be connected to the Earth. Grounding is easy for them, they enjoy an unfailing dynamism, and their vital force is out of the ordinary. Even if at times they feel some reluctance to truly incarnate, they are gifted with an extraordinary capacity to materialize abundance, and they draw to themselves a bit more each day the perfect situations in which to experience their predisposition to be businesspeople.

Third and Fourth Chakras: The Artisans Family

The following soul family is the Artisans, also called the Artisans of Peace, because more than anything they aspire to live in a world of harmony and constant felicity. Their ruling chakra is identified as either the third (solar plexus or yellow) or the fourth (heart or green). Their incarnation contract consists of celebrating life by investing themselves with passion in everything they believe in: charity, causes, artistic creation, and so on.

They are generous and caring beings who need to learn to get more involved and to develop the personal power of creating their lives, for in past lives they have often been scared to reveal themselves or to open up to others. Just like Gerard in the example used in the last chapter ("Activating the Ruling Chakra"), they often choose to be part of a human family in which the predominant values will be essentially material or intellectual in order to bring to those close to them a different, more lighthearted vision of three-dimensional reality.

They are usually gifted with an extreme sensitivity and an intensely artistic nature, along with everything that entails: overflowing creativity, excessive emotionality, mood swings, disturbing originality, esthetic quests, over-the-top perfectionism; and evidently they are always big-hearted. They will thus have much more facility in giving rather than in receiving, in doing rather than in being. Everything within them simply aspires to be loved, cuddled, reassured, and comforted. Their greatest challenge remains helping their inner child to grow in stability as well as in wisdom.

Fifth and Sixth Chakras: The Visionaries Family

The Visionaries have the ability to connect to their soul family through the fifth (throat or sky blue) or the sixth (third-eye or indigo) chakras. They are called "visionary" because their priority in this life is to aid the evolution of humanity through the transmission of scientific or universal knowledge via communications (the media, computers, or other means) or the creation of pertinent technological innovations (inventions, scientific discoveries, quantum research, and so on).

Their biggest strength, naturally, is an overdeveloped intellect. They possess an incredible analytical capacity matched only by their exceptional reasoning faculties. While they are known for their good judgment and discerning nature, it is nevertheless their integrity, frankness, and authenticity that make them remarkable beings. When they learn to listen to their intuition, they become geniuses like Albert Einstein or Leonardo da Vinci, who enlightened their contemporaries with their important discoveries.

Seventh Chakra: The Facilitators Family

The Facilitators family consists of those who endeavor to bring to Earth the divine light to heal others through traditional, natural, or energetic medicine by exploring their psychic gifts—clairvoyance, clairaudience, mediumship—or else by offering their fellow human beings spiritual teachings or personalized accompaniment like coaching and spiritual guidance.

They aspire to awaken the human consciousnesses in order to help people integrate the spiritual dimension of their being. Because their ruling chakra is the seventh (crown or violet), they seem constantly connected to the higher dimensions, with the feeling of always living with one foot "on the other side." Therefore they sometimes feel some difficulties incarnating within the limitations of a physical body, and the material world often seems quite futile to them.

On the other hand, Facilitators have most probably been considered mystics, "crazy," or heretical during their past lives, and thus they fear being tortured, burned, or crucified once again by populist prosecution. Knowing that we have already entered the golden age of our civilization, at the time of their present incarnation they were aware that there was nothing to fear in that regard; it is therefore in their interest to divulge their profound nature in order to encourage the emergence of the divine spark present in us all, for the much-awaited coming of the new world.

All Chakras Aligned: The Sages Family

Finally, the Sages are those who have gone through all the previous soul families and succeeded in aligning and integrating all the dimensions of their being. They have understood that it is no longer necessary to work hard on themselves, nor to try constantly to evolve, for they are and always have been children of God, accomplished and sovereign.

This is why they radiate love, joy, and light no matter where they are or what they are doing. They are simply applying themselves as a living example for others. For the most part they are realized beings who come back to Earth to accompany humanity on the way to ascension, or they are pure and simple souls who have just finished their terrestrial journey but who haven't yet left the three-dimensional plane.

The Sages are easily distinguished from ordinary mortals because they emit a powerful luminous energy and elevate souls by their radiant, attentive, and serene presence alone. They live continuously in the present moment and remain permanently at the service of their higher selves. Their ultimate challenge can be in managing to recognize themselves as such, for in their great humility they will tend to minimize their primacy and reject their skills.

Note: there isn't necessarily a link between the symbol associated with your soul family and the usual shape of your energy field or light cocoon. The former reveals your incarnation contract as a soul, and the latter is influenced by your ego or dominant personality.

The Incarnation Contract

It is important to mention that even if you have never come into contact with your soul family before, or you believe that you haven't yet succeeded in fulfilling the objectives you gave yourself in accepting your incarnation contract, it is never too late to reactivate within you the qualities and virtues of your real soul family.

Even if your original family hasn't recognized or welcomed the Builder, Artisan of Peace, Visionary, Facilitator, or Sage in you, you now hold the secret to regularly reconnect with your own soul family through your ruling chakra. By activating this luminous portal daily, you can benefit from all the help and support you need to discover who you really are, and thus reintegrate one or many of the dimensions of your being that until today may have remained latent or asleep deep within.

Your soul family watches over you. This has always been so, ever since you were born. As a child you could probably feel this loving and reassuring presence that accompanied you. However, the three-dimensional density you progressively became caught up in quickly weakened this privileged link with the hereafter. Alternately, your parents were amused at seeing you communicate with an invisible friend, only later to denigrate these "childish fantasies" by affirming that you were too old to have an "imaginary" companion.

By this very act, they contributed to cutting you off from your true nature. When the hazards of life thus turned you away from your engagement toward yourself, you ended up rallying with the surrounding family values and social norms.

Choosing to adopt more "reasonable" and acceptable attitudes, according to the criteria of the authority figures present in the milieu where they grow up, some people then come to seriously alter their personalities, even losing their own identity by succeeding in totally smothering the fire of passion that once burned inside them.

Take the example of one of my friends, Joseph, who has a base (root or red) ruling chakra. When he was very young he had a tendency to contest everything and frequently to question the established rules and his father's arbitrary whims. His mother quickly brought him back into line by telling him that not only did he owe his father respect, but it was especially wrong to confront an adult, especially an elder and your progenitor. She thereby drained all the ardor and self-confidence from her child, manipulating him and causing guilt to rise within him.

From that moment on, Joseph applied himself in any way he could to prove to his father that he was a good guy, that he could accomplish countless feats, and that he would succeed in life even more than his father had. He involved himself exclusively in large-scale projects, neglecting to look after himself or to spend time with his own family. Because he never accepted the Builder within, he wasn't able to capitalize on the gifts of materialization from his soul family to do well and build a comfortable life for himself.

As for Mireille, she was born into a dysfunctional family where she was confronted with countless forms of suffering, including extreme poverty, physical violence, and sexual abuse at the hands of relatives. Even though her ruling chakra was the second (sacral or orange) chakra, she ended up succumbing to the pressure she was submitted to, failing to maintain her natural enthusiasm that would have allowed her to influence those around her positively. The deprivations she endured temporarily blinded her to the meaning of her life. After lengthy therapy, Mireille succeeded in handing back to her parents the heavy burden that belonged to them. She thus managed to reclaim her freedom and finally reclaimed her joie de vivre.

No matter what soul family you come from, you will no doubt find, at some time or another on your path, people who will try to break you, make you conform, or get you back in step.

I discovered I was different from others—a Facilitator—at the age of seven, during my first year in primary school, when my teacher started talking about God as a big bearded man seated on a cloud and judging and condemning our every doing. I enjoyed a specific connection to the invisible world, so I couldn't help but share with her my perspective on the subject, perceiving God as an invisible energy current, intense and palpable at once, resembling more the electromagnetic power emitted by a nuclear reactor. You can imagine the consternation of my poor parents when they were called in by the principal to discuss my discipline problem and religious-belief issues.

Traumatizing experiences like this take us away from what we have come into this life to accomplish. However, the essence of our incarnation contract itself lies in managing to overcome those difficulties to firm up the vulnerable aspects of our personality, dissolve the illusions of fragility we maintain about ourselves, and once and for all balance the five energetic dimensions within us.

A metal chain is only as strong as its weakest link, and so it is for our luminous radiance: the parts we consider to be the darkest, that we imagine to be tainted with negativity, are the ones that prevent us from recognizing the wonderful being that we are. The fragments of us that we have forgotten, neglected, or denied are what constitute the real obstacle within us to the ascension process.

The Soul's Mission

By exploring the qualities and virtues specific to each of the five great soul families, you will surely recognize within you some affinities with several of them. This is completely normal, as many parts of you are already well aligned and integrated.

Are you perhaps already part of the Builders, Artisans of Peace, Visionaries, Facilitators, or even Sages families? Have you perhaps opted into some life choices that point you toward a specific soul mission that makes you vibrate?

You can take this opportunity to check whether you already possess the qualities and virtues of the soul family corresponding to the ambitions of your soul. To do so, simply identify in the third column of the chart below the "life choice" that most appeals to you, and verify the presence of the distinctive competencies of the related soul family in the baggage of your incarnation.

Knowing that you won't be able to fully devote yourself to your ideal vocation until you have managed to welcome and accept all the aspects of your personality, it is important to focus your attention on the qualities and virtues of the members of the soul family to which you are now connected through your ruling chakra. They are essential to balancing and strengthening the weakest or most fragile links in your constitution.

In order to help you actualize these specific characteristics in your life, the universe will certainly tend to send you challenges relative to your resistance so that you may discover unsuspected resources within you. At times in your existence, this is how you have had to, or will have to, make certain life choices that will allow you to concretely assume those powerful attributes by playing a specific role with the people around you.

This is what is popularly called call the "soul mission." In reality this phase is quite often a temporary function, a challenge to overcome, simply helping you to discover some new talents and stabilize within you the character traits of your soul family.

Soul Families and Life Choices

SOUL FAMILY	QUALITIES AND VIRTUES (INCARNATION BUNDLE)	LIFE CHOICES (SOUL MISSION)
Builders	Confidence, strength, courage, leadership, endurance, perseverance, stability, dynamism, and ease in materializing one's goals	**Yang** (root chakra) Entrepreneurs, explorers, chiefs, leaders **Yin** (sacral chakra) Peacemakers, conciliators, procreators
Artisans	Sensitivity, creativity, artistic talents, originality, spontaneity, simplicity, kindness, generosity, helpfulness, and ease in weaving connections	**Yin** (solar plexus chakra) Artists, artisans, creators **Yang** (heart chakra) Humanists, missionaries, therapists, environmentalists
Visionaries	Great analytic and reasoning capacity, authenticity, sincerity, autonomy, astuteness, intuition, clairvoyance, and communication abilities	**Yang** (throat chakra) Communicators, mediators, defenders **Yin** (third-eye chakra) Thinkers, dreamers, idea people, inventors
Facilitators	Enthusiasm, pep, positiveness, predisposition to compassion, social consciousness, relieving depression, and gifts of healing	**In balance** (crown chakra) Caregivers, healers, teachers
Sages	Capacity to remain centered, balance oneself, harmonize oneself, live in the present, easily let go, trust life, and accept guidance from the higher self	**In balance** (all chakras) Contemplative, radiate through the Christic grid, "I am who I am"

First and Second Chakras: Builders

Those who belong to the Builders family might see the following qualities kindle in them through their ruling chakra: confidence, strength, courage, leadership, endurance, perseverance, stability, dynamism, and ease in materializing your goals.

To help you integrate these qualities in you, if your ruling chakra is the first or root chakra, you can exteriorize the entrepreneur, explorer, chief, or decision-maker in you.

If your ruling chakra is the second or sacral chakra, your challenge will consist of acting discreetly among those around you as a peacemaker, conciliator, or simply a procreator, by contributing the best you can to the creation of a couple, a family, a project, and so on.

Third and Fourth Chakras: Artisans

If you are an Artisan, the qualities and virtues your soul family inspires in you are sensitivity, creativity, artistic talents, originality, spontaneity, simplicity, kindness, generosity, helpfulness, and ease in weaving connections.

By reconnecting to your soul family through the third or solar plexus chakra, you may explore your creative talents as an artist (painter, musician, actor, etc.), artisan (sculptor, carpenter, gardener, cook, etc.), or creator (hairdresser, designer, decorator, writer, and so on).

Those whose ruling chakra is the fourth or heart chakra will instead tackle the great causes of humanity as humanists, missionaries, therapists, or naturalists: protectors of the fauna, flora, and of the environment overall.

Fifth and Sixth Chakras: Visionaries

The Visionaries benefit from the precious contributions of their soul family in several areas of subtle experimentation: great analytic and reasoning capacity, authenticity, sincerity, autonomy, astuteness, intuition, clairvoyance, and communication abilities.

Extroverts, connected to their soul family at the level of the fifth or throat chakra, will have many opportunities to express themselves verbally as communicators, mediators, or defenders.

Being connected to the sixth or third-eye chakra will feed the fertile imagination of thinkers, dreamers, idea people, and inventors.

Seventh Chakra: Facilitators

If you are one of those Facilitators who tends to deny their extrasensory perceptions due to a fear of being rejected by their peers, you will be thrilled to note that it is not necessary to present yourself as a mystic to benefit from the constructive energies of your soul family: enthusiasm, pep, positiveness, predisposition to compassion, social consciousness, relieving depression, and gifts of healing.

You may nevertheless intervene around individuals or groups as a guide, caregiver, healer, or teacher, since your ruling chakra, the seventh or crown chakra, remains essentially connected to heaven and constantly prompts you to spread the divine light all around you.

All Chakras Aligned: Sages

Without exception, we may all discover the great Sages in us. They invite us to welcome those unsuspected virtues and qualities that lay dormant within: the capacity to remain centered, balance oneself, and harmonize oneself. Sages live in the present, easily let go of things, trust life, and accept guidance from the higher self.

It is our inner Sage, our superior consciousness, the radiant angel present within us, that sometimes prompts us to meditate, to be more contemplative, and to radiate actively and effortlessly through the Christic grid simply by recognizing "who I am."

Once more, at the risk of repeating myself, in order for all those fabulous harmonizing characteristics and properties to settle in, all you have to do is say "*yes.*"

Integration: *Radiating*

Our deepest fear is not that we are inadequate.
Our deepest fear is that we are powerful beyond measure.
It is our light, not our darkness, that most frightens us.
We ask ourselves, Who am I to be brilliant, gorgeous, talented, fabulous?
Actually, who are you not to be?
You are a child of God. Your playing small does not serve the world.
There is nothing enlightened about shrinking
so that other people won't feel insecure around you.
We are all meant to shine, as children do.
We were born to make manifest the glory of God that is within us.
It's not just in some of us; it is in everyone.
And as we let our own light shine,
we unconsciously give other people permission to do the same.
As we are liberated from our own fear, our presence
automatically liberates others.

> *—Incorrectly credited to Nelson Mandela as an excerpt*
> *from his 1994 inaugural speech, this was in fact written*
> *by Marianne Williamson in her book* A Return to Love:
> Reflections on the Principles of "A Course in Miracles."

CHAPTER 5

Aiming for Balance

An Angel Dressed Up as a Human Being

Message from December 13, 2004

Did you know that you are an angel? By incarnating, you have the feeling that you lost your wings and severed your ability to elevate yourself toward the light. However, that is far from true. You are an angel dressed up as a human being—you have only folded your wings for them to be less cumbersome on this planet that appeared so dense and limited to you.

Those wings are a symbol, an image of what many of you call Merkaba. It is indeed your unlimited vital energy that, once spread, allows your vibrations to rise, giving you access to the higher dimensions. Forget complicated techniques and mental methods. You are pure love. You simply have to reactivate this love in all your cells really to feel its presence in your heart, and this extraordinary energy will completely wrap you up and spread around you like the wings of the angel that you truly are.

Some claim that angels don't have gender. However, they seem to emit mainly feminine or masculine vibrations according to the individual. Yes, the angels from heaven are themselves on their own course toward absolute divine fusion; there may still remain inside them some subtle sparks looking to be complemented. But it is said of them that "they do not have a gender" because they hold the power of creation through thought. The process of fertilization and cellular division as you know it has its vibratory equivalent in the angel's capacity to model a new soul just by the fusion of two angelic energies that complement each other.

Humans can also proceed in the same way, by joining through spirit rather than through the physical body; some have done it already. But you tend to let yourself be imprisoned and restrained by your corporeal dimension. You think you master your body, when actually it controls your destiny. The proof: notice how vulnera-

ble you become when your health fails you. However, you are immortal, and it is possible for you not to go through death to get a taste of eternal life. What are you waiting for? Say "yes" to who you really are.

Why not choose, once and for all, to give yourself the best present: a moment of intimacy with yourself, to forgive yourself for all your lack of love toward yourself, in order then to be able to finally celebrate your angel life in communion with all the beings of creation you are universally one with. With your soul family, the angels, the archangels, the ascended masters, and all of your light brothers and sisters, start to sing songs of bliss to elevate and maintain you in this perpetual state of grace, the song of all the beings of the fifth dimension—from which you originate and toward which you are walking back at this very moment.

It is never too late to give back all this healing love to your body and soul, spirit and consciousness. You are children of God; you originate from the same unlimited creative energy. Feel this liberating love; feel how you are one with the angels and the whole of creation. Say this essential "yes" to who you really are, and see to what extent this information frees the love energy that was dormant in your heart. Welcome this love as purification, as a miraculous healing. Feel how all of your cells regenerate with love, activate and elevate themselves to the light, to this sacred place in your heart where you know you are an angel.

—Bianca Gaia

Saying "Yes" to the Best Part of Ourselves

Here we will address the question of angels. As you see in the following chart, every soul family benefits from the protection of a specific archangel. You probably know them already: Gabriel, Michael, Raphael, Uriel, and Metatron are the patriarchs of each of the five great soul families.

Let's consider the following question: is Mr. Smith's grandson less of a Smith than his father or his grandfather? Imagine that the archangel corresponding to your soul family is your real ancestor and that you carry the same last name. Would you be less of an angel because you have accepted returning to Earth? Aren't you carrying the same celestial vibrations, and aren't you united energetically to the same vibratory family through your ruling chakra?

Gaia claims that a spark of love toward yourself is enough to awaken you to who you really are. Every spark of love in oneself is a parcel of divinity, the proclamation of your angelic lineage, and the recognition of the multidimensional being that you truly are.

You can reconnect to your soul family to access the transcendental energy of your guardian angels and also the beneficial vibrations of one of the five archangels: the one who rallies all the members of your soul family under his protective wing, you included, as a divine spark from the same celestial affiliation.

The archangels feel toward you the same love a mother or father experiences when holding their newborn child in their arms for the first time. Their affection for you is unalterable. They only aspire to your happiness on Earth as in heaven. So why hold back from asking them to give you their backing, support, and comfort when you need it?

We tend to think that our soul family, our guides, and our guardian angels stand at a certain distance behind us, sending us positive thoughts so that we can keep sailing serenely and arrive at our destination without hurdles. We picture ourselves walking alone in the jungle, machete in hand, thinking that we are the ones making our path or finding the most auspicious way for us.

Effectively, our soul family is present all around us: in front, behind, and on each side of us. It doesn't only act as a muse or a scout; on the contrary, our brothers and sisters of light simply want to contribute to making us happy. We are the ones who choose not to have the courage to ask them for help or favors from time to time.

Perhaps once or twice some of you have attempted to say a prayer to them. Surely you may have asked them for a parking space or to help get a good grade in math. Do you believe it is harder for them to answer those humble requests than to make your dearest wishes come true? What if it was enough simply to trust in them?

Daring to Ask

Having had the privilege of being contacted by my father-in-law, Conrad, after his death, one of the first bits of information he passed on to me was his disappointment in realizing that he had deprived himself all his life without any valid reason.

"I would never have believed the reserves of the universe were infinite," he confided to me one day. I grew up with the feeling that the resources surrounding me were limited and that I should content myself with what was at my disposal, being thankful for what life could bring me every day. My life experience convinced me that I had to manage on my own, that I shouldn't ask for help from those around me. If only I had known then what I know today."

In order to demonstrate to my husband and me that we could dare to ask at all times for the best for ourselves, Conrad warned us that we would be stunned by several major surprises in the year following his death.

Thus when we decided to sell the family house, which belonged to us, he claimed that we would get a much higher price than what we expected. Indeed, a few weeks later when we contacted our real estate agent, we learned that a similar house in a neighboring area had sold for fifty percent more than what we had thought of asking for our house. Not only did the house sell for a much higher price than we thought of asking for, but we received four offers in less than a week.

Pleased to have succeeded in getting our attention, my father-in-law added that we would sign the contract to sell on March 13, his birthday. This is when the story got weirder. Doubt started to grow in our minds when the buyers told us it would be almost impossible to sort out all the legal and mortgage documents by that date. They asked for an extension, which was finally agreed on as March 20, enough time for them to complete their paperwork. The notary was then advised accordingly.

"You will see that I'm right," my husband's father declared.

Allow me an aside to explain that the husband in question, Serge, the man who has shared my life for over twenty years now, is a true hockey fan, like most Quebecers. Because he had attended a few Montreal Canadiens games with his dad when he had been alive, months earlier in his father's memory he had bought himself a great seat for a game that was to take place a few days later, specifically on March 13. He was therefore relieved to find out that he wouldn't have to give up the precious ticket since the house transaction was postponed to the following week.

However, it seems that my father-in-law had decided that he would move heaven and Earth for everything to happen according to his predictions. The following day, we found out that the notary chosen by the buyers was only available on the evening of the 13th because subsequently he had to be out of town for fifteen days. I thought I heard a burst of laughter from the beyond; it was probably Conrad laughing out loud.

At the time, Serge was rather disappointed because he understood it meant sacrificing his exciting hockey evening. "If I could at least give my ticket away to Charles-Antoine rather than selling it," he said.

Once more, the wheel of destiny (perhaps with Conrad's support, I don't really know) seemed to turn in our favor. Only an hour after finding out about the change of events, Charles-Antoine, our eldest son, a huge hockey fan like his dad but who was living outside the Montreal area for a few months, called us to announce he would be briefly passing through the city on March 13, and was wondering if we could have dinner with him, since he was free for the evening.

You can guess the next part; Serge regretfully but proudly offered him his hockey ticket, which had been purchased at top price, nevertheless happy that his son could enjoy it in his place. The rest of the story seems incredible: not only did the signing with the notary take place earlier in the day on the 13th, but Serge decided to go in to Montreal anyway in case there were some tickets left for sale for the game, even though in principle none had been available since the beginning of the hockey season five months earlier. Getting there at the end of the first period of a three-period game, he was offered a ticket similar to the one he had offered Charles-Antoine, and for a fraction of the price.

The tradition therefore carried on, father and son assisting each other at a game of their favorite sport, all under the protective approval of the grandfather, Conrad, who incidentally invited me to relate this absolutely true story for all those he left behind to understand that they only need to ask in order for blessings to rain on them.

Aiming for Balance

SOUL FAMILY	HOW TO RECONNECT AND REBALANCE YOURSELF ON A DAILY BASIS
Builders	Protector: Archangel Uriel Chakra: root and sacral Colors: red and orange Vibration: Earth Therapeutic tools: physical exercise, grounding
Artisans	Protector: Archangel Gabriel Chakra: solar plexus and heart Colors: yellow and green Vibration: water Therapeutic tools: verbalizing, socializing, creating
Visionaries	Protector: Archangel Raphael Chakra: throat and third eye Colors: blue and indigo Vibration: air Therapeutic tools: nourishing your brain, reading, understanding
Facilitators	Protector: Archangel Michael Chakra: crown Color: violet Vibration: fire Therapeutic tools: respecting yourself, relaxing, harmonizing yourself
Sages	Protector: Archangel Metatron and the ascended masters Chakra: all Colors: white and gold Vibration: ether Therapeutic tools: meditating, praying, being centered or unified, "radiating"

Reconnecting and Harmonizing Daily

The chart above invites us to consider the different resources specific to each soul family that will allow us to focus and harmonize ourselves every time we need it.

Builders

The patriarch of the Builders family is Archangel Uriel. Because he is related to the physical dimension of your being, it is appropriate to invoke him for all your incarnation or grounding issues, as well as all your material or financial worries. He invites you to look after yourself, to stand up for yourself, to take the right means to get to your ends, and to do everything that is needed to maintain the buoyancy of your vital energy level.

By reconnecting to your soul family through your ruling chakra, the first or root chakra or the second or sacral chakra, you allow to be instilled and reactivated within you all the qualities and virtues specific to the members of this dynamic family. The red and orange colors can also contribute to balancing or revitalizing your global energy, while the Earth element brings you a vibration of backing and support in recognizing who you really are. This is also why the shape of the light cocoon is an equilateral triangle, illustrating the strength drawn from the Earth, grounding, and incarnation.

The therapeutic tools most suited to replenish your energy when it is low are, of course, grounding exercises: physical activity, sports, martial arts, and yoga; in brief, anything that puts your body in motion.

Artisans

The archangel spokesperson of the Artisans family is named Gabriel. Because he governs the emotional dimension of our being, he inspires in us the power to create our lives as we want. He is an endless source of inspiration for artists and creators, and his contribution proves to be precious in maintaining serene and harmonious interpersonal relationships.

You can of course reconnect to the soul family of the Artisans of Peace through your ruling chakra: the third (solar plexus) chakra or the fourth (heart) chakra, which will allow you to access the generous qualities and virtues provided by all of those benevolent souls. Because the chakras best fed by the luminous energy of this soul family are located in the upper part of the trunk, the light cocoon radiates particularly at this level, which explains its diamond shape. Also, carrying with you or surrounding yourself with bright yellow and emerald green will contribute to appeasing your soul, to freeing you from tumultuous emotions, and to healing certain illnesses in you.

Everything related to water—a hot bath, a boat ride on the ocean, or hydrotherapy—will be most beneficial to you. Add to this a few therapeutic tools to lighten things up on a psychological level, verbalize your feelings, stimulate your creativity, and socialize; basically, do anything that allows you to remain in contact with the heart of your being.

Visionaries

The patriarch of the Visionaries family is Archangel Raphael. He connects you to the intellectual dimension of your being, therefore dealing with your state of mind. Not only does he contribute to regenerating cerebral tissues, he can bring back dormant memories. His vibrations increase your reasoning abilities, bring you wisdom, and can bring out the necessary confidence for you to trust your intuition.

By reconnecting to your soul family through your ruling chakra, the fifth (throat) or sixth (third-eye) chakra, you have access to all the qualities and virtues as well as the mental faculties and countless skills accumulated through the centuries by scholars of this luminous family. The preferred playground of this family is essentially the intellect; the light cocoon of the Visionaries is therefore usually the shape of an inverted triangle. The colors sky blue and indigo will contribute to calming your overstimulated mind or prepare your body for relaxation. The element air allows you to lighten your mind and to breathe through you nose, meaning to center yourself, at times when you feel overexcited.

Your personal therapeutic tools are leisure and nourishment activities, reading, and the judicious understanding of things, because your brain will only be able to integrate what it has completely understood and assimilated.

Facilitators

The Archangel Michael is the protector and reference for the Facilitators family. From time immemorial he has been associated with the spiritual dimension of the being. Therefore it is relevant to invoke him for anything relating to moral, social, religious, or metaphysical questions. He contributes to awakening the consciousness, and when it is needed, protection against malicious supernatural influences.

By reconnecting to your soul family through the seventh or crown chakra, not only do you instill within you all the qualities and virtues specific to this family, but this can allow you, if you so desire, to reactivate your psychic gifts and extrasensory faculties. Because the interrelational dimension eases opening up toward others and the expansion of consciousness, it is no surprise that the light cocoon of the members of this family usually has a square shape. Additionally, as violet is recognized as a typical spiritual color, this vibration promotes access to higher dimensions, while the element fire revives in you the spark of your intrinsic divinity.

The Facilitators don't need therapeutic tools, strictly speaking, to rebalance themselves, but because they have a tendency to give a lot of themselves to others, it is important that they learn to respect themselves more, to relax, and to harmonize regularly with awareness of their subtle energies.

Sages

While the Archangel Metatron is the patriarch of the
Sages family, he is accompanied by several sidekicks,
for all the ascended masters also belong to this radiant family. It is said that like Saint Peter, Metatron
opens the gates of heaven to the most deserving souls.
But he also hears pleas on the most desperate causes
and resolves inextricable situations by inspiring hope,
restoring confidence, and allowing each of us to find
peace within ourselves.

Because it is possible to reconnect to this soul family through all the chakras,
from the first to the seventh, you have the potential to integrate within you all
the qualities and virtues of this radiant brotherhood, as well as all those of the
previous soul families.

The colors that harmonize the whole being are white and gold, for they help
to rebalance all the dimensions of the self. This balance reached, all the energetic bodies of the members of this soul family align to form a luminous iridescent cocoon, similar to a sun or a huge halo that is at times golden, at times
multicolored. It is in unconditional love that this powerful Merkaba is created.
Finally, ether, constituting the fifth element, represents all the energy that flows
in you, as it does in all living things. You thus have access to it regardless of
which soul family is originally your own.

In fact, you can meditate, center yourself, be united, and merge with all the
soul families to radiate like a thousand suns, finally to taste the plenitude of the
soul, the divine quintessence, the absolute state of grace that opens the gates to
the fifth dimension. What more could you ask for? Everything is already there
inside of you.

The Protective Prayer

May Gaia, our Mother Earth

Watch over my every step.

May the angel Michael secure my right

Gabriel my left

May Uriel walk in front of me

Raphael behind me

And may God almighty

Protect the top of my head.

PART TWO

The Human Experience

CHAPTER 6

The Five Dimensions of the Human Brain

The Brain, the Most Powerful of Computers

Imagine your brain as the most powerfully performing computer in the whole world. At the same time, like a computer, it simply stores and sorts out data. It can neither judge whether that data is good or bad nor whether it is pertinent or not. It simply writes down what it's told and proceeds as it is asked to.

Thus the brain does not make the distinction between a positive and a negative action. For that matter, it only retains the word, the verb used. As with a computer, for which one cannot write negative programming instructions like "do not do x" (only the positive version, "do x," can be coded), the brain does not attach any consideration to "cannot." This is why, if I tell my child, "Most importantly, don't lose your new hat," I can be sure he will misplace it, perhaps not that day but soon, in a few days or weeks—especially if I keep repeating the same thing to him.

This is why it is important to weigh our intentions and words carefully, especially when addressing those around us. It is much more efficient and judicious to use expressions such as "be careful" or "take good care of your new hat" to allow the brain to align with the action we are asking it to perform, rather than having it try to understand what we really mean or what is really expected of it.

Similarly, because the brain remembers every verb used as an action to undertake or set in motion, when I tell myself, *I am scared of losing my job,* all the brain will retain is "losing my job," and it will try to obtain this result by any means. Thoughts create. This is why all the great wise people of this world encourage us to be vigilant in our thoughts and to choose them with care. In the present example, it is better to tell myself, *I'll do everything to keep my job, even if I am scared.* The brain then understands that it has a right to "be scared" (state), but that it must however ensure that I "keep my job" (action).

The Brain Is Reprogrammable

Among other amazing abilities of our brain, like a computer it has access to a considerable amount of "software" and "programming" of all sorts, stored on its "hard drive" (the conscious, unconscious, and subconscious parts of the memory). Thus any information or experience acquired at any moment in our lives is forever available, even if we do not know how long it has been recorded. We can simply remind the brain that we possess that information and it will become available again, ready to be reactivated.

For instance, when we go through a difficult period, it is as if we are starting a digression, a "program" that monopolizes a big part of our internal resources. But we can simply ask the brain to end the digression, to stop the programming, to automatically come back to the state we were in before it started.

Not only is it possible, it is easy. In the same way that we can format a computer hard disk when it has been corrupted, we can do the same with our brains. We simply have to ask that all the negative harmful experiences we have suffered be erased from our memory. However, for this to work, it is important to "reprogram" the whole system by reactivating the memories of our positive experiences, choosing to keep only the pleasant memories and positive lessons we have derived from them.

Imagine that you have recorded a horror movie on tape, but that you hated this movie because you found it much too violent and bloody. Later on, every time you pass your bookshelf, just the sight of this tape puts you in the same state of unease as when you first watched the movie, without even taking it off the shelf. You will probably be tempted to destroy it. But for the tape to stop carrying this vibration that affects you, erasing it won't be enough; you need to record something pleasant over it (your favorite movie, for instance) and replace the label. From this moment on, when you see the tape on the shelf, it will put you in a beautiful state of energy that will brighten your day.

The same thing has to be done for our brains: reformat, then reprogram. If we simply eliminate the negative programming without replacing it with something else, the process is doomed. If, for instance, you would like to stop smoking, but you only suppress the use of cigarettes, your brain will attempt to replace what it has lost with any available compensation. You might then feel like nibbling, be grumpy, have a sleeping disorder, or something else. But if you choose to replace it with something pleasant and beneficial instead, the old programming will be erased and the new will take over.

The brain is so powerful that it can overcome the worst situations. In his book *Unconditional Life,* Deepak Chopra relates an experience he had in Los Angeles with about twenty compulsive drug users, for years hooked on cocaine, heroin, valium, and other drugs. During a therapy session, they were asked to visualize that they were mentally creating a massive dose of their drug of choice and that they were releasing it in their brains. The results were dazzling: in addition to realizing that they could themselves reproduce at will that same state of lightness and beatitude in their metabolism as when they were using, they totally freed, healed, and liberated themselves from their drug dependency.

Plugging into the Celestial Web

The brain's potential is infinite. One extraordinary example is that through the brain, we have the ability to connect to the Christic grid, an energetic web surrounding our planet. Like computers connected to the Internet, some children, commonly called "indigo children" because this color predominates in their supracausal energetic field, communicate among themselves through this celestial grid and use it to transmit the energy of light and healing to those who need it. More on the indigo children will be revealed in Chapter 14, "The Divine Cocreating Expression."

It is not necessary to be a psychic kid, however, to have access to the wisdom of the universe, to the information and solutions required for us to grow and recognize ourselves; that wisdom is registered in the fiber of our own being, in the neurons of our brains, in our genetic baggage, and in our cellular memory. It can be reactivated whenever we feel like it through opening up to the higher dimensions of our being and the practice of very simple decoding exercises, such as the muscle test exercise in Chapter 3, or listening to our soul's song, as described in Chapter 1.

We can also trust our brains to draw what it needs directly from the collective unconscious that connects us to one another. It is said that learning is done from generation to generation and eventually enters our genetic code.

The typical example of this, a variation of the hundredth monkey theory presented in Chapter 1, is an analogy involving chickens. When the automobile was first invented, chickens would almost always get run over when they would venture onto the road because they had never seen a car before. But a few generations later it seems that the sound of cars had become easily identifiable by their brains. As soon as their collective unconscious encrypted this piece of information in their "internal computer," they developed the ability to escape any time they sensed a vehicle approaching.

The same goes for us. For example, look at today's children, who seem to have extraordinary capacities to operate electronic devices. Why is that? Because these objects are part of their daily lives, they are so familiar with them that they have integrated them and classified them among their innate knowledge.

For older people, it's completely the opposite. They struggle to acquire skills that aren't yet part of their usual baggage. They have spent several decades of their lives exclusively using pens to write and their fingers to count; they don't really know what to do with a computer, nor how to use a bank card, or program the recording of a TV show on their video recorder. In brief, their brains need to be trained in order to be able to harness those new technologies.

Fortunately, all things are possible, for them as well as for us. The brain is so very powerful—we can't even begin to imagine the extent of its potential. In fact, it seems that we only use a small fraction of our brain capacity. We therefore have many more dimensions of our brain to discover and explore. Here are a few:

The Five Dimensions of the Human Brain

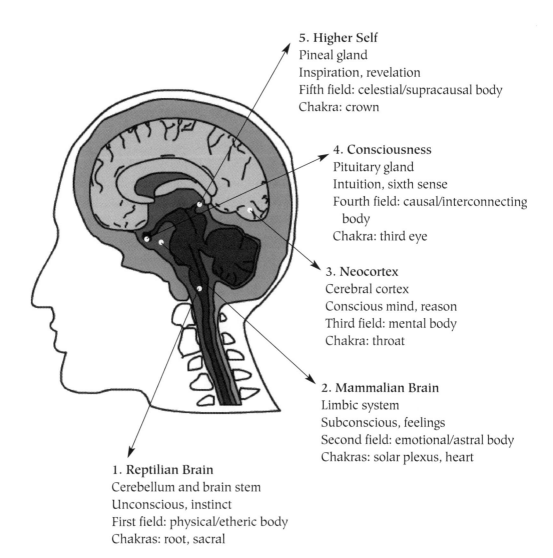

5. Higher Self
Pineal gland
Inspiration, revelation
Fifth field: celestial/supracausal body
Chakra: crown

4. Consciousness
Pituitary gland
Intuition, sixth sense
Fourth field: causal/interconnecting
  body
Chakra: third eye

3. Neocortex
Cerebral cortex
Conscious mind, reason
Third field: mental body
Chakra: throat

2. Mammalian Brain
Limbic system
Subconscious, feelings
Second field: emotional/astral body
Chakras: solar plexus, heart

1. Reptilian Brain
Cerebellum and brain stem
Unconscious, instinct
First field: physical/etheric body
Chakras: root, sacral

1. The Reptilian Brain

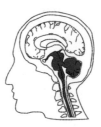

Scientifically, it is commonly understood that the brain is composed of three specific parts. The first dimension of the human brain would therefore be the cerebellum and brain stem, also called the reptilian brain. Without going into overly medical or anatomical considerations, let's say that it is the so-called primary part of our brain, the most ancient, resembling a long cord unrolling from a bulge situated on top of the medulla oblongata and going all the way down the spine to merge with the bone marrow.

It is said of the reptilian brain that it is of reptilian origin, because according to the theory of evolution it corresponds to the part of us that goes back to prehistoric times when we were still cold-blooded animals, reacting exclusively on instinct.

Visually, the sacral vertebrae, located at the bottom of our spine between the iliac bones, suggest that like most animals, we did indeed have tails ages ago. After all, the sacral plexus (or sacrum) is considered the place where the snake of the kundalini (according to the Hindu tradition, the source of both sexual and spiritual energy) is nestled.

The energetic part of the reptilian brain, therefore, deals with the first two chakras, the first or root chakra and the second or sacral, coincidentally also called the sexual chakra. This is where we find the seat of the unconscious.

It is the reptilian brain that regulates all the body's basic functions and automatic systems: blood circulation, breathing, sweating, the immune system, etc. It is therefore the reptile in us that regulates all our instinctive impulses, protecting us from external attack and fighting viruses and bacteria in order to ensure our survival.

2. The Mammalian Brain

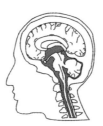

The origins of the mammalian brain, also called the limbic brain, correspond to the second phase of evolution, during which animals went from being cold-blooded to warm-blooded. While reptiles lay eggs and leave their offspring to their own devices, female mammals insure the gestation of their babies by keeping them warm and cozy in their bellies. This allows them not only to protect them more effectively against potential predators but also to move more easily outside the family nest.

It would seem that the moment we became warm-blooded animals coincides with our discovery of attachment to one another. By taking care of their offspring, breastfeeding them, and teaching them to hunt, mammals felt the first feeling of belonging and the primary emotions of fear, anger, pleasure, and so on. This is how the emotional dimension of our brain developed: a layer shaped like a ring (the limbic system) gradually overlapped the reptilian brain.

The mammalian brain thus represents the part of us connected to our feelings. We associate it with sensory perceptions (taste, sight, hearing, touch, smell) and to the subconscious, the part of us that, among other things, dreams at night. On the energetic level, it is connected to the third or solar plexus chakra and to the fourth or heart chakra.

3. The Neocortex

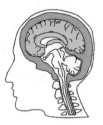

The superior layer of our brain, essentially composed of two large hemispheres, is called the cerebral cortex. It is the seat of intelligence, the part of us that thinks, reasons, analyses, makes decisions, and acts accordingly. The neocortex thus regulates all the cognitive functions of the individual.

Psychology very often associates the conscious aspect of the cerebral cortex with all of the acquired knowledge, past experiences, comprehension of what we experience, and lessons drawn from them.

On the energetic level it is associated with the fifth or throat chakra.

4. Consciousness

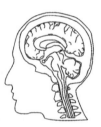

We get off the beaten track when we examine the fourth dimension of the human brain, consciousness. Unlike conscious intelligence, here we are talking about a global universal consciousness, the belief that we are part of a whole connected through an invisible thread to all that lives in the universe.

Scientists generally recognize the first three parts of the brain, although it is still a very delicate matter to have them admit the existence of a soul and the fact that it might be located in the brain.

Indeed, we can't really say what consciousness is made of nor exactly where it is located. But is it really important? The question is similar to operating a switch to turn on a light. We can't really say where the electricity is coming from; a windmill, a hydroelectric dam, or a nuclear plant. Similarly, we can't explain how electric current circulates inside a circuit, but it doesn't matter. The main thing is the result: the light comes on.

The same applies to this invisible dimension in us: we know it exists, that it connects us to God or to the universal energy, whatever you call it, and that it manifests in us through our intuition, our sixth sense. But how does it function? That's hard to explain.

At the frontal extremity of the medulla oblongata lies a small circular gland, situated directly at the junction of the two eyes and the temples, behind the bridge of the nose. Contrary to what I have always believed, it isn't the pineal gland but the pituitary gland. It has the shape of an eye, but instead of being directed forward, this "eye" is orientated upward, providing peripheral vision, enabling it to see at a distance, to perceive, or to have visions without the use of the eyes. It is the part of us that, when activated, manages to see the invisible very clearly.

Of course, the pituitary, also called hypophysis in medical terms, merges with the sixth chakra, the third eye. So, if I had to point out where my soul is located, the place where I have stored celestial information beyond the conscious, unconscious, and subconscious minds, I would say it is probably at the level of the pituitary gland.

Finally, because the pituitary is intrinsically part of the medulla oblongata, thus of the reptilian brain common to all vertebrates, I affirm that this is indisputable evidence that animals have souls too.

5. The Higher Self

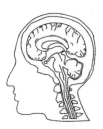

According to the teachings I have received in channeling, the fifth dimension of the brain is also situated in a tiny, barely perceptible little gland located on a posterior protrusion of the medulla oblongata.

It is possible to find its location by visualizing a stem going through the brain starting from the top of the forehead, just at the hairline, and coming out between the two first cervical vertebrae, with an inclination of roughly 45 degrees from the top of the skull. In the middle, halfway between the entry point and the exit point, we find the pineal gland, called the epiphysis in physiology.

Ayurvedic traditions have always considered the pineal gland, which owes its name to its pinecone shape, as the master gland of the body, the seat of our higher self. It is connected to the seventh chakra, the crown, and therefore to the celestial dimensions: inspiration, revelation, and illumination. In traditional medicine it has been difficult to establish the precise role of the pineal gland, the epiphysis, in the human organism. When I look up *epiphysis* in a medical dictionary, I find the following definition: "A little gland situated inside the brain, the function of which is not really known, but the ablation of which is fatal."

Therefore, if I had to point out a place in my body where the spark of life is found, my divine quintessence, the part of me that makes me alive or not, I would say the pineal gland definitely carries in it some vibrations of eternity. It plays the role of a condenser or a catalyst in an electrical system: it regulates the energetic sphere of the human body and harmonizes the whole of the subtle bodies.

Exercise: Introduction to the Brain Gym

Are you familiar with the "brain gym"? This technique is also called "kinesthetic education" or "applied educational kinesiology" because it stimulates cerebral functions with the help of some simple and judicious coordination exercises that encourage better communication among the different parts of the brain.

Practically, only a few "corporal remodeling" and "lateral rebalancing" movements are necessary to allow the body and mind to become better centered, brighter, and better performing. It is therefore ideal for children with concentration or attention-deficit issues.

The following seven exercises have been selected because they not only allow the energetic dimensions of the brain but also the seven related chakras to be balanced for a better overall harmonization. In order to integrate the exercises well, it is suggested that you drink a large glass of water before doing them.

1. The Lumberjack

Imagine picking up an ax from the floor: bend forward while bringing your hands together, then slowly rise until your arms are above your head. Keeping your feet firmly on the ground, throw your body forward, as if you were chopping wood placed between your legs, swinging your arms in between your legs while at the same time letting out a deep sound from the depth of the belly: "ha!" Once head-down, breathe out deeply three times. Do the exercise two more times.

2. Frontal Cross-crawl

Standing straight, lift the left knee to waist height and lay the right hand on it, then lift the right knee and lay the left hand on it, each movement alternating quickly for about a minute.

3. Back Cross-crawl

This is the same exercise but toward the back: lift the right heel up to the buttocks and touch it with the left hand, then lift the left heel and touch it with the right hand, alternating quickly for about a minute.

4. Contrary Rubbing

Rest your left hand on the top of your head and rub it around your skull clockwise (as seen from above). At the same time, your right hand rubs your abdomen, but in the opposite direction (counterclockwise). Reverse the hands after about thirty seconds, and start the exercise in the other direction.

5. The Hook

Stretch your right arm out in front of you, cross your arms, and join your hands together, palm to palm, fingers interlaced. Then slowly fold your elbows to bring your joined hands toward you, and finally, turn them back on themselves to rest them on your chest at the level of your heart. Hold this position for about a minute with your eyes closed and your tongue pressed to the roof of your mouth.

6. Visualization

Place your fingers on each side of your head and imagine that you are activating the two hemispheres of your brain while slowly moving the tips of your fingers. Then visualize that your left hand grabs the left part of the brain and your right hand takes the right. Slowly your hands move down in front of you at the height of the solar plexus, taking care of their precious cargo. Then bring your hands back to face each other while connecting the tips of the fingers, left and right. They touch to form a ball in front of you and reunite the two parts of the brain. Hold this position for a minute, tongue pointed to the roof of your mouth.

7. Harmonization

Finish by resting your hands on your forehead for a few moments, and relax while breathing deeply.

Total time required: 8 to 10 minutes maximum. For better results, these exercises can be done regularly, even daily, ideally at the same time each day for greater efficiency for the brain.

Aligning Your Creative Thoughts

Now that you have rebalanced all the parts of your brain and realigned all the dimensions of your being, you are ready to put into practice your cocreating potential. You know that thoughts create and that you can manifest the best in your life. Simply really believing it allows your wildest dreams to come true and your most treasured wishes to manifest.

At the moment, however, countless thoughts charged with duality and conflict proliferate around you. When you are preoccupied or confronted with situations that unsettle you, without knowing it you also emit negative thoughts that feed the gray cloud suspended above your head. It is therefore normal to look for a means to evacuate those thoughts that torment you and to try to push them as far away from you as possible.

If you simply attempt to make all those harmful thoughts abstract or to eliminate them by chasing them from your mind, they continue to hang around you and pollute the mental spheres of humanity. You may already know it, but these thoughts end up creating entities, "critical masses" of negative thoughts that unconsciously keep people in fear, disturb them, and influence their daily decisions.

Without you noticing it, all those thoughts of separation from your divine self, all those illusions you entertain of not yet being luminous or "perfect" enough as you are, contribute to slowing down the global ascension process.

All your self-criticism, judgments of others, and altered perceptions of the pseudoreality in which you imprison yourself act on the balance of the planetary system like viruses and parasites that weaken and delay its ultimate healing, the coming of the new world we so aspire to. These limiting thoughts that abound in your energetic environment form a dump of disturbing and alienating energies that regularly contaminate you without your knowledge.

This also explains why it is that certain people who meditate regularly, reach some powerful energetic peaks, or assiduously communicate with the higher dimensions feel at times out of balance or weakened on the human level: if they are not anchored enough yet, if they haven't made peace with their incarnation choices, or if they mull over the past from time to time, they become vulnerable to this collective unconscious that irreparably connects them to each other.

Fortunately, you can do something about it. You have everything you need within yourself to recycle those thoughts and turn them into a formidable energetic planetary fuel. Imagine for a moment that all the polarized thoughts of humanity floating in the fourth dimension could be caught, concentrated, transmuted, and transformed into luminous energy. The garbage bins of fears, worries, limits, and undisclosed resistance could be purified by the collective intervention of all the light workers, who would choose to act like powerful interdimensional compost in order to reduce the whole thing into energetic fertilizer and thus contribute to speeding up the ascension process rather than holding it back.

Your thoughts create. Choose them with care. Feed them with peace, love, and light. Surround them with joy and simplicity. See all the resistance and blockages in and around you turn into compost, which you can bury deep in the Earth to enrich the quality of the soil and fertilize the transmutation efforts of the entire planet.

You are the salt of the Earth. Your intervention makes all the difference. It is therefore you who decides what the future will be like—yours as well as that of future generations. Through your pure channel of light, you have the possibility to reconnect, align, and unify with all the parts of yourself, interior and exterior. The world that surrounds you is nothing but the reflection of you: purify yourself, illuminate yourself, ground the ascension energy in the depth of your being, and it will be the same for all the dimensions you are connected to.

Integration: *Method to Manifest Wonders*

No matter what you want to manifest in your life, chances are that everything you think of is still filled with duality. Its origin is written at the heart of your two brain hemispheres and therefore necessarily functions in binary mode, emitting at the same time every thought and its opposite.

On the energetic level, it often happens that the intensity and power of your aspirations are smaller than those of the doubts, resistance, and fears that plague you. That's why some of your dreams and secret desires are never fulfilled. If the negative thought patterns that your brain emits are more frequent than the positive thought patterns, the former will surely have the advantage and will determine what will happen in your life; hence the expression "to be at the mercy" of events, meaning not to have a hold on them.

The brain therefore remains the hardest part of the body to master. As for the rest of the metabolism, the only way to become an "athlete" or a champion of creative thinking consists of training fervently every day to improve the brain's programming. It is a long and demanding process that may well be called into question every time an unexpected and unsettling event happens in your life.

Fortunately, there is another path available: that of the heart's intelligence. In love, no duality is possible. Would a loving mother refuse to give milk to her baby, a loving father to open his consoling arms to his upset child, or a suitor to grant any favor to the love of his life? Even if you had a tough childhood, you know what love is. It is impossible that you have never felt it, even for a brief moment.

Love can accomplish anything, overcome and materialize anything—even the impossible. That's why any request made in sincere love toward yourself and in communion with the divine love present in the entire universe will necessarily be fulfilled. It is possible to find a way of expression to eliminate the mind's duality by neutralizing the positive and negative forces that oppose each other to leave space for the power of love.

From the start, you know that regardless of the essence of your request, doubts, anxieties, and resistance may appear. Name them: enunciate them in the formulation of your request itself so as to tell them; "Ha! I see and recognize you, and you no longer scare me." Choose the words that suit you best and that reflect the level of trust that you have in the power of materialization from the greatest source that is: universal love (also called energy, the source of life, mother-father God, according to the name you choose to give the source of infinite love).

Your wording could sound like this: "Since I have love toward myself and all that lives, I choose to manifest my creating power by bringing forth [specify your request] here and now in my life, even though fears, doubts, or resistance may remain in my personality." You can also let yourself be guided by the heart's intelligence, also known as intuition, to find the words that resonate best within you.

For the wording to work, what matters is that it is felt deeply in all your being, so that the message sinks into all of your cells and is sealed in by the fire of love. The best approach is first to connect to the universal energy, to the creator of all life, to your father-mother God with whom you enjoy a special relationship, or simply to your soul family, the one that is most familiar to you.

Take the time to settle comfortably in a quiet place. Breathe deeply and try as best you can to disregard any parasitic thoughts by focusing on a sacred space inside your heart. Visualize yourself going down a staircase within yourself to this peaceful place no one can disturb. Settle in total tranquility and arrange a cozy little nest for yourself filled with the loving presence of the divine creator, this father-mother who created you with love.

Feel the intensity of this love comforting you and a soft warmth settling everywhere in your body, from top to bottom. Say out loud that you are loved and are fully vibrating in this living flame of love that grows in you and is recorded in your every cell. If you need to, visualize this flame like a soft golden glow enveloping your whole body from the inside out.

Feel how your father-mother only wishes the best for you, anticipating with joy that he-she won't be able to resist the love that you feel in return. Like a child fulfilled and appreciated by his parents, visualize that your request receives an unconditional welcome even before being heard, and that the gift is already there, ready to be unwrapped.

Then formulate your request in total trust. Say out loud the sentence you have constructed, and visualize the message spreading in your entire being, engraving deeply in all your cells. Like a powerful laser, make sure every word penetrates everywhere in and around you, radiating out for thousands of miles.

Then visualize that the ray of transmutation, the violet flame, descends on you, producing a powerful alchemy in all of your cells. You yourself become the creator of all things. You become one with the source of all life. You melt in infinite celestial love. You know you are unlimited. Your cellular memory recalls having already accomplished miracles, having already manifested this request, in other times and places. It's as if you are waking up from a long sleep to become yourself again, the divine alchemist that you are.

The power of materialization has been awakened in all your being, and all is now accomplished according to your will, in love and respect of yourself and all that lives. Allow yourself to feel a deep sense of gratitude for this renewed opening to the creating love, and enjoy the surge of bliss filling your heart to communicate itself to your whole being, then to spread through your own luminous radiance to all that lives.

In order to keep this new programming in your consciousness, it is recommended that you write it down on a piece of paper and place it under a burning candle for twenty-four hours. Then notice the wonders that come forth in your life that are even beyond your expectations. Accumulating the written record of your successful materializations will have the same effect on the two hemispheres of your brain as if you were programming them positively on a daily basis. This way, in the long run, your brain will also become a champion at manifestation in love.

CHAPTER 7

Becoming Attuned to the Messages of Our Bodies

Seven Angry Men

Message from April 26, 2007

This is a story of seven friends who worked together at the same firm for over twenty years. One day when they arrived at work they found themselves in front of a locked door. The factory had gone bankrupt, and the owners had run away during the night without even warning their employees. Everyone was appalled.

The first man worked as a foreman, managing the group. As soon as he became aware of what was happening to him, he flew into a wild rage. Unable to tolerate the despicable treatment from his bosses after so many years of service, he attempted to convince his unfortunate friends to sue the company. Rather than look for a solution to his problem by searching for a new job, he went around in circles, fuming and blaming the company for what it had put him through. After a few months he ended up in hospital with severe leg problems that degenerated into phlebitis.

The second worker, the "clown" of the group, the one who usually turned everything into a joke, found himself at a standstill. With his children studying and renovations at his country house in the making, he felt financially trapped. He was overcome with panic and started going around to job centers, distributing his résumé without even taking the time to wonder what would be of interest to him or what would be the best thing for him. Shaken, he started to believe he might soon lose all of his possessions and end up in the street. Weakened by his self-imposed pressure and the feeling that he wasn't fit to overcome such a challenge, he required an urgent operation to remove kidney stones.

The third man had always been a very emotional person. He was ridden with shame and worry and became withdrawn. Feeling sorry for himself, he opted for unemployment benefits rather than making the effort to look for a new job. Worn down by anxiety, he quickly developed a stomach ulcer.

The fourth worker was a tall, warm guy who was always big-hearted. To him the factory was more than a workplace; it was where he met with his friends every day. In the evenings after work, he used to go out for a drink with his coworkers. So, more than just losing a job, he lost his joie de vivre and motivation to get out of bed every day. From one day to the next he felt as if his heart had been ripped out. What do you think happened to him? He died of a heart attack.

The fifth was the youngest of the group. Eager, efficient, and discreet, he didn't dare tell his wife he had lost his job. Every morning he carried on preparing his lunch box and left home for the day so as not to raise any suspicion. He was hoping to find another job quickly, and for everything to be as it was before. Not daring to express his anxiety, holding back his tears and sadness, he tried as best he could to keep his chin up. After a few months he got throat cancer.

The sixth man seemed to be in perfect control of the situation. He immediately declared that it wasn't serious, and because he was the best of the bunch and had had the biggest income as a manager, he was sure to find a new job "in a jiffy." Yet he was struck down by an aneurism. You might ask why, when he was so positive; but you're wrong: he was in denial. He told everyone that the loss of his job had not affected him, but deep down he was under extreme, nearly unbearable internal pressure.

The seventh man first thought to himself, This is not good news. It's no fun at all. But I still believe that I should get through it anyway. *When he got back home, he discussed the situation at length with his family, taking the time to express his feelings and asking them all for their support. He explained that the coming months might be difficult, but that by tightening their belts they would surely manage to overcome this challenge together. He didn't have any health problems except an occasional migraine, toward the end of the month when he was going through the bills, but generally speaking he remained healthy. He simply accepted the situation and did the best he could on a daily basis.*

And you: how would you react if you lost your job?

—Bianca Gaia

The Impact of Moods on Health

Do you sometimes have physical symptoms that disturb you inner serenity—a mild uneasiness that suddenly appears without any apparent reason and seems difficult to treat or is totally unexplainable, even when you consult a professional? Calm down: it is your body talking to you.

These days more and more people are claiming that the body is a reflection of the unconscious mind. Of course, poor eating habits or an unhealthy lifestyle surely contribute to creating health problems. However, it is accepted nowadays that conflicting states of mind or spirit also affect the organism, superficially as well as deeply. Open wounds, unresolved conflicts, or a lack of love toward yourself are all reasons for your body to be crying out for help. In this case, before running to the nearest health professional, why not simply look inward and ask what your body is trying to tell you?

There are numerous books available that explore these new aspects of medicine, called "of the soul." Whether they call it "wellness through awareness," "biological decoding," or "naturogenesis of illness," these different techniques can help you to identify the mental and psychological causes of your illness.

The Law of Attraction

What we do not express

Gets imprinted in us.

What we resist persists.

What affects us infects us.

What we flee pursues us.

On the other hand, fortunately,

What we face fades away.

What we visualize materializes,

And what we bless delights us.

This little poem outlining the law of attraction highlights the impact of our thoughts on our life and state of health. It is easy to realize that it is the pressure and stress that we put on ourselves that ends up causing our demise and making us ill. We could also use another significant saying: "What we do not succeed in expressing in words will probably be translated by our bodies into a world of troubles."

What if we were asked to stop considering illness as an attack against our metabolism, to see it rather as a block preventing the simple flow of information and its assimilation by the brain? Here is what really happens inside us whenever a major event unsettles our inner harmony:

1. Pressure: Initial Shock

At first, a stress trigger appears, the initial shock: an unexpected event, some bad news, a conflicting situation, or some hurtful words. Shaken, you first try to deny its reality: "It can't be! This is impossible. This can't be happening to me." Rather than welcome that new information, the brain rejects it or "hides" it in a lost corner of consciousness in order to continue with business as usual.

At times, we consciously keep mulling over the situation, trying to find its meaning or a solution. Very often, we try our best to put our attention elsewhere, to think of something else, and to ignore anything that could hurt us.

This is a very normal reflex: who would choose to deliberately rub salt into a wound or to suffer? "If I can't do anything about it, why worry?" If we could indeed shrug off everything that compromises our well-being, it would be truly amazing. In reality, our mind continues to be affected and even disturbed by what is troubling us.

2. Repression: The Small Inconveniences

Although we may not be aware of it, we are like a computer that has to run several programs at the same time. We continue to pretend that nothing has happened, get busy with other things, but within us our "processor" works very hard, stubbornly wondering, *But what can I do with this?*

In the long run, this takes more and more space in our virtual memory. Our brain, caught up in its need to actualize its data, could well turn out to be increasingly distracted. This is the second stage: the attention deficit. These little moments of distraction create various hassles. We cut ourselves on a sheet of paper, stub a toe against the furniture, burn ourselves accidentally.

But because these are things that do happen, we don't pay attention to them, forgetting these little troubles as quickly as they appear.

3. Impression: The Call to Order

After a few days, however, this ignored uneasiness starts to leave its mark, to become imprinted in our brain, which really wants to stop and focus our attention on what is latent within us (pain, dissatisfaction, a feeling of powerlessness). We can then see further troubling events happen in life: a minor collision with the car, losing objects we are attached to, or neglecting to repair a dripping faucet only to end up with the kitchen inadvertently flooded.

Again, we still have a choice: take the time to be introspective in order to contemplate what is wrong with us, or maintain our attention on what is happening outside of us, going on our way as if all these incidents were merely coincidences.

4. Compression: The Small Emergencies

Frustrated by our evasion, this is when our brain starts to seethe with impatience. It now sends us a distress signal: "Hey, there is something that you haven't yet 'digested' in your life, a state of mind you haven't taken the time to welcome, a feeling you didn't give the attention it deserves. You are going to end up stopping for a while to take the time to think about it, whether you want to or not."

This is the fourth step for information that has not been welcomed. Our unconscious mind is too busy juggling what is troubling us, and some of our primitive functions are put on hold. Our immune system weakens, our internal organs work in slow motion, and old aches and pains reappear. We unwittingly allow these troubling thoughts to invade us, and this makes us more vulnerable to the viruses and bacteria around us.

This is when we catch the flu, have gastroenteritis, dislocate a shoulder, create an allergic reaction in our bodies, have terrible migraines, and so on. It is always quite possible to bury those symptoms and pretend that they have no connection to reality while suppressing them with the help of medications or other treatments. But could this be like cleaning up by simply sweeping the dust under the carpet? If the dust makes too big a lump, we flatten it with a foot, but in reality it just spreads to other places.

5. Oppression: More Serious Ailments

Indeed, after a few weeks, if the conflict still isn't resolved, certain areas of the brain begin to set into necrosis. The zone that is normally irrigated by the brain is no longer fed because it is now incapable of assuming its usual functions: its entire attention is mobilized to attempt to deal with the extreme internal tension it is submitted to.

Since the supply of energy coming from the brain is no longer going to certain organs or systems, they will end up suffering and thus generate uncontrollable crises like asthma, eczema, arthritis, angina, or degenerative illnesses like diabetes, multiple sclerosis, or Parkinson's.

6. Depression: General Exhaustion

After two or three months, other intermittent ailments, all quite unpleasant, will add to the previous ones: insomnia, nausea, dizziness, tinnitus, inner trembling, or uncontrollable weeping. Because the neurosensory system has been troubled for too long, the vital energy of the whole metabolism decreases considerably, leading to the appearance of symptoms of extreme fatigue, depression, or exhaustion.

The overall situation worsens considerably, for now the whole system is affected and the brain no longer manages to get the upper hand: going around in circles has worn it out.

7. Suppression: Survival in Question

As a last resort, when despite all the warnings given by the body the problem still hasn't been resolved, the individual's survival itself is threatened.

This is the final step, suppression. The pressure has done so much damage inside us that the brain can no longer function at all; it is forced to admit defeat. The unresolved conflict has ended up crystallizing itself somewhere in the body (as an aneurysm, tumor, or something else), putting our life at risk and sometimes inexorably sealing our destiny.

8. Expression: The Best Solution

Imagine that at the beginning, when the unsettling element intervened, you'd had the chance there and then to express the troubling effect that this unsettling news was having on you. Imagine that you had had someone with whom to share your worries and your fears, someone who would have helped you dedramatize the situation. Can you see how everything would have happened in a different way, simply by welcoming the situation with more distance or detachment?

It is possible to overcome the stress inherent in a major disturbance. We can simply admit that we've been there before, and that until now we have always managed to get out of bad situations without losing our life. The proof? We are still here, aren't we?

Stress Management, a Question of Survival

A few years ago, while attending a conference hosted by a French Canadian doctor, Serge Marquis, a most interesting brief story about stress came up. According to him, in these situations, the brain reacts in the same way that it did in prehistoric times. Its reactions haven't evolved a bit since then.

Imagine a cave woman strolling through the woods to collect fruit. The sky is blue, and life is beautiful. She is unaware that in a moment, her entire life will change. Hearing a noise behind her, she turns around and sees a huge tyrannosaur charging at her with its jaws open wide, showing its sharp teeth. In the blink of an eye a rush of adrenaline puts all of her systems on alert: her survival is threatened. It goes without saying that she is no longer hungry or thirsty, and isn't really driven to reproduce; she has only one thought: to flee.

In your own life, when a stressful situation occurs (you haven't taken responsibility for your actions, you are in a bad situation, you have made a massive error that may put your job at risk, etc.), the chemical reaction produced inside you is exactly the same as for the prehistoric woman. It is the same adrenaline rush: the heart beats fast, and nervous tension settles into your entire body so that you can flee as quickly as possible. The brain reacts as dramatically as if your very survival was threatened. But does the present situation require such a strong reaction?

The brain doesn't differentiate between very small and very large fear. It reacts in the same way whether a car unexpectedly passes you on the road or a truck driver has lost control of his vehicle and is heading straight at you.

This is why it is essential, no matter what situation you are in, to learn to dedramatize and put into perspective the stress that you impose on yourself. To help you unwind, Dr. Marquis makes an amusing suggestion: simply ask yourself, "Will I die from it?"

One of my friends is upset with me; will I die from it? I didn't get the job I was hoping for; will I die from it? A faucet is leaking; will I die from it? And so on.

In some troubling situations, when we first feel that the tension is rising or that a hot flash is taking hold of us as if our life were in danger, it is useful to wonder whether we truly, concretely run the risk of losing our life. The simple fact of realizing that our survival as such is not threatened brings the stress level down a notch and reduces the adrenaline rush. As Dr. Marquis would say, this allows us to maintain our reserves in the event that we meet a tyrannosaur.

After realizing that our life is not truly in danger, it is easier to envisage looking at things differently, perceiving the situation from another angle. What if life is sending us challenges as a gift to allow us to reveal ourselves to ourselves, to show us that we can act on our environment and choose to make things happen differently?

If I lose the relationship with a friend, I still have all those other friends who adore me. If I do not obtain the job I had hoped for, then life has much more appropriate things in store to fill my needs, and so on.

Since we tend to tell ourselves stories, why not chose to make them funny ones? Isn't humor the universal panacea, the best way to free ourselves from the tensions that oppress us and to lower our stress level? It is up to you to learn to dedramatize by cultivating the pleasure of laughing—at yourself.

"Everything Is in the Eye of the Beholder"

This old American Indian saying reveals with accuracy the extent to which appearances can be deceiving. You know that a situation is not always as painful as you believe it to be, and that it is rare that a person truly has the intentions toward you that you assume they do. Everything is a matter of perception.

For instance, when you enter into a conflict with someone, mildly harsh words are exchanged, and this creates a chill, an insurmountable gap between the two of you. You take for granted that the person is angry with you, or that you have disappointed him or her, and that he or she has remained in that frame of mind ever since. However, have you remained in exactly the same frame of mind as when the incident happened? Do you still harbor the same anger, sadness, or guilt as on that day? Be honest; isn't it just a trick that your mind is playing on you? Emotions come and go, and perhaps they reappear when you think again about what happened, but does it still really vibrate with the same intensity as before?

Isn't the remaining pain instead connected to the disappointment and regret of no longer enjoying a good relationship with that person? It might be that it is you who is upset and closed toward him. It is normal: you've been wounded, and from that point you are suspicious and want to protect yourself from that person so that he won't be able to get to you anymore. But the opposite thing happens: he continues to get to you, even from a distance, through the bitterness and the uneasiness that you harbor toward that person.

Blinded by Pain

When you are eaten at by pain, paralyzed by fear, or closed to any possibility of reconciliation, who does it hurt the most? Is it you, or the other person? And if this person truly means harm, doesn't giving her power over your life only make things worse? What if it wasn't this person torturing you from a distance but you yourself, through the thoughts you entertain toward the other person? Are those thoughts real, or could they be stories you are telling yourself?

You think that person holds a grudge against you, that she doesn't want to hear about you anymore, that the crisis you went through has left a scar that may never heal. Is that the truth? Really, do you have any proof of it? Have you double-checked? Most importantly, how do you feel inside when you feed those limiting thoughts? Is it your past wound hurting and imprisoning you or, on the contrary, could it simply be the negative perceptions that you harbor that are wearing you down from inside?

Have you ever wondered what this person truly thought of you? Could it be that she has been affected by the same disappointment, suffering the same wounds as you, and that she may be paralyzed by the same fear to reestablish contact? The problem with telling stories to ourselves in order to protect ourselves is that all they do is entertain the pain. Just like a woman enduring domestic violence, the fear is of what would happen if she were to be on her own. The anxiety of the unknown paralyzes her to the point that she prefers to accept hell on a daily basis rather than taking the risk of leaving. The same goes for the man who continues to go to work in an office where the atmosphere is horrible; he goes because he fears he will not be able to find anything better elsewhere. Although these fears prevent us from moving forward, daily torment generates much more discomfort and unease.

Seeing Beyond Appearances

Human beings seem to be made this way: we create our convictions and don't stray from them unless we have no other choice. It is easy to judge from outside, however. The battered woman has many brothers and sisters who would be only too happy to give her a hand to rebuild her life; why doesn't she ask them for help? The man has good credentials and undeniable expertise in his field; why doesn't he look for another job rather than making himself unhappy and continually complaining? And you, why have you not made any attempt to get back in touch or make peace with the person who has wounded you?

Forgiveness benefits us even more than those we forgive. It is not just about "turning the page" or "getting over" the events of the past. On the contrary, it is about going to see what is hiding behind the pain. What has hurt you the most during this quarrel? When you think back on what this person said to you, have his hurtful words offended you because they were not true, or because they were too true? Didn't a part of you believe you deserved to hear such things? Perhaps you already had similar thoughts concerning yourself—that you were good for nothing, that you had your head in the clouds, that you were not open enough to others, or any other criticism that you silently entertain in your mind.

Why did you feel attacked? If there was indeed no kernel of truth in what this individual told you, you wouldn't have taken it so personally. You would have found it so far-fetched that you would have laughed. And you would have told yourself, *No, that's not true. I don't know who this person is talking about, but it's not me. Something must be going wrong in his life, and he is looking for a scape-goat. This doesn't belong to me.* And you would have gotten over it. Really. Think about it; this has probably happened to you before: a stranger has an angry outburst in front of you and verbally attacks you for no reason. What do you say to yourself then? *This guy really has a problem.* And you go on your way without giving his words any credence.

Isn't it when the words thrown at you touch on some truth that they hurt? When they resonate with you, do they not awaken something that was already dormant? It is not the words that hurt you, but rather the pain that they invoke. Because nobody aspires to emotional unease, rather than welcoming the words as part of ourselves, it is much easier to bury them and to close ourselves to the person who has brought them to our consciousness.

What if that person had given you the most fabulous gift that exists: the opportunity to become aware of those judgments and self-criticisms that you entertain within yourself, in order to free yourself from them once and for all? Think about it for a moment. Go back to your own intentions toward the person concerned: were you deliberately trying to hurt, wound, or torture him with your words? Despite your intentions, did you not use some offending words? Were you not simply trying to make the other person see some sense?

Seeing Some Sense

Which is the voice of reason—the voice that silently and destructively takes pleasure at denigrating, criticizing, and bringing you down, or the voice of the friend, parent, or colleague that invites you to consider that you are more than those limitations or weaknesses that inhabit you?

Often it is the people you love the most who hurt you the most. Why is this? Because you stop at the words, details, and criticisms without taking the time to see the intention hidden behind their clumsy interventions. The other person isn't just trying to be right, to take power over you, or to be superior. She believes she has detected a breach in you that could harm you in the long run, and clumsily, perhaps, attempts to make you aware of it so that you can change.

Don't change who you are, because you know that it is nearly impossible to do so. But you can change your way of perceiving yourself through this experience. The other person has highlighted your own tendency to denigrate and lower yourself. Caught up in her own vulnerabilities, her soul and heart ask you to consider that you are much more than those defects you attribute to yourself, than those silly things you tell yourself.

This may not be easy to accept, but what if the only way to heal these wounds from the past was simply to admit that this person could have said something truthful about you? She may have exaggerated, but deep down it was only the reflection of the thoughts you entertain toward yourself, as if that person read the information that you yourself had written right in the middle of your forehead: "I'm not worthy," "I'm a loser," "I don't trust myself." What if the story you were telling yourself was, "I don't deserve other people's trust"? That might explain why the conflict happened in your life. The other person perceived this vulnerability unconsciously and attempted to verify whether it was real or imaginary.

You Have the Choice

How to get out of such a dead end? There is only one solution: getting back to the now. To free yourself from all the emotional weight that has been indulged and that has created this gap between you and the other person, it is important to take some time to ponder the real intention hidden behind the words and to get back to the now to consider what thoughts and what attitudes you are choosing to adopt here and now.

It isn't necessary to go back to the past and to take everything from the start; it is only necessary to accept seeing things differently, with different eyes. You have pretended to know what the other person thinks of you, and you have built a fortress for yourself in order to protect yourself from his attacks, but what was it like in reality? Just opening yourself up to moving forward and moving beyond appearances can change the quality of your relationship with that person.

By forgiving yourself for your blindness, you open the door to the possibility of really perceiving yourself as you are: with your defects, certainly, but also with your countless qualities, strengths, and talents. You are more than the criticism formulated within and outside of you. Perhaps, in some cases, is it too late to rekindle your relationship with the other person, but nevertheless, by freeing yourself from the weight of this conflict, you can only come out a winner on all levels.

And who knows, you could be surprised to realize that the person you thought you had a conflict with in fact harbors much nicer thoughts about you than you had imagined, and that he only wants what is good for you. Even if that person got carried away in a heated moment, it is never too late to reclaim a better connection if the feelings of love and friendship are still present between you.

Making Peace within Ourselves

Some time ago my daughter Marlène started seeing an absolutely adorable young man. She was his first true sweetheart. Because they were spending lots of time together, he was away from home more and more frequently for long periods of time, and his mother started to feel that her son was seeing a bit too much of my daughter. The boy reported this to Marlène, who took it very personally.

She started to tell herself the following story: it was possible that her new "mother-in-law" didn't love her or didn't want her. Without even taking the time to check whether her assumptions were true, she claimed that she was the source of the problem. Suddenly she felt hopeless, not knowing how to deal with her boyfriend. Could she continue seeing him? Could she call him, or did she have to wait for him to call? She went as far as to question the relationship, ending up making herself ill over it, both figuratively and literally: she caught a bad flu combined with sinusitis.

When I talked with her, Marlène was able to become aware of the fact that what her boyfriend was going through with his mother did not belong to her, and it wasn't really even any of her business. She could admit that she had created a tempest in a tea pot for herself.

Once she recovered from her ailment, she was invited for dinner at her sweetheart's house, and she quickly realized that the boy's mother, even though she was very happy with her two sons, was in fact excited to welcome Marlène and to have found a new female accomplice to bring some balance back into her home, where the men outnumbered the women.

It is therefore always possible to make peace within yourself, despite your worries and storms. You can accept in advance that there are some situations that happen around you regardless of what you do and which you cannot change, and that some life experiences, even if they appear inextricable at first, allow you to grow, evolve, and draw life lessons that have made you the wonderful being that you are today.

As a consequence, if you take the time to take a deep breath when some internal trouble arises, chances are that through the events you might distinguish the challenges that your soul has chosen in order to help you recognize yourself and reveal your true inner power.

This doesn't mean that we shouldn't treat illnesses when they appear or take the time to alleviate the symptoms that are affecting us. However, medications, treatments of all kinds, and natural remedies should not be perceived as the only possible path to healing but rather as tools, crutches on which to lean that indicate the time to return to our mastery and for peace to settle in all the parts of ourselves that we sometimes tend to neglect.

Wouldn't it be fabulous to grant ourselves some time to go inside and have a gentle look at what is hiding behind a health problem in order to sort it out before it degenerates into some more serious illness? Next time a symptom appears in your body, rather than pretending that nothing is happening and going to fetch the aspirin, here is a very simple exercise that will allow you to reestablish you energy and find peace within yourself:

Integration: *Breathing Better to Live Better*

If you can, take the time to lie on a bed or on the floor so as to be totally relaxed. Settle in comfortably and grant yourself some time to unwind.

Then, taking three very deep abdominal breaths, visualize that you are in contact with your soul family through your ruling chakra (see Chapter 3). Invoke the presence of your guardian angels, guides, and of all your celestial protectors. If this is difficult for you, you may also think of the people you sincerely love, or of some happy memories that have marked your life. Allow your-

self to reconnect with any form of love and plenitude energy that you have felt before.

Again, take some deep breaths, floating in this beautiful love energy. Grant yourself the right to taste and fully enjoy this intimate privileged moment with your brothers and sisters of light.

Then, try to imagine how much God (or energy, or life, according to your beliefs) loves and accepts you as you are. Visualize that a gentle breeze filled with divine love reaches you and warms up your heart, or else fills the most uneasy part of your body.

With every inhalation, visualize divine light flooding more and more deeply within your body, and with every exhalation feel all the accumulated stress and all your uneasiness being expelled. If some discordant thoughts come to disturb your state of plenitude, love them too and see them melt in the light of absolute love.

Now visualize that many hands of light cover your entire body and take away the tensions, unlocking all the blockages that might remain in you, that the energy penetrates through all the pores of your skin and regenerates all your cells, that there is no more resistance nor limits to who you really are, and that any extra energy present in you is directly transmitted to the Earth to touch all those who, like you, are ready to welcome this wave of divine love pouring into all your being.

Illuminate your entire body and see it with the eyes of your own divine essence. With every inhalation, repeat "I am love" and with every exhalation "I am light." Notice that you become one with all that lives and that love now circulates in all of your being.

From now on, every time your body manifests any signs of fragility, weakness, or pain, you have the possibility of doing this exercise again. To refuse yourself this regenerating infusion would be like depriving your body of the food it needs for its survival. You are entitled to it. Let yourself be filled with the love and light of the entire universe.

CHAPTER 8

Vibrating in Love

The Physical Body: Privileged Ascension Vehicle

Message from October 20, 2005

The more your vibrations rise, the more sensitive you become to the energetic fluctuations that surround you. You may not always be aware of it consciously, but when you don't take the time daily to properly ground and create your field of protection, you remain more vulnerable to external disturbances. Indeed, if your energetic bodies are not perfectly aligned and harmonized, they can act like sponges and absorb various energies surrounding you, originating from all over the world.

Thus if you are affected by the passage of a hurricane, if you have sympathized with the pain or sickness of one of those dear to you, if your compassion over a social injustice has moved you to tears, chances are good that you have allowed yourself to be invaded by discordant energies that, even though they did not come directly from you, have found some resonance somewhere in one of your subtle bodies.

The unique solution available is the following: to recenter yourself and to listen to your inner state. Your body is talking to you; it invites you to channel the energy of love rather than those of dispersion and duality. Even if chaos is present all around you, letting it disturb you will not free humanity of it; this will be achieved by making the effort to remain centered and choosing to radiate love and peace no matter what seems to be surrounding you.

Remember this: even when a storm is raging on the surface, in the depths the ocean is calm and imperturbable. The same goes for your divine essence: it knows that everything you go through in the third dimension is an experience and an invitation to merge with your inner wisdom. This is why any minor disturbance, any symptom, any emotion, and any discordant thoughts must be treated first and foremost for what they are: a lack of love toward yourself, the reflection of your disconnection from your eternal self.

Any time you feel a discomfort, whatever it may be, go within and take the time to meditate and to replenish yourself at the heart of this ocean of infinite love that is perpetually available within you as well as around you. To do so, you must put aside all thought, positive as well as negative, to get back to who you really are: a light being, eternal and unlimited, becoming one with all that lives.

Deep down, know that beyond what you say or do, what will bring the most benefit to the world really is who you are at the depth of your being. Even if you are a champion at recycling, have adopted all the humanitarian causes, or spend all your money to get things moving, if in your heart there remains a single particle of resentment, dissatisfaction, or anger, these emotions will communicate to the whole of humanity through the energetic grid that surrounds the planet, and this will generate new energetic disturbances, surely leading to disastrous consequences for your world.

This goes to show the importance of what our thoughts create. This is the origin of the theory affirming that the fluttering of a butterfly's wings emits vibrations that can have repercussions in China, even causing a tsunami. You are all connected to each other; you are one in the planetary ascension process. It is no longer enough to work hard for a better world to manifest: you need to carry the new world within you, in every particle of your being.

No part of your body, neither your limbs nor your organs nor even your seven chakras, can tolerate imbalance or neglect from you. Because the fifth dimension is one of sovereign plenitude, it is crucial to pay attention at every moment to your privileged ascension vehicle, your physical body. The more it radiates health and harmony, the more luminous it will be. The more you manage to love and appreciate yourself as you are, the more you will elevate your vibration and subtle energies.

Hence the importance once again of mastering your thoughts and emotions. When these are repressed or submitted to your inner duality, they create a distortion in your subtle bodies. This distortion may eventually create a blockage in your internal circuits (energetic meridians) that will momentarily stop being properly supplied. If the brain, which acts as a transformer or catalyst of these energies, experiences a lack of electric fluidity, the neurons will be short-circuited. After a while this can translate into a deficiency affecting the corresponding part of the body.

Fortunately, you now know that it is easy to untie an energetic blockage before having felt its effects in your physical body: you simply need to make peace within you. Breathe deeply. Visualize yourself bathing in a sea of complete and total bliss. Recenter yourself in the energy of love emanating from your heart. Love heals everything. This is the absolute secret of healing: unconditional love toward yourself. It is the most powerful healing tool a healer can be equipped with: not an energetic technique or a capacity to achieve miracles, but rather a complete and total openness to the divine love present within, an unlimited faith in the love that God has for His creation, and in love as an energy of transformation that manifests even the impossible.

A lack of love toward yourself is therefore a lack of faith, or simply a lack—the feeling of not being fulfilled or of being incomplete. Dissatisfaction is one of the main causes of unease and sickness on Earth. Plenitude and love toward yourself are therefore the best possible remedies. How can this be put into practice? By applying yourself to living exclusively in the now. Ask yourself the following questions: Here and now, am I lacking anything? Here and now, can I choose to be happy, if only for a few seconds? Here and now, will my life stop if I take the time to breathe deeply and appreciate this incredible world that surrounds me?

Cultivating gratitude at every instant of your life is surely the best way to live in a permanent state of grace and to remain in good health. Reconnect to the celestial energy of healing and protection available in the whole universe. Say "yes" to who you really are, in unconditional love and infinite bliss. This is one of the best presents you can give yourself—and the entire planet.

—Bianca Gaia

The Body Needs Love Too

For several months, even years, countless messages tell of vibratory changes affecting your physical body. More and more discomforts are associated with the rise of your cosmic energies, and as a consequence, many of you don't even consult health professionals anymore, ignoring or denying the existence of any symptoms in yourselves.

In reality, while the actual planetary changes have a direct impact on your individual vibrations, this isn't a reason to neglect your health or your body.

When it feels pain, minor though it may be, it is because an energetic block lies somewhere within you, demanding immediate attention on your part.

If, however, despite your search you really cannot find the cause of these minor symptoms, it may be that an energetic cleansing is happening in your DNA, bringing up to your unconscious mind darkness that had been deeply buried. This is why even the most precise manuals on discomforts and illnesses leave you perplexed: your purification doesn't happen on the emotional, mental, or karmic planes, but rather at a cellular level.

Of course, you may ask your soul family or the celestial source for some help to alleviate these symptoms. You can also choose to simply trust and believe that they will go away just like they came, but isn't there the danger of overlooking some important information or crucial messages sent by your body?

Does This Belong to You?

It is true that people who are most sensitive to energy can easily perceive the influence of transmutation energies coming from various corners of the universe to help our beautiful planet complete this fantastic transition to higher dimensions. However, there is a big difference between feeling and being affected.

The same goes for energetic harmonization practitioners: some perceive the discordant energies of their clients, while others feel them in their own bodies. The latter are like sponges and see their own energy fluctuate according to the people who come through their offices or whom they encounter on the street.

If you feel any discomfort, you can ask yourself the following question: "Does this belong to me?" This query is legitimate; it is absolutely not necessary to suffer in order to coach, heal, or transmit healing energy to others. Similarly, working with light doesn't mean you have to work hard.

The more centered you remain and the more you apply yourself to living in the present, the more available and open you will be to harmonize nimbly the powerful transmutation energies presently working in and around you. But there is no reason for this to bring you any suffering or pain on a personal level. On the contrary, if you have the ability to perceive these energies, it is because you also have the capacity to channel, catalyze, or even recycle them for the benefit of all that lives in and around you. There is not, therefore, any reason for this to disturb you, because you can control the flow and choose your degree of openness to these luminous energies.

But could it be that in your work with light, you happen to forget to recharge your own batteries, to illuminate and feed your own subtle bodies before transmitting the energy around you? This could partially explain those physical symptoms felt from time to time. Some people pretend that their discomforts are only energetic because they are temporary, that these pains in the head, the back, the stomach, or elsewhere come and go. Mainly they minimize these pains because they don't understand, or do not want to take the time to understand, their presence and their reason for being there.

"My life is going well, I eat well, I meditate regularly, I am following the teachings I am given, there is no reason for me to be sick." The only possible explanation seems to be those infamous planetary vibratory changes and the cosmic energy transmitted by your celestial brothers and sisters.

But do you sincerely believe that in the higher dimensions, some energy capable of shaking your metabolism and affecting your state of health would intentionally be sent to you? Don't you think your soul families are somewhat wiser than this?

Loving Oneself

Some will say, "If you feel discomfort, it means your body or your personality is resisting." Consciously or otherwise, you translate this as, "This is my fault." Can you see that this is the kind of response that keeps you anchored in duality and guilt, giving you the feeling that you haven't yet arrived at the end of your troubles, that you are not being good enough or pure enough yet for the light to softly incarnate in you?

As soon as we establish comparisons or evaluations, the power that some people have over others is still prevalent. You have a right to wonder who those people are who dare to say that you still have a long way to go to access total bliss. Don't ever forget that ascension is not a goal to reach but a state of being, a permanent state of grace, and that a spark of love is enough to rekindle this infinite celestial fire within you.

Returning to your discomforts: when a symptom or pain manifests itself, it is probably only because there is still a lack of love toward yourself remaining somewhere in your conscious or unconscious mind, and your body wants you to become aware of it by manifesting itself lightly or firmly, according to the circumstances.

By being true to yourself and constantly remaining aware of the thoughts that you entertain within, you will be better disposed to catching those thoughts and choosing to transform them inside you before they crystallize in the shape of external problems or physical discomfort.

From now on, you will no longer feel that you are at the mercy of the planetary vibratory elevation, but rather you will have the privilege of contributing to it, gently and harmoniously, in peace in your soul, body, and heart. By maintaining your own energy level to its full capacity, you will no longer allow your surroundings to drain or parasitize you: there can only be space in you for the outer disturbances when your "inside," your soul, is in need or feels dissatisfaction at any level.

Hence the importance of loving oneself at every second, more and more each day. Love your body, look after it, take some time to rest, and replenish yourself daily. When you feel "invaded," send that discordant energy back where it came from, without judging it or trying to analyze it. When you feel drained by someone else, no matter who it is stealing your energy, visualize him or her also surrounded by a soul family that just wants to nourish and fulfill that person energetically, without needing your involvement to achieve it.

You know that you no longer need to "work hard"; you simply need to allow the love energy to flow freely in your life. You can make this conscious choice every time you inhale and exhale; it only requires a bit of practice. The benefits are not only immediate but increase with use. Isn't that wonderful? The more you love yourself, the happier and healthier you are, and the better the whole planet will feel.

Your body is the sacred vessel of your divinity, the physical vehicle that you have chosen for this unique experience in existence. The way you look after it reflects the way you treat the part of God present within you: the more your love grows toward yourself as you are, the more your quintessence manages to imprint itself deeply within your cells, your DNA, and your subtle bodies.

Bioenergetic Correspondence
How the chakras correspond to the different parts of the metabolism

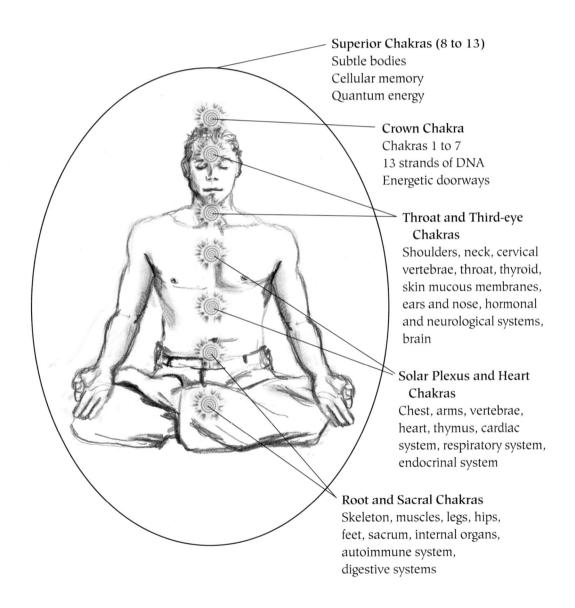

Superior Chakras (8 to 13)
Subtle bodies
Cellular memory
Quantum energy

Crown Chakra
Chakras 1 to 7
13 strands of DNA
Energetic doorways

**Throat and Third-eye
Chakras**
Shoulders, neck, cervical
vertebrae, throat, thyroid,
skin mucous membranes,
ears and nose, hormonal
and neurological systems,
brain

**Solar Plexus and Heart
Chakras**
Chest, arms, vertebrae,
heart, thymus, cardiac
system, respiratory system,
endocrinal system

Root and Sacral Chakras
Skeleton, muscles, legs, hips,
feet, sacrum, internal organs,
autoimmune system,
digestive systems

Love opens the way for the ascension energy to diffuse itself into all the particles of your being, including your body. Merge in love, both with your essence and your terrestrial vehicle, for it is by unifying all the parts of yourself that you will know the feeling of ultimate plenitude: access to the higher dimensions present first and foremost in yourself.

To help you circulate the energy adequately in your body, the following is an overview of the connections between the chakras, the areas of life, and the different parts of the physical body.

With the exception of the Facilitators and the Sages, we know that each soul family is connected to two specific chakras covering a particular area of the body. Therefore, when a block or a lack affects an area of your life ruled by these chakras, there is most probably part of the physical body corresponding to these chakras that is affected too. This is what is known as a bioenergetic correspondence.

1. Root and Sacral

Starting from the bottom of the illustration, we find the first two chakras, the root (red) and sacral (orange). Physical problems connected to these energy centers concern the skeleton, muscles, legs, hips, feet, sacrum, and internal organs, as well as the immune and digestive systems.

Generally speaking, when health problems appear in the lower part of your body, it means that you have some difficulties in grounding, incarnating, or insuring your survival: material security and comfort, hygiene, personal or professional worth, self-esteem, procreation or matters concerning your descendants, etc.

The soul family most likely to help you overcome these problems is the Builders.

2. Solar Plexus and Heart

Let us next examine what is connected to the solar plexus (yellow) and heart (green) chakras. The problems encountered will essentially be of an emotional nature and will present themselves in the chest, arms, vertebrae, and thymus, as well as the cardiac, respiratory, and endocrine systems.

As most of the discomforts in this area are related to the heart dimension, the areas affected will involve emotions and interpersonal relationships: expressing one's feelings, inspiration and creativity, settling conflicts, emotional development, social belonging, sentimental experiences, and so on.

The soul family to invoke for these kinds of troubles is, of course, the Artisans.

3. Throat and Third Eye

Regarding the next two chakras, the throat (sky blue) and the third eye (indigo), as you might expect the discomfort connected to the intellectual sphere of being is mostly found from the shoulders to the brain: the shoulders, neck, cervical vertebrae, throat, thyroid, skin, mucus membranes, ears and nose, the hormonal and neurological systems, and the brain.

These chakras are connected to existential questions and mental preoccupations: truth, authenticity, respect, communication, verbal expression, evolution and personal growth, concentration, attention, and learning ability, as well as recognition of one's skills.

The corresponding soul family is the Visionaries.

4. The Crown

The crown chakra (violet) is connected to the spiritual dimension of being. The problems encountered are more difficult to define because they are located in the energetic sphere and concern the first to seventh chakras, thirteen strands of DNA, and the energetic doorways.

Even if we don't manage to clearly perceive those areas of energy in the subtle bodies, the consequences of any energetic disturbance are tangible on a conscious level. They affect the capacity to recenter oneself, to relax, to appease oneself, to go inward, to connect both among ourselves and to the great whole, to find one's life mission, and similar matters.

To realign on the energetic level, it is useful to call on the Facilitators soul family.

5. Higher Chakras

Even though very few people manage to visualize them, the higher chakras remain our privileged connection to our higher self. They evolve in the higher cosmic and celestial spheres from which it is possible to work on the subtle bodies, cellular memories, and quantum energy.

Although it is overly esoteric for some, those energetic vibrations allow us to intervene on the causal level, also called karma in the ancient scriptures of Hinduism: the holistic perspective of the individual, his or her past lives, transgenerational baggage, and so on.

The soul family that inspires and supervises those energetic reharmonizations is the Sages, including all the archangels, in particular Metatron, and the ascended masters invoked on such occasions.

Celebrating Life while Cultivating Love

When you reconnect to your inner light, to your soul family, and to the five dimensions of your being, you revive the essence of who you really are. It is therefore no longer necessary to "work hard" on yourself.

Rather than constantly splitting hairs or trying to understand the how and the why or the ins and outs of all your discomforts and illnesses, the great soul families invite you instead to celebrate life.

The more you cultivate love toward yourself and all that lives, the more you remain centered in the present moment, the more you apply yourself to living in gratitude from the depth of your heart, and the more life will appear beautiful and luminous to you.

This is what you have heard, read, and applied for years, but have you really integrated it in your whole being? Ascension, as you know, is only possible in this state.

The best part about all this is that from now on, you are receiving help. You are no longer alone. By feeling more and more the acting, loving, and beneficial presence of your soul family, you will feel more in harmony internally and learn to truly love life, present in all the dimensions.

Asking to Be Protected by Our Soul Family

I would like to share a true story that I was told a few years ago about help from our soul families. You have probably heard of people who have had extraordinary experiences in which angels have intervened in their favor at a time when their life was in danger. Most of the time the intervention took place in the invisible realm, and the person rescued was only able to feel or hear the presence of their protectors. This account is astonishing in that the person concerned didn't perceive anything.

A young woman was returning home very late on a dark night. At one point she had to pass through a rather dark alley that always gave her a chill. That evening a man was standing at the entrance to the alley. Hidden in the shadows, he seemed to be waiting for something, but his dubious appearance immediately raised the young woman's suspicions.

Before entering the alley, she called on her guardian angels, asking them for protection and reassurance. Then, knowing she had no other choice, she walked down the alley. She felt the intense dark look of the man go through her, but he made no attempt to attack her.

Some days later, to her surprise, the young woman discovered a photograph of the man in question in the local paper. He had been arrested for a rape committed the very same night she had encountered him on the street. The tragedy had happened at the same spot only a few minutes after she had passed by.

Intrigued, she couldn't help but want to get to the bottom of the story. Since she was a journalist, she was allowed to enter the jail to question the offender. "Why her, and not me?" she asked him. The man answered, "Aren't you that woman who passed by a bit earlier that night, escorted by those two tall muscular guys? I knew I wasn't strong enough to go up against those guys."

While the woman hadn't perceived anything, the attacker had indeed seen the angels that were protecting her.

Since the day I heard that story, I have never again questioned the capacity of my guardian angels to ensure my protection. You too can appeal to your soul family not only to protect you but also to accompany you in all your life experiences, open the way for you, smooth out your difficulties, resolve your existential worries, and heal your health problems.

All you need to do is to trust them, but mainly to have the courage to ask them for help when you need it. They are waiting for you just there, very near, in the silence of your heart.

Exercise: *Recreating Unity in Ourselves*

There is a simple energetic technique to consciously undo any energetic blockage before it imprints itself in your physical body as a discomfort. This body-mind-soul reunification tool originates from the Buddhist philosophy that aims at remaining on the "middle path," put simply, to reestablish the balance between extremes and thereby bring the personality to a feeling of security and move forward in confidence toward the light.

The visualization exercise suggested below is inspired by an exercise offered by the Canadian psychologist Jean Monbourquette in his book À Chacun Sa Mission. *It helps to realign energetically the two cerebral hemispheres toward a pacifying and reunifying symbolic consensus, thus establishing a bridge between reality as it is perceived in a limited way by the mind, and the ideal, aimed at by the soul in constant evolution.*

Settle comfortably in a quiet place where you won't be disturbed. Take some time to relax and center yourself. Invite your guides, your guardian angels, and your celestial family to accompany you on this journey. Try to create a void in yourself and to be aware of your breathing in the present moment. Inhale and exhale deeply numerous times.

Now, try to visualize the state of peace and well-being to which you aspire with your entire self. If you were living in an ideal world, if you were a "perfect" being, what would you look like? How would you feel in all your cells, thoughts, and emotions? If you asked your subconscious to find a symbol (an animal, an object, a famous mythical or fictional character) to represent your ideal self, what would it be? Take the time to visualize this symbol, describe its characteristics, and identify the qualities you like about it.

Then consider a fear, a conflict, a wound, or a negative thought currently present in you. For example: what part of your personality or your body do you dislike most? Or else, what most affects you within or around you? What effect does it have in you? By going in and taking a deep breath again, ask yourself if there is a part of your body in which you can feel a certain tension or uneasiness. If there is, put your hands on that spot and let the purification and relief energy flow through your hands.

Then ask your subconscious mind to inspire you with a second symbol (an animal, an object, a famous mythical or fictional character), an image that evokes the fear, wound, or other matter that you have identified. Describe the characteristic of this symbol and the negative aspects it conjures without judging yourself or holding back. Let your imagination flow freely.

Finally, ask your higher self—the part of you that knows how to harmonize the two psychic poles, your mind and soul—to synthesize those two symbols.

Hold your arms out straight on each side of your body at the height of your shoulders. Turn your gaze toward your wide-open right hand, and imagine that you see your first symbol, the positive one, materialize in this hand. Then see the second, negative symbol appear similarly in your left hand, the heart one.

Gently, slowly, bring your hands together while asking your higher self, your divine essence, to integrate the symbols within you by merging them into a third symbol, one that illustrates the harmonization of the soul and spirit in its proper regenerating balance. Join your hands to signify your tangible intention to welcome this balance and this peace within yourself, and let yourself be filled by what this new symbol evokes in you.

Could it be that this integrating symbol invites you to unconditionally welcome yourself, to find harmony and serenity within? Generally, it will have a spiritual, sacred, or precious meaning to you; it is an inspiration, a model to follow for your life path.

You can find a way to integrate this symbol into your everyday life. Find an illustration or an object to place in an obvious spot where you spend the majority of your time. This will allow your consciousness to remain aligned and centered on this opening you have created within yourself, which has managed to undo the energetic block in your mind, or even liberate your body from the physical symptoms that may have been attached to it.

I would be pleased to hear how it went.

Integration: *The Healing Love*
Ho'oponopono

By Joe Vitale

Two years ago, I heard about a therapist in Hawaii who cured a complete ward of criminally insane patients—without ever seeing any of them. The psychologist would study an inmate's chart and then look within himself to see how he created that person's illness. As he improved himself, the patient improved.

When I first heard this story, I thought it was an urban legend. How could anyone heal anyone else by healing himself? How could even the best self-improvement master cure the criminally insane? It didn't make any sense. It wasn't logical, so I dismissed the story.

However, I heard it again a year later. I heard that the therapist had used a Hawaiian healing process called ho'oponopono, which means "straitening," "rectifying," and "correcting" in Hawaiian. I had never heard of it, yet I couldn't get it out of my mind. If the story was at all true, I had to know more. I had always understood "total responsibility" to mean that I am responsible for what I think and do. Beyond that, it's out of my hands. I think that most people think of total responsibility that way. We're responsible for what we do, not what anyone else does—but that's wrong.

The Hawaiian therapist who healed those mentally ill people would teach me an advanced new perspective about total responsibility. His name is Dr. Ihaleakala Hew Len. We probably spent an hour talking during our first phone call. I asked him to tell me the complete story of his work as a therapist.

He explained that he worked at Hawaii State Hospital for four years. That ward where they kept the criminally insane was dangerous. Psychologists quit on a monthly basis. The staff called in sick a lot or simply quit. People would walk through the ward with their backs against the wall, afraid of being attacked by patients. It was not a pleasant place to live, work, or visit.

Dr. Len told me that he never saw patients. He agreed to have an office and to review their files. While he looked at those files, he would work on himself. As he worked on himself, patients began to heal.

"After a few months, patients that had to be shackled were being allowed to walk freely," he told me. "Others who had to be heavily medicated were getting off their medications. And those who had no chance of ever being released were being freed." I was in awe. "Not only that," he went on, "but the staff began to enjoy coming to work. Absenteeism and turnover disappeared. We ended up with more staff than we needed because patients were being released, and all the staff was showing up to work. Today, that ward is closed."

This is when I had to ask the million-dollar question: "What were you doing within yourself that caused those people to change?"

"I was simply healing the part of me that created them," he said. I didn't understand. Dr. Len explained that total responsibility for your life means that everything in your life—simply because it is in your life—is your responsibility. In a literal sense, the entire world is your creation.

Whew. That is tough to swallow. Being responsible for what I say or do is one thing; being responsible for what everyone in my life says or does is quite another. Yet the truth is this: if you take complete responsibility for your life, then everything you see, hear, taste, touch, or in any way experience is your responsibility because it is in your life. This means that terrorist activity, the president, the economy, or anything you experience and don't like is up to you to heal. They don't exist, in a manner of speaking, except as projections from inside you. The problem isn't with them, it's with you, and to change them, you have to change you.

I know this is tough to grasp, let alone accept or actually live. Blame is far easier than total responsibility, but as I spoke with Dr. Len, I began to realize that healing for him and in ho'oponopono means loving yourself.

If you want to improve your life, you have to heal your life. If you want to cure anyone, even a mentally ill criminal, you do it by healing you.

I asked Dr. Len how he went about healing himself. What was he doing, exactly, when he looked at those patients' files?

"I just kept saying 'I'm sorry' and 'I love you' over and over again," he explained.

"That's it?"

"That's it."

It turns out that loving yourself is the greatest way to improve yourself, and as you improve yourself, you improve your world.

Let me give you a quick example of how this works: one day someone sent me an e-mail that upset me. In the past I would have handled it by working on my emotional hot buttons or by trying to reason with the person who sent the nasty message. This time I decided to try Dr. Len's method. I kept silently saying "I'm sorry" and "I love you." I didn't say it to anyone in particular. I was simply evoking the spirit of love to heal within me what was creating the outer circumstances.

Within an hour I got an e-mail from the same person. He apologized for his previous message. Keep in mind that I didn't take any outward action to get that apology; I didn't even write him back. Yet by saying "I love you," I somehow healed within me what was creating him.

I later attended a ho'oponopono workshop run by Dr. Len. He's now seventy years old, considered a grandfatherly shaman, and is somewhat reclusive.

He praised my book, The Attractor Factor. *He told me that as I improve myself, my book's vibration will rise, and everyone will feel it when they read it. In short, as I improve, my readers will improve.*

"What about the books that are already sold and out there?" I asked.

"They aren't out there," he explained, once again blowing my mind with his mystic wisdom. "They are still in you." In short, there is no "out there." It would take a whole book to explain this advanced technique with the depth it deserves.

Suffice it to say that whenever you want to improve anything in your life, there's only one place to look: inside you. When you look, do it with love.

Source: http://healingdrummer.blogspot.com/2006/07/hooponopono-by-joe-vitale.html

CHAPTER 9

The Five Ways of Acquiring Energy

Where to Find Light?

Message from October 9, 2006

Why do human beings spend so much time in front of their televisions, computer screens, or video game consoles? Simply because they need light in order to live, and even a dim artificial light turns out to be preferable to total darkness or solitude of the heart.

Human beings need light the way plants need the sun and water to survive. Light is a form of energy that feeds and revitalizes all of your being. It allows you to recharge your batteries and especially to reconnect with who you really are. This light, or prana *as the Hindus call it, is the source of every living thing. It is the electricity freely flowing through your inner circuits: your synapses, your meridians, your chakras, feeding and regenerating both your physical and energetic bodies.*

It is impossible for any living being to live without light. This is why you spend your life finding a way to get this light, make it yours, and store it in all your cells. Just like sunflowers at the end of the summer, you ceaselessly sway from left to right, back to front, constantly looking for the tiniest ray of sun shining from the sky. It is so simple, though, to find the light inside of you: you simply have to connect to your own inner sun, the light of divine love alive in all your being.

So many people have forgotten that they are themselves light. They don't know how to rekindle their inner fire, and they find themselves having to compensate for it through resources outside of themselves. Are you one of those people looking for a particle of light in the eyes of every person you meet, to quench your thirst, as if you'd been lost in the desert? Just like the child who catches a glimpse of pride in his parents' eyes, do you spend your life trying to find that spark of approval and love from those near you to ease your lonely soul?

By trying to nourish yourself through the recognition and admiration of your peers or by waiting for a moment of attention from them every time you accomplish something, you remain primarily turned outward. You have encoded the fact that anything spectacular you do will be rewarded by the luminous gaze of the other, just like a brief ray of sun that will momentarily brighten your inner sky. What you have accomplished no longer needs to be good or beneficial to your fellow human beings; each and every glance is filled with energy, and it briefly suffices to sustain your inner thirst.

In reality, let's ask ourselves: what if all those games of power, war, and control taking place everywhere on the planet were nothing more than the reflection of this massive need for every individual to get energy from others? Whether this energy is positive or negative matters little, as long as you are satiated, even for a brief moment. So goes your world. You think you are no more than light "vacuums," always looking for more energy, ready to drain it from those around you, with or without their consent.

Even worse, if you don't manage to get the attention of your peers, any other luminous source will do. Like moths attracted to a flame, you gather around those luminous screens of all sizes that diffuse pale reflections night and day, keeping you in the illusion of being in communion with the light of others.

You must admit that those who have learned to synthesize light and lock it into a tube are clever: they have understood that an artificial ray of sun is preferable to life in darkness. If you can't illuminate your entire being, if your eyes manage to grab even a few weak rays of light, this will give the brain the momentary illusion of being fulfilled.

This isn't about denying the importance of those powerful technological tools that have in many ways contributed to humanity's progress. But as in all things, it is excess that causes harm. How many of your children are now obsessed by machines that keep them in a parallel universe outside of time and reality? Who among you can spend a day without checking your e-mail? How many of you come back from work and settle in front of the television for the rest of the evening?

Why satisfy yourself with a mere illusion when you can taste the real light, the light that illuminates and transforms the entire being?

Since time immemorial, all civilizations have taught human beings how to gain access to this unlimited inner light. Whether through meditation, prayer, yoga, or martial arts, it is easy to find the inner peace that allows light to flow inside of you, for this light is very much here and present. You know it, and you have always known it. The sacred fire vibrates in all of your being, and you occasionally access it through a brief moment of amorous, sexual, or mystic ecstasy. Imagine that you could recreate at will this magical moment of fusion with your divine self through some very simple breathing exercises. Isn't that what the yogis have practiced for millennia? Nowadays, meditation is more and more in fashion; bringing calm to your agitated mind can only be beneficial on all levels. But what about the rest of the body? It is through breathing and harmonious movements that light can circulate and spread into all of your being.

Tai chi, as well as other practices aimed at amplifying the life energy that supplies your body, turns out to be an excellent illumination technique. But you could also practice walking, dancing, or swimming. What matters is the motivation, the purpose for which you move. Is it only to keep yourself in shape, or do you truly apply yourself to reconnecting with your flamboyant essence?

Would you like to find the light and make it yours at any given moment? Do you want to enjoy perfect health and to live many happy years at peace with yourself? It is possible for you to achieve this by unifying with all the different aspects of yourself. Recenter on your own inner sun, at the height of the solar plexus, and breathe deeply while visualizing the luminous energy increasing and intensifying until it encompasses you fully.

"You are the light of the world." Does this sound familiar? If you take the time to reconnect to your inner light and increase your energetic vitality, you will no longer be light "vacuums" but rather torch bearers. Be the ones who transmit the divine flame rather than the ones who hoard it. You just have to remember who you are.

You are light.

You are energy.

You are love.

Love, indeed, remains the best tool of integration of your inner light. The more you love and accept yourself as you are, the more your inner light will grow and shine everywhere within and around you.

Say "yes" to the wonderful being that you are. Breathe deeply and see your vital energy grow and vitalize your body and your mind. Let your inner sun warm up and illuminate your entire being. Connect to the sky, to the Earth, and to everything that lives. From now on, you become one with the universal energy. Your light not only revitalizes and regenerates all your living cells, it emanates well beyond your body, shining like a thousand suns and being transmitted to the entire planet.

You are an enlightened being. You have always been so. Nothing will take you away from the light that you come from and that pours out of you here and now, and for eternity, in the sacred fire of universal love.

—*Bianca Gaia*

Living in Light

Wouldn't it be amazing if, at every moment of every day, we lived in light, and we took the time to meditate and center ourselves at every moment in order to acquire the universal energy that maintains us in perfect balance in all the dimensions of ourselves? Of course, that would be ideal. In reality, we are regularly confronted with complex situations that unsettle us. Daily we are surrounded by people who invade our light cocoon, trying to bring us down or to squeeze us like lemons.

In a perfect world, we would only have to go back inside ourselves and feel that it is just an illusion for everything to return to its optimum state. However, we are at times tired, unsettled, or worried. Because our soul aspires to make us recognize the divine and wonderful being that we are, it will attract events and opportunities to reveal our unlimited inner potential to us. All these problems, conflicts, and dramas we encounter are indeed the challenges sent by the most luminous part of ourselves to encourage the emergence of all the energetic power that inhabits us.

Our soul, our sixth sense, the part of our brain that only wants to be developed acknowledges the presence of the energy of light trapped inside us, and it will do everything to allow it to come out into the light of day; hence all the apparently problematic situations that happen when we least expect them.

Thierry, one of my clients, was very disappointed because his girlfriend and most of his friends had forgotten his birthday. Sure, it had snowed a lot that day and a few days previously, and snowstorms tend to affect the mood of the population in general because they limit movement. Thierry therefore thought that he was wrong to be saddened for so little and was thinking that his ego had expectations that he needed my help to get rid of.

During our consultation, I invited him to examine the days that had preceded his birthday: what state of mind was he in? Was he looking forward to this beautiful moment to arrive? Was he really expecting, "demanding," a special celebration? "On the contrary," he answered, "I was very absorbed with my job. I spent the week on the road trying to catch up on delivery delays caused by the snowstorms. I didn't have a minute to myself. I worked over sixty hours straight, and when I got back home, I went directly to bed."

The law of attraction means that in life, people have a natural tendency to treat us not the way we treat them but rather the way we treat ourselves. Thierry's problem, therefore, wasn't his expectations of the events to come but rather the fact that he had forgotten himself and neglected his own essential needs. His soul then helped bring him back to his senses by making him aware of his negligence in the only way available to it: other people's attitudes.

The best way to live a fulfilled life and to live in harmony with those around us is taking good care of yourself so that others will do the same with you. Once again, this is not being selfish, but rather it is keeping a balance between outer reality (responsibilities, work, and survival) and inner needs (fulfillment, quality of life, and replenishment).

Stealing Other People's Light

It is only when we neglect our own essential needs that it becomes necessary to go get energy outside ourselves to compensate for the inner void. This is what we call a survival reaction: desperately needing energy to survive, the personality will try to grab it by any means available, even if it means stealing it from others.

There are various ways of taking energy from our fellow human beings. We are not always aware of it, but the way that we react to mishaps in our lives is dictated by this intense need to get the maximum energy to keep ourselves afloat internally. Our primary reactions—anger, sadness, denial, and guilt—reveal our recurrent stratagems of choice when it comes to recharging our energetic batteries in our daily lives and our relations with those around us.

The following exercise allows you to become aware of your various unconscious mechanisms. Without judging yourself or trying to overrationalize each of the following affirmations, consider the way you spontaneously react to everyday situations. This test will allow you to identify what your true values are, which behaviors you generally adopt in your life, and the methods you use to get energy from others.

Exercise: *Test Your Egogram*

For each of the following affirmations, check "Somewhat True" each time you recognize yourself or mostly agree with what is described. Otherwise, check "Somewhat False." Answer spontaneously, without taking time to think it over. When you can't decide, simply jump to the next affirmation. It doesn't matter if some lines are left blank.

AFFIRMATION	Somewhat True	Somewhat False
1. It is easy for me to express my point of view and bring forth my opinions. ▲		
2. Faced with a problem, I don't hesitate to admit my limitations and ask for help if I need it. ◆		
3. In my family, we were not allowed to show our emotions; we had to be reserved and polite. ▼		
4. With my friends, lending a helping hand doesn't bother me. I readily volunteer to help out. ■		
5. I am not afraid to tell people what I think. Sincerity is crucial in human relationships. ●		

AFFIRMATION	Somewhat True	Somewhat False
6. I very much enjoy physical activity (walking, tennis, swimming, gardening, etc.). It gives me a lot of energy. ▲		
7. I am rather submissive and obedient. ◆		
8. I am generally on time for meetings, and in turn I avoid keeping people waiting. ▼		
9. I readily lend people my things without worrying about whether they will be returned to me or not. ■		
10. I feel at ease, tranquil, and comfortable in my skin. ●		
11. I have a tendency to get angry and to be impatient more often that I would like. ▲		
12. Giving orders scares me, and I do not like to take on responsibilities. ◆		
13. I like a job that is done well, done precisely, and is completed on time. ▼		
14. When a work colleague asks me for information, I do not hesitate to provide it, even if we are in competition. ■		
15. I feel free in my life choices and in the decisions that I make. ●		
16. In a group, I like to take the lead and direct operations. ▲		

AFFIRMATION	Somewhat True	Somewhat False
17. When I share something, I readily accept the smaller part. ◆		
18. I suffer easily from the criticisms others make about my behavior. ▼		
19. I enjoy contact with people and have a tendency to favor the social element of my professional activities, even if I don't always know where this will lead. ■		
20. I like a job done well; this is why I apply myself to respect the procedures and deadlines that need to be followed. ●		
21. I drive fast whenever I can because I enjoy speed. ▲		
22. I think I lack confidence in myself and often doubt my abilities. ◆		
23. My parents brought me up strictly and with respect for principles. ▼		
24. I am very comfortable with everyone, even strangers. ■		
25. I always make decisions quickly, even on important matters or in difficult situations, because I do not like things to drag out. ▲		
26. I find it hard to put an end to some relationships, even if I know they are not good for me. ◆		

AFFIRMATION	Somewhat True	Somewhat False
27. I have been accused of being a bit of a moralist and of preaching. ▼		
28. I readily lend a hand to my coworkers and collaborators, even if I don't have much spare time. ■		
29. Unlike many children my age, my parents encouraged me to think for myself. ●		
30. I am often told that I have quite a temper; it is true that I do not let people step all over me. ▲		
31. I try to give my children the affection that I didn't get. ◆		
32. I like methodical work; I can be picky in making sure the instructions are respected. ▼		
33. I am a good negotiator, and I have been called on many times to resolve difficult problems between people efficiently. ■		
34. I manage to cooperate well with my boss, without necessarily being in agreement with him on many points. ●		
35. I am often impatient with people who don't understand me well right away. ▲		
36. I have a tendency to find that others are better than me. ◆		

AFFIRMATION	Somewhat True	Somewhat False
37. I am more logical than intuitive, which facilitates the detailed analysis of problems to draw out useful solutions. ▼		
38. I want to help young people blossom and be happy. ●		
39. Whatever people say, children need us much longer than it seems, and you need to be ready.■		
40. When I feel someone is trying to put pressure on me, I see red. ▲		
41. I keep thankless or difficult tasks to myself so as not to burden others. ◆		
42. I enjoy explaining things and helping people understand and discover new things. ▼		
43. I love my partner and my children very much; family has a very important place in my life. ■		
44. In everything, you need to know how to maintain the right balance. ●		
45. When I am criticized, I respond straight away.▲		
46. To please my boss and finish what she asks me to do, I have at times canceled a dinner or worked on a weekend, even if she had not asked me to.◆		
47. When I need to make a decision in a tricky situation, I try to get the proper information and accumulate indisputable facts. ▼		

AFFIRMATION	Somewhat True	Somewhat False
48. I think it is important to be esteemed by the people around us, and I work at it more efficiently than the average person. ■		
49. I like to meet people, but I also need quiet and solitude. I am not afraid to live on my own. ●		
50. I love competition, and I usually manage to do better than others. ▲		
51. I am very tolerant of other people's mistakes. After all, nobody is perfect. ◆		
52. Those around me find me a bit cold and distant at times. ▼		
53. I am rather generous. I like to give presents, but I often spend too much. ■		
54. I balance my time between work and hobbies quite well; both interest me. ●		
55. To manage people is to make everyone give the maximum of their potential. ▲		
56. I prefer to ask trusted people for their advice before making any decisions. ◆		
57. I never get angry, and my mood is constant even if I am annoyed by the situation. ▼		
58. It is normal to sacrifice ourselves for the happiness of our children. ■		

AFFIRMATION	Somewhat True	Somewhat False
59. I have a happy family life: I have built and I continue building positive relationships with my partner and my children. ●		
60. It is true that I can be jealous in my romantic relationships and in friendships. ▲		
61. I still remember clearly the shame I experienced in childhood, in my family, or at school. ◆		
62. During my life I have often changed my opinion on essential issues, after reading and seeking information on the subject. ▼		
63. I like having contact with foreigners and feel at ease with people who are different from me. ■		
64. Life changes and evolves constantly; I need to adjust to it rather than trying to change others. ●		
65. I don't really believe in recipes and methods; I prefer to experiment for myself. ▲		
66. Too often I continue to follow certain principles even though I increasingly doubt their relevance, but this is how I was brought up, and there is nothing I can do about it. ◆		
67. I am used to foreseeing and planning my professional work and my private life; this allows me to be more relaxed and tranquil. ▼		
68. One needs to learn to devote oneself to the right causes; this is what gives life a meaning. ■		

AFFIRMATION	Somewhat True	Somewhat False
69. In education, it is crucial to have trusting relationships with one's children.	●	
70. I sometimes honk, gesture, or flash my lights at drivers who do not respect the rules of the road.	▲	
71. I easily get the feeling that I do not have any luck.	◆	
72. Faced with a difficult decision, I will go with what my reason tells me, because I am a reasonable person.	▼	
73. It is not possible to live a tranquil and carefree life while more than a quarter of the world's population suffers from hunger.	■	
74. I regularly make blunders like forgetting an appointment or arriving late.	●	
75. It is true that I have difficulty delegating because I don't always trust the way others do things.	▲	
76. I don't like conflict, and in order to avoid it, when I have a problem with someone, I prefer to give in.	◆	
77. I like to be told very clearly what is expected of me and what I need to do. Thus I am efficient in my work because I don't like to take much initiative.	▼	
78. The war on poverty and hunger worldwide is the biggest challenge of our time.	■	

AFFIRMATION	Somewhat True	Somewhat False
79. I do not fear silence when I'm talking to someone or in a group; on the contrary, this aids us in reflection and communication. ●		
80. I admit that I don't always trust the capacity of others, and I have a tendency to check what they have done. ▲		
81. I don't like it when people sulk because I sometimes think they are angry with me or that I am the cause. ◆		
82. I love precise things, rules, and procedures, and it is true that at times I get lost in procedures and lose sight of my objectives. ▼		
83. I like to thank people and show them my gratitude. ■		
84. I prefer for people to form their own opinions rather than giving them advice; it is better for them to learn through their own experiences. ●		
85. I sometimes raise my voice, and it is true that I have a tendency to blow up easily. ▲		
86. My attic is full of old stuff and old clothes; I find it hard to throw away things I no longer use. ◆		
87. It is true that I find it hard to show interest in people, even when I appreciate them. I don't have a very demonstrative personality, and I rarely give compliments. ▼		

AFFIRMATION	Somewhat True	Somewhat False
88. I have a tendency to be too good; when I am asked for a favor, I can't say no.	■	
89. I try to look on the bright side of life; I always end up fine and am able to draw some profitable lessons.	●	
90. I find that people who are too kind are often boring or uninteresting.	▼	
91. I don't like to get criticism because it hurts me. I find it difficult to detach from it and not let it affect me personally.	◆	
92. I like to take risks, and conflicts don't scare me; I enjoy having an adrenaline rush from time to time.	▲	
93. I have a tendency to take things in hand and to master all situations well.	■	
94. I have learned to define my priorities and to take them into account in the decisions I make; this way I am less spread out.	●	
95. I like competition, especially when I am winning.	▲	
96. When I think about my life, I see that I have often changed ideas and perspectives on fundamental issues.	●	
97. Outside of my area of expertise, I feel neither the right nor the ability to judge, and I trust the specialists.	▼	

AFFIRMATION	Somewhat True	Somewhat False
98. I can pretty much predict what is going to happen when I start an action; I always have a few possible solutions in mind. ■		
99. At times I am pessimistic or depressed when things are not going well. ◆		
100. My material environment is at least as important as moral and spiritual values; we need some balance in life. ●		

Once you have completed the test, add up the number of "Somewhat True" answers according to these categories:

Number of ▲: _____
Number of ◆: _____
Number of ▼: _____
Number of ■: _____
Number of ●: _____

After taking the test and adding up your answers, transfer the total of each life position to the corresponding columns in the following table. You simply need to fill each column up to the level corresponding to the results obtained, according to the points you accumulated for each type of personality.

Portrait of the Five Defense Mechanisms

What are your favorite ways to acquire energy?

▲	◆	▼	■	●
----20----	----20----	----20----	----20----	----20----
----18----	----18----	----18----	----18----	----18----
----15----	----15----	----15----	----15----	----15----
----12----	----12----	----12----	----12----	----12----
----9----	----9----	----9----	----9----	----9----
----6----	----6----	----6----	----6----	----6----
----3----	----3----	----3----	----3----	----3----
----0----	----0----	----0----	----0----	----0----
Perpetrator/ Intimidator	Victim/ "Poor Me"	Indifferent Aloof	Savior/ Interrogator	Witness/ Centered

Results

Generally speaking, if your number of "somewhat true" answers varies between nine and twelve in each column, you are a rather balanced person. You know how to adjust and react differently according to the situations you are exposed to. You allow yourself to get the energy available around you in the way that most benefits your balance in the moment without getting caught up in a specific typology.

If, on the other hand, the total of one or several columns stands out considerably from the others, if the number of responses seems much higher or much lower in some categories, it is a sign of some imbalance at the level of your personality.

The different affirmations you read during the test reflect your primary reactions, those that characterize you when your survival instinct is threatened. The typology with the highest score represents your most common way of stealing or draining energy from others. This is what is called a defense mechanism or control drama, as identified by author James Redfield in his book *The Celestine Prophecy*. The lowest total corresponds to the repressed part of your personality, the one you may not allow yourself to freely express.

To better understand each of these instinctive mechanisms, it is important to let go of any notion of judgment or moralizing criticism. You must remember that it is impossible for any human being to survive without vital energy, and that it is not always easy in a conflicting situation to recenter yourself in order to get back to your inner balance without soliciting those around you.

In an ideal world, meditation would be taught to children from an early age, and three deep breaths would be enough for anyone to reconnect to the feeling of inner peace. In reality, most modern societies live in an endless power struggle to obtain the energy of others—willingly or forcibly.

When a technique to obtain energy works well, it then becomes easy to repeat the process and for it to become a means to an end. A particular typology then overtakes the others, shaping the personality and character of an individual until this structurally repetitive and limited pattern becomes predominant, thus smothering the person's real inner light. Below is an overview of the five favored ways used by humans to revitalize their energetic bodies.

The Five Ways to Acquire Energy
From *The Celestine Prophecy*'s "Control Dramas"

1. By Frontal Confrontation

The Perpetrator or Intimidator

Motivation: anger

Imposes, controls, threatens, attacks

The energy leaps forward from the top of the body, and
jumps toward others like a predator on prey.

1. By Frontal Confrontation: The Perpetrator

The first way of acquiring energy from others is by forcing them to give it to us by imposing ourselves on them. We may do this by being charming, by manipulating, or by convincing the other person that we deserve his support. Such charisma is typical of politicians and people in positions of power.

It is the constructive aspect that Redfield calls the Intimidator: he or she uses his power of persuasion to maintain control over situations, events, and people around him. He affirms himself and knows how to get ahead, has the courage to make decisions, and generally gets everyone to follow him. He makes a good army general: he knows how to take advantage of any situation to get to the top and obtain the most prestigious medals.

On the negative side, this type of person will have a tendency to disregard other people's opinions. He tends to put his own ideas first. He won't hesitate, if need be, to use his physical strength in order to impose his will. This is why he can easily be called a perpetrator in popular psychology. He is the mean one, the bad guy in every action movie and children's tale, the one without whom the adventure couldn't happen.

His way of functioning is, "It is me who decides, and if it doesn't work out as I intended, I will impose, control, threaten, aggress, and if need be, punch."

According to his vision of things, he is right, and you are wrong. The Perpetrator's message is that he is superior, and that others are therefore inferior to him. As Eric Berne, creator of transactional analysis, would say, his life position is, "I'm OK; you're not OK."

What characterizes the Perpetrator is anger. On the vibratory level, his way of getting energy is by extracting it from others, willingly or by force, the way we squeeze a lemon. In his energetic fields, he gets power from his grounding to jump forward out of his body and pounce on others like a predator on prey. His strategy is to dominate others in order to obtain his energy.

What we need to understand is that deep down, the Perpetrator is shaking with fear that his weaknesses or vulnerabilities might be uncovered. He is suspicious of others, and this is what makes him angry: he is afraid to be betrayed. By maintaining and imposing his control, he then believes he is mastering the situation and keeping the upper hand.

One part of the Perpetrator imagines that the best way to silence his fear is to impose it on others by generating fear in them. The problem is that it remains present inside him anyway. On top of that, the energy he is draining from others is never quite enough to totally reassure him. And even if he excels at getting respect and getting other people's attention, he remains constantly unhappy and unsatisfied.

If your higher score is in the column of the Perpetrator, there is a good chance that you were brought up in a family where you had to fight to survive. One of your parents was probably controlling and dominating, and you understood that the best way to gain respect was to ensure that you mastered any situation you were confronted with.

This also explains why people who suffer from violence during childhood have a tendency to recreate the same pattern with their own children. Because it is the only role model they had, it remains the only way they know to acquire energy, attention, and respect from others.

In the following chapter, we will talk about some practical solutions to undo this alienating typology, but for now, it is better to consider the space that other defense mechanisms have in your life. Could there be one in particular that you haven't experimented very well with until now?

2. From the Left

The Victim: "Poor Me"

Motivation: sadness

Complains, despairs, begs, implores

Weakness of the solar plexus, caving in with self pity;
energy leaks downward on the left side.

2. From the Left: The Victim

The second way of acquiring energy from others consists of appealing to their natural empathy. As the left is said to be the side of the heart, a simple way to rob the energy of others is to do so through feelings; in other words, to induce compassion or sympathy in others.

On the positive side, it is easy for a very sensitive person to generate these emotions in others, allowing him or her to open up and express what he feels. Generosity, humanity, and sentimentality are characteristics of these people, and they are often idealists, aspiring to make a more beautiful or more serene world in the surroundings of their lives. They do not always find ways to materialize their dreams, which often leads to them feel powerless.

This is when they tend to feel sorry for themselves, seeing problems rather than solutions, negative aspects rather than positive ones, weaknesses rather than strengths. Because they always need to express their emotions, even the most negative ones, Redfield names them Plaintives: to get energy from others they will complain, despair, beg for attention, and implore others for help.

It seems that people who are sensitive and apparently vulnerable usually have greater abilities to attract protectors—people who need to feel useful and worthwhile through the help they provide. However, it is true that at times we all need a hand, but some individuals have developed a particular talent at exploiting others by becoming dependent on their generosity, strengths, and the resources extended to them.

They are complacent in their role as victim. They need others because on their own they cannot manage to take control over their lives. They feel that their past wounds or failures are too heavy to bear and that they are simply subjected to what happens to them without being able to change anything about it. The Victim is easy to spot; no matter what reassurance or help we try to give them, their response always starts with the same words, "Yes, but ...": "Yes, but, you know, for me it's different, it's much more serious, it never works, it always gets worse."

Deep down, the Victim does not want to be helped in finding solutions. She just wants to complain, and she is constantly burdened by sadness. Feeling destitute and devalued, she lacks self-confidence and would like someone to make up for her own weakness. She would like to be supported, consoled, "pepped up"—in brief, to have others sacrifice themselves for her the way she believes she is sacrificing herself for others.

The Victim's life position, according to transactional analysis, is, "I am not OK; you are OK." In other words, "Since you have extra energy, and I don't have enough to keep myself afloat, I beg you to give me yours."

The Victim draws to her the energy of any person who gives her attention. She inspires pity and hangs on to others as to a life ring while draining others of the vital energy she pretends to need to get her balance back.

In reality, because her solar plexus, seat of the emotions, is constantly made more bitter and weakened, a leak remains at this level that doesn't permit energy to be stored efficiently. To the contrary, self-pity and withdrawal maintain the global vitality of the person at a minimum, and her energetic field gets deflated and wasted and flees downward, to the left of the body.

If the typology of the Victim is the one for which you have obtained the highest score, it means that a part of you regularly feels overwhelmed by events or burdened by the weight of a heavy or painful past. Your self-esteem is often low, and you consider others to be better, stronger, or happier than you.

You find it hard to understand that you create your life and that it is possible to change things on the condition that you believe sufficiently in yourself. You probably felt abandoned in your youth, and your inner child constantly needs to be reassured and secured rather than going forward and exploring his inner unlimited potential to create.

In the following chapter we will explain the benefits of a change of attitude rather than trying to solve the external problems that afflict your existence. However, in the following pages, you can meditate on the positive aspects of the other defense mechanisms that perhaps could allow you to let some other parts of you emerge: parts that know you have everything you need within you to manifest the most fulfilled of lives.

3. From the Right

The Savior or Interrogator

Motivation: bargaining and guilt

Makes herself indispensable, can't say "no,"
forgets to take care of herself

The energy leans to the right side and slightly downward
because of a tendency to take others on her shoulders.

3. From the Right: The Savior

This way to obtain energy from others is much more subtle because in appearance the Savior is the one who gives his energy to others. He is the person who is always helpful, attentive, resourceful, and available to help others or give advice.

In a group, she is an excellent right hand, the one we can always count on, who never lets us down, assumes responsibility diligently, and ensures that everyone is well. In fairy tales he is the hero, the charming prince who rescues the beautiful princess in distress. This is why, almost unanimously, he is appreciated by those around him.

But one might wonder what his real motivations are for devoting himself in that way. In fairy tales, the one who intervenes as a hero usually obtains all the honor: he is given the hand of the princess, inherits from her a kingdom, and becomes a king acclaimed by all. Could it be that the Savior, deep down, perhaps needs to feel that he is appreciated, recognized, even acclaimed, if not by jubilant crowds then by those close to her?

His life position would ideally be, "I'm OK; you're OK," or, in reality, if we extrapolate a little, "I'm OK, and thanks to me, you will be OK." All in all, he adopts a pretty condescending attitude motivated by bargaining. He has others believe that they won't make it unless they give all their trust and energy. By acting as a protector, mediator, counselor, or therapist, he makes sure that his peers cannot do without him, nor act without first consulting him.

Put simply, the Savior has a tendency to drain people of their own self-confidence in order to get a leg up on them. He drains others' energy by destabilizing them and questioning their ability to find their own solutions. This is why Redfield calls him the Interrogator: he spends his time questioning others, interrogating them on what is wrong in their lives, and grilling them to always find out more about them. Under the pretense of being concerned about those close to his heart, he does all he can to become indispensable in their eyes.

However, in the long run this becomes a dangerous game. Always ready to do a favor and feeling that he never does enough, he gives of himself without keeping track, forgets himself, feels it more and more difficult to say "no" at the risk of being eaten away by guilt, and eventually empties himself of his vital energy.

The Savior is therefore the one who is always turned toward others, with his hands extended and open to give. Her energetic body is slightly bent toward the front, slightly to the right and downward, because he has a tendency to bear others on his shoulders.

Nevertheless, although he obtains his energy through the value he draws from his relationships with others, he doesn't manage to truly accept the love and tenderness of those close to him. He always gives more than he receives.

If the Savior profile was dominant in your results in the previous test, you know from experience that the major problems of this type of personality are that when you yourself need to be "saved" or at least comforted, it seems like there is never anyone able, or even available, to reciprocate.

Once again, it's the law of attraction that applies: others won't feel obliged to help you just because you have been there for them when they needed it. They will treat you the way you treat yourself: if you put yourself last in your life, the same will apply in your relationships with others.

Of course, the solution remains to maintain a good balance between giving and receiving. However, this defense mechanism often goes back to childhood, when you understood that you needed to prove your true value in the eyes of those you loved. Either someone around you found themselves distraught and you felt you had to make up for their vulnerability, or you felt, at some point, devalued, humiliated, or denigrated, and you haven't managed to overcome your need for approval since.

Your challenge is to learn to create a bit of distance and to be less preoccupied by what others think of you, the way the Indifferents are so apt at doing: by using another method of acquiring energy, but without having to work so hard.

4. From Behind

The Indifferent or Aloof

Motivation: state of shock, denial

Feels paralyzed, escapes reality, stays out of reach

Mental energy leaks toward the head, pushing all the
subtle energy outside the body backward and slightly to the right.

4. From Behind: The Indifferent

We have talked about the Perpetrator, the Victim, and the Savior, the eternal triangle found in any good action movie. Who, then, is the fourth musketeer that we have yet to discover? It is impossible to imagine a children's tale without the classic Narrator, the indefinable character, a total stranger to the story who simply relates it without taking part in it. Isn't this the typical attitude of the Indifferent?

The Indifferent is the one who always remains at a distance, lost in thought, unaffected by what surrounds him or her. Her biggest strength is her ability to pull back in the mental sphere: she is generally very smart, enjoying great abilities for analysis and reasoning. With a strong critical mind she can quickly evaluate the situation she is in, not wasting time in hypothetical considerations and sticking to the facts. She is looking for perfection, to surpass the self, and for ultimate efficiency.

On the other hand, this way of being also allows her to play devil's advocate. In a group she is able to discover problems before anyone else and draw attention to the procedures to be followed. She doesn't hesitate to bring others back in line if they lose focus or get carried away by their emotions. Very attached to structure, she is excellent at dealing with time, deadlines, and anything that is factual.

On the negative side, such a person is never satisfied. Meticulous to a fault, she is always splitting hairs, preferring to juggle with ideas and concepts rather than to look for practical solutions. The Indifferent tends to demotivate her surroundings by constantly discussing and questioning everything. Constantly looking for the impossible, she drains the Energy of everyone around her without ever being satisfied.

Her life position, as described by Eric Berne, could be summed up as, "I'm not OK, but neither are you." She can appear intolerant, skeptical, defeatist, or even disdainful toward emotional people, to the point of retracting into her own bubble when people express their feelings and emotions too openly.

In any situation, whether joyous or troubling, she will at some point feel the need to create some distance. She systematically cuts herself off from her emotions, her feelings, and even her pain to remain within analysis, objectivity, and observable facts, even if it paralyzes her inside; therefore she is, generally speaking, in denial. To remain in her mental universe, the Indifferent will tend to disconnect from what is happening around her. Because her spirit leaves her body, it then becomes difficult for anyone to join her or to drain her: her energy field remains out of reach, projected upwards, backward, to the right of the body. In fact, she is like a bar of soap in the bathtub: the more one tries to get hold of her, the more she slips, dodges, and escapes.

Her favorite way of obtaining energy consists of appearing partly inaccessible. This way, she forces others to come to her and to put everything in action to try to get her attention while she casually keeps her distance.

If you have a high score in this sphere of experimentation, there is a good chance that you have been subjected to some major trauma in your childhood or that you may have felt strongly repressed in your need for autonomy or independence. It is as if your personality remains in a state of shock, imprisoned in a shell.

Hence there is much insecurity when it comes to taking initiative, expressing bold opinions, or investing yourself in intimate relationships. You don't dare spread your wings for fear of having them clipped. You continually refer to outside norms, conventions, and objective reasoning rather than considering the call of your heart, your intuition, and your feelings.

Because you constantly doubt yourself, you don't have the courage to search for ways to improve the situation or to change your attitude; the notion of change itself scares you too much. More than anything, it is important to understand that you are not exempt from emotions. On the contrary, it is your hypersensitivity that pushes you to protect yourself excessively.

By going back inside and asking yourself what you feel on the emotional level, bit by bit and day by day you will be able to reconnect with the wonderful being that you truly are.

If you are uneasy with the idea of letting others into your personal bubble, you can always turn toward you soul family. Their subtle luminous presence will feel less invasive to you, while allowing you to open yourself to energy that is both beneficial and reassuring on all levels.

5. Through Your Ruling Chakra

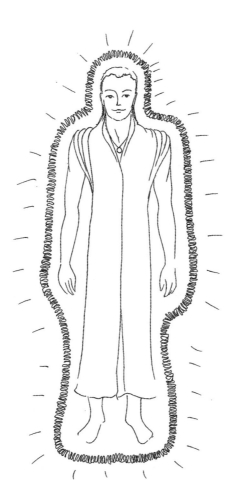

The Witness or Centered

Motivation: acceptance, detachment

Remains centered, allows himself to let go, lives in the now

The energy is stable, luminous, and balanced because the individual
is open and radiating, connected to the ground as well as the heavens.

5. Through Your Ruling Chakra: The Witness or Centered

No matter what your usual primary reactions are and which domination mechanisms characterize you, there is a simple, easy, and joyous way to obtain energy without having to drain it from others: you can connect to your soul family through your ruling chakra.

As discussed in Chapter 3, the ruling chakra is our privileged connection to our guardian angels, guides, and the light beings that accompany us. At any moment, no matter what the situation, they will be happy to give us energy, revitalize our energetic bodies, and rebalance all of our being, for they are themselves perpetually unified with the celestial source: eternal, infinite, and unlimited.

Among humans, power struggles push you to drain your peers in order to increase your own vital energy level. The members of your soul family, on the other hand, are always ready and available to recharge your batteries without ever asking for anything in return. Quite the contrary, they hope that you will appeal to them because well before your birth they committed to supporting you whenever you feel weakened on an energetic level.

In fact, the very mission of your soul family is to heighten your vibratory level so that you have at your disposal the maximum energetic potential finally to recognize yourself and remember who you really are. They are part of you, and you are part of them. By connecting to them you plug directly into the divine universal energy you originate from.

Your light cocoon then returns to its original ovoid shape: stable, luminous, and balanced, favoring your openness to others, thus allowing you to radiate like a thousand suns to be fully in harmony with heaven and earth and connected to all that lives.

There is no danger of weakening or undermine anyone: the light beings are made of incomparable energy that regenerates itself and is entirely renewable at any moment. Hence there is the possibility of being revitalized on demand at every second by simply taking three deep breaths while visualizing your ruling chakra opening to receive all the energy you need to reharmonize yourself.

It is important to point out that in daily life, not all circumstances affect us. Some people come into our lives without necessarily exploiting or draining our energies every time we are in their presence. We are therefore regularly able to recenter ourselves without any help or effort, to get caught up in unexpected events, or to go through tumultuous times while remaining calm and poised. This is why many people end up with a high score in the Witness or Centered column.

These people manage to remain centered by living day to day in the present moment. In their eyes, "everything is OK here and now." They apply themselves to seeing only the good side of things, accepting what they cannot change and letting go, meaning trusting and believing that everything happens for a good reason and that time heals all. They take for granted that life wishes them well and that God is on their side, no matter how things appear to be. Just like Tibetan monks, they look for detachment and aim for transcendence beyond the illusions of this world.

Living Here and Now

However, we all know it is illusory to believe that we can remain permanently detached without getting involved personally in anything at all. We might aim for balance, but from that to a continual state of grace there is a gap. Furthermore, if you visualize a scale in perfect balance, what do you see? The two trays are perfectly level, forming a line parallel to the ground that extends in length without any fluctuation or difference: put simply, it is a flat line. Who truly wants their life always to be flat, stable, straight, and without flavor, just to be a witness to events without ever taking part in them?

It isn't necessary to detach from everything and to be in constant meditation in order to live in harmony. You can go with the flow, and if need be, courageously face the waves of chaos that hit us at times, knowing that even when a tempest is brewing on the surface, in the depths of the ocean, as in the depths of ourselves, everything remains unchanged, calm, and serene, unperturbed by what is happening on the surface.

The same applies to your soul. No matter what has happened in this or any previous life—family burdens, wounds from your past, mistakes, or failures—this divine spark remains intact, integral, and filled with purity. Just as one could not condemn a child victim of incest, your past experiences have no damning or karmic value against you unless you give them alienating importance.

Again, at any time you can choose to unburden yourself from the weight of the past, to drop your backpack, and to set the meter back to zero simply by repositioning yourself here and now in the present moment and making some new choices for the future.

This is the best way to preserve and maintain the energy within you: become aware that nothing and no one can harm your divine essence, nor rob you of it, weaken it, or take it over. People will try to grab your energy, but in no way can they ever manage to diminish or extinguish your inner light.

Your childhood experiences may have largely contributed to forging your character, to crystallizing in you the defense mechanisms most likely to allow you to be recognized and accepted by others, but in no way do they define who you are deep within.

Even if a part of you believes that it must suffer the assaults of people who are lacking in light and that if need be it must fight back by instinctively draining the energy of others, you now know that another choice is available to you: to benefit from a serene and luminous energy that is totally accessible and has no limits.

Your soul family is always beside you, and you can connect to it in order to enjoy once again absolute plenitude in all spheres of your being.

Exercise: *Choosing to Let Go*

Here's a simple exercise that you can do at will any time a problematic situation appears in your life. It was inspired in me by my yoga teacher, Lucie Geoffroy, whom I thank from the bottom of my heart for her openness and her ever-warm simplicity.

With your arm extended out in front of you, the back of your hand facing the sky, imagine that you hold a precious diamond in your palm. You will keep your fist tightly clenched, of course, your fingers holding onto the jewel so as not to let it slip.

If someone asked you to let go, what would you do? Would you open your hand at the risk of letting the diamond drop?

What goes on in your head if you tell yourself that you have to let go of the most precious thing that you have? Do you believe that letting go means dropping, renouncing, capitulating, throwing in the towel, losing face, or abandoning the game? If this is the case, it is no wonder you refuse to submit to it.

Truly letting go instead implies seeing things differently, opening up to new avenues you had not thought of on your own.

In this particular case, it isn't necessary to keep your hand facing downward to open it. You can turn it upward, your palm facing the sky, and open your fingers, thus creating space for the new opportunities that present themselves to you.

Letting go is simply dropping control, trusting life, and opening up to receiving the countless benefits that rain on you.

Next time you feel that you need to let go, do this symbolic little gesture: free yourself from your worries by offering them to God, extend your hands out in front of you, open and ready to welcome divine jewels in the form of providential blessings and perfect solutions.

CHAPTER 10

Ensuring Survival, or Living Fully?

The Five Suitors

Message from April 3, 2007

When his only daughter finally reached marriageable age, the sovereign of a powerful kingdom called his most loyal subjects, all noblemen and notables who were still unmarried, in order to choose the one who, in his eyes, would be worthy of the hand of the charming princess.

The first man to appear in front of the king was a duke whose wealth was considerable. He told the king, "I will put my wealth at the service of the kingdom, and our alliance will be more than prosperous. Everyone will benefit from this abundance."

Before the duke had finished speaking, music started playing from the other end of the room. A young troubadour with a melodious voice walked toward them, singing the praises of the sweet princess. Addressing the king, he said, "With me, the princess will never know boredom. I will know how to ravish her heart and teach her the arts and music so that her talents will be recognized throughout the world."

The king's adviser leaned in and said in the king's ear, "The princess need not display her gifts. Her beauty is already so perfect that she is admired without limit throughout the world. Sire, if you will allow me, I too would like to ask humbly for your daughter's hand. She will need assistance when she ascends to the throne, and having been your right hand, am I not the one who knows the affairs of the kingdom best?"

At that moment, in the courtyard, trumpets blared. A valiant knight made a remarkable entrance, proudly displaying the head of a dragon he had just vanquished. The whole audience acclaimed him. The captain of the guard addressed the king to praise his favorite: "Can't you see, sire, that what your daughter needs, just like the rest of the kingdom, is to be well protected? Here is my most valiant warrior. He alone will be able to offer the protection and efficient strategies to maintain and even extend our borders."

The king's gaze went from one suitor to the next, unsure of what to do. Then, turning toward his daughter, he noticed that she had eyes only for a young squire standing next to the knight. He was in turn staring at her with eyes filled with ardent love. Outraged, the king stood up from his throne and said to the squire in a demeaning tone, "How dare you cast such a glance on my daughter? You don't even know how to hold a sword or charm her with your singing or your scholarly knowledge, and furthermore you have no riches other than what you have in your pockets."

"Please forgive me, sire," the squire replied. "My love for the princess is greater than my love for life itself. For years we have met and talked at length every time she comes to the stables. I am the one who saddles her horse and make sure that nothing happens to her during her rides in the forest. I know that I am in no way worthy of asking for her hand, but I can't help loving her with all my heart, and this is why I dare to ask you: since it is your daughter who will have to share the rest of her life with the man she will marry, why not let her choose the one most suited to her?"

The crowd could not help but react to the audacity of the young squire. No one could deny his obvious wisdom. Magnanimously the king then asked his daughter about the suitor of her choice. Intimidated, staring at the ground, the princess asked her father, "Will you respect my decision, whatever it might be, even if it does not suit you?" Her father agreed: "We have assembled before us a group of suitors full of diverse qualities and competencies. Your wish will be mine."

"Father," the princess said, "with all due respect, I feel obliged to listen to my heart, and for a long time I have offered it to Christian, the young squire who has been for many years my dearest friend and confidant. For me, his love is the greatest wealth there is. My heart dances and my soul sings every time he enters the room. Often his comforting words have managed to appease my spirit tormented or heated by the injustices of this kingdom. Only in his arms will I find the protection my whole being needs to be assisted as a queen and supported as a woman."

Faced with such a demonstration of attachment and affection, the king decided to agree to his daughter's choice. After all, isn't a man who only desires the happiness of the woman he loves the best suitor of all?

—Bianca Gaia

Some Typical Human Power Games

If the suitors in this allegory were in competition among themselves for the hand of a beautiful princess in real life, their defense mechanisms would rival to obtain a ray of light, no matter how futile or brief it might be.

In daily life, as in this beautiful story, every person puts forth his or her strengths and talents in order to get attention and to be appreciated, or so he believes, for his just value. Thus the Savior personality will come to the rescue of the most destitute. The Indifferent will shine through her intelligence and her erudition; the Victim through his great sensitivity, extreme vulnerability, and heightened sensuality that will bewitch the knights and other weak spirits. Finally, the Perpetrator will convince everyone, through her charm or her powers of manipulation, to choose her as leader.

The Centered person simply looks on from afar, as a witness and an observer, and there is a good chance that one day he or she too may be invited to take part in this seduction game, which always ends up degenerating into a power struggle.

The Ups and Downs of Married Life

Let's take the example of Winifred and Robert. When they met, it was love at first sight. Winifred, reserved and shy, admired Robert's charisma. Always up for a laugh, Robert was the center of attention in their group of common friends. Robert felt safe around this charming brunet, who was at the same time serious, silent, and very attentive to him. After a few months of seeing each other, they ended up getting married, and they settled in the suburbs, halfway between their respective workplaces.

The young woman would have loved to confide her concerns to her new husband, but he always seemed to take everything so lightly, telling her every time not to worry and to think of other things, to leave her worries at the doorstep before entering the house.

Although Winnie had initially coveted the unflinching optimism and nonchalance of her beloved, after a few months she started to find that these attitudes resembled absentmindedness and irresponsibility. Couldn't her husband see the extent to which the future of the company she was working for was at risk as more and more people around her were losing their jobs?

Robert, for his part, openly mocked the anxious nature of his partner, often reproaching her for inventing torments for herself out of sheer pessimism, encouraging her to be complacent in her anxieties. And this is how the dark dance of the defense mechanisms started.

Lacking attention and validation, because all the attention was naturally directed toward her husband, Winnie started to feel a void or weakness on the energetic level. Because she had devoted herself totally to Robert's happiness, wasn't it normal that in all fairness he would in turn look after her?

From being poised and introverted, according to her partner, Winifred became first indifferent and then a victim. While she used to appreciate Robert's audacity back in the day, the hero or Savior that he had once been in her eyes became a Perpetrator, constantly plaguing her with disapproval. This anecdote demonstrates that it is possible to adopt several different life positions according to the context and situations encountered.

For this young couple, the dance was only starting. A simple weakness of one of the two partners, in this case Winifred, was enough to initiate a power struggle that could have no winner. In turn, each partner will try to unsettle the other to gain their vital energy without ever being fulfilled, because the other will fight back immediately, adopting another attack position in order to regain the lost energy.

Inner Duality

Do you recognize part of yourself in this example? Here is another anecdote that is just as eloquent.

Jeanne is a warm dynamic person who adores working with the public. Hired as a receptionist at a public relations firm, she quickly got noticed by her boss for her ease in taking initiative and her aptitude at comforting people when their expectations had not been met. He offered her a job as an assistant in charge of accompanying clients in their mundane activities.

Jeanne's engaging and naturally honest nature allowed her to win the trust of the personalities she was in charge of, so they regularly asked her for her opinion on what decisions to make regarding their artistic or media careers. While the young woman was attentive to the needs of her clients and applied herself to advising them exclusively on the best path to follow for their success on all levels, this did not please her boss, who accused her of not having the interests of the company at heart.

Jeanne was split between her sincere affection for the people she was entrusted with and her duty toward her employer. Her Savior tendency first led her to side with her clients, potential victims of an intimidating Perpetrator boss. By doing so, however, she risked losing her job, thus becoming a Victim herself. She then tried to play Indifferent, being just an attentive ear for her clients without getting involved; but some then accused her of keeping her distance and got offended by what they perceived as a lack of concern on her part.

After a few weeks, Jeanne started to doubt herself. Had she made the right choice? Did she truly have the talent and qualifications for such a job? She had no degree that qualified her to assume such complex responsibilities. She wasn't strong enough to be submitted to such pressure and answer efficiently the increasingly demanding requests of her clients. Without noticing it, Jeanne had become a Perpetrator to herself.

Thus two people aren't needed to enter the dance of defense mechanisms; different parts of us may well oppose each other and tear us apart. A breach in a moment of weakness or vulnerability can cause everything inside us to collapse.

Adapting to Our Environment

But, you say, it is so easy to reconnect to divine energy in order to reestablish the balance within ourselves, without ever having to fight to feel valued, both in our eyes and in those of others. It is very true and so easy to comprehend, but how difficult it is to put into practice.

From a very young age, you have been exposed to power struggles playing out between your parents, your brothers and sisters, or those close to you. You have experienced the pressure of your peers, and the control exerted by a strict parental authority or a severe teacher. You have been submitted to social conditioning with its norms to respect and its laws to follow. Unknowingly, you have been programmed to react to the slightest energetic fluctuations around you. You have unconsciously allowed yourself to be manipulated over the years, becoming not what you were dreaming of being but instead becoming a good little soldier, one among many, an anonymous face in the crowd.

It isn't surprising then that you rebel in order to find your place in the sun. And because it is much easier to find light around us than within ourselves, the next best option seems to be to rob others who are accessible and engaging.

Judging ourselves or feeling bad about this does not help. It is like criticizing ourselves because we need to kill plants to eat. The primary reaction is a necessary evil, an existential obligation for anyone who has not found another way of nourishing himself energetically.

To illustrate this, imagine that you had to move to China. Initially the culture, the people, and the language would feel strange, almost hermetic. Then, little by little, you would learn to express yourself in Chinese. After a length of time of complete immersion you would find yourself thinking in Chinese and acting like the people of that country. Habit and routine would then have won over your differences. You would have assimilated the energy of the place in order to feel more at ease there by conforming to the rituals that you would have taken on through mimicry.

But would you have lost your ability to express yourself in your native tongue? Would it be impossible for you to return to your country of origin and get back into your old typically Western behavior?

The same goes for a soul newly incarnated in a physical body. It has to learn the language of humans and, to be understood and accepted by its surroundings, adopt the same rules of conduct. Isn't there a saying that goes, "When in Rome ..."?

Just like a newborn adopted at birth by Chinese people, you have made the language, values, and customs of your parents your own, forgetting your celestial origins in this three-dimensional world that is so different from the one your originate in. Luckily it is never too late for an adopted child to claim the right to know his biological parents. You can reconnect with your soul family through your ruling chakra to get all your divine faculties back and to fill with luminous energy at every moment.

What matters is love. As in the metaphor of the five suitors, a pure heart open to love can only attract the best for ourselves and for others. It is important to accept and to love ourselves as we are. After all, each of those defense mechanisms is in reality a challenge that our soul hands us in order to overcome our fears and win back who we really are.

Below is a summary chart allowing you to identify which attitude, more positive and more luminous, would be the best one for you to adopt in order to lower the impact of the predominant typologies of your personality and, by consequence, encourage the preservation of a good vital energy level that is harmonious and balanced.

Every time an unpredictable event comes along or a conflict occurs in your relationships, you have a choice: fight to ensure your survival by robbing your neighbors of vital energy, or decide to undertake a completely new challenge by overcoming your old programming to finally live fully in the now in recognition of your divine unchangeable nature.

In order to reach inner plenitude, every defense mechanism has the possibility of opening up to a new life experience, allowing it to simultaneously heal childhood traumas and definitively turn the page on the past. This is the secret of letting go: no matter what baggage we carry—that of our parents, ancestors, nations, or even our past lives—it is possible to choose to get rid of it here and now, to start anew, and to make peace within ourselves.

If you feel burdened by the past or by some current problem, one question can get you out of it: "Will I die from it?" Is your life in danger? Are you at risk of being eaten alive by a tyrannosaur in the next few minutes? If not, just relax. Take three deep breaths and come back to the essential, to the now. Every life experience isn't a threat, provocation, or danger to overcome. Rather, they are challenges and new adventures that open to you in order to allow you to learn to acquire luminous energy in some other way, from the inside out, rather than the other way around. Life constantly invites you to discover your inner potential to enjoy a simple, easy, and happy existence, including in your relationships with others, no matter what your dominant typology is.

Ensuring Survival or Living Fully

DEFENSE, MECHANISM	CONTROL DRAMA WAY TO ACQUIRE	LIFE CHALLENGE ENERGY
Perpetrator or Intimidator	Anger: imposes, controls, threatens, attacks the top of the body and jumps toward others like a predator on prey.	"I am learning to let the universe and the people around me support me. I am more trusting in others."
Victim, "Poor Me"	Sadness: complains, despairs, begs, implores Weakness of the solar plexus, caving in with self pity; energy leaks downward on the left side.	"I say 'thank you' for all the benefits of every day. I acknowledge in myself the power to create the life that I deserve."
Savior or Interrogator	Blackmail/Guilt: makes himself indispensable, unable to say "no," forgets to take care of himself. The energy leans to the right side and slightly downward because of a tendency to take others on his shoulders.	"I am learning to love who I am instead of what I'm able to do. I choose to take care of myself first."
Indifferent or Aloof	State of Shock/Denial: feels paralyzed, escapes reality, stays out of reach Mental energy leaks toward the head, pushing all the subtle energy outside the body backward and slightly to the right.	"I am learning to verbalize my emotions and to express what I feel in the present moment."

DEFENSE, MECHANISM	CONTROL DRAMA WAY TO ACQUIRE	LIFE CHALLENGE ENERGY
Witness or Centered	Acceptance/Detachment: remains centered, allows himself to let go, lives in the now. The energy is stable, luminous, and balanced because the individual is open and radiating, connected to the ground as well as the heavens.	"I welcome my inner wisdom and the divine dwelling in me. I acknowledge who I really am."

1. The Perpetrator

Having felt betrayed or threatened by your peers as a child, it may at times be difficult for you, once reaching adulthood, to trust others. If on top of that you have been treated badly or have been the victim of violence or aggression, there surely remains in you a certain anger, a legitimate bitterness that prevents you from letting down your guard and opening yourself to others.

In such circumstances, it is normal to remain on the defensive and to want to keep control of your life at all costs. Part of you remains constantly on the alert. You are ready to face any eventuality and to fight potential enemies, if necessary with your own hands if not with your power of persuasion.

If anyone pushes you around or confronts you, you do not hesitate to strike and crush your adversary immediately. This is why your Perpetrator instinct is perceptible in your energy field when it leaps forward from the top of your body and jumps toward others like a predator on prey.

Rather than acquiring the energy of others from the front by confronting them, here is what would allow you instead to make peace with the past and overcome your intrinsic insecurity: "I am learning to let the universe and the people around me support me. I am more trusting in others."

Will you have the courage to overcome this challenge? No matter what has happened earlier, here and now the people you encounter aren't potential nemies. To the contrary, some turn out to be powerful allies, helping you discover what softness, human warmth, and nonthreatening intimacy really are, without a power struggle. Although it may appear impossible to overcome for the moment, your fear can progressively decrease if you allow yourself to experiment with opening up to others.

If the people around you seem too threatening to you, you can always call on your soul family: visualize the guardian angel that watches over you coming near you and holding you in his arms. In the invisible realm, it is easier to get used to contact with others simply by opening yourself to welcome his benevolent presence.

2. The Victim

The feeling of powerlessness and vulnerability that regularly oppresses some people has its origins in the deep feeling of having been abandoned by one's mother or father during the first years of life. The Victim is burdened by sadness because he or she feels that people who mattered to him have not been there for him; they were absent, unavailable, or blatantly indifferent to his plight. Hence he has the constant need to find someone who will at last give him the attention and affection he needs to live and to feel that he exists.

If you are one of the people who find it hard to believe that they deserve to be loved, it is normal that you don't know how to define your own value except through the eyes of another person. The safest way for you to be valued lies in your ability to attract sympathy and pity by emphasizing your fragility and your need to be supported by others.

This is why your energy field always seems to leak downward on the left side of the body. Part of you believes that by taking up so little space and by acting like a child, you will awaken the maternal instinct in a trusted person, who will know how to make up your lack of affection.

If the emotional part of your being has not been properly nourished while you were young, it doesn't mean that it is impossible for you to grow and become a fulfilled adult. What if your challenge was no longer to have your happiness depend on anyone but yourself, becoming the loving parent of your own inner child to help her consolidate her base and catch up on her growth?

No matter what challenges and failures have accumulated, here and now you have the choice to go within and awaken the wonderful, luminous, and remarkable being that you are. Decide to reveal to the world your natural inner power, shining and unlimited. Life is so beautiful when you recognize that "I am the person who can make all the difference."

Again, the secret of happiness consists of recentering yourself and remaining in the now to realize that you are never completely alone. So many people around you love you, accompany you, and admire you, even if only in the invisible realm.

So, if you have the feeling that you are no longer able to count on people, turn to your soul family. Ask it for some signs of care toward you. Open yourself a bit more each day to the gifts of life and welcome the little joys that your guardian angels and guides place on your path.

"I give thanks for all the benefits of every day. I acknowledge in myself the power to create the life that I deserve."

Look at yourself in the mirror and contemplate the intense light that shines in your eyes. You don't need anyone to recognize you and give you the right to exist. Make this choice for yourself. Make the decision to love yourself and to look after yourself. You will discover that you have accomplished a large part of the journey up to now. After all, you have always managed until now, haven't you?

Be proud of your achievements. Rather than keeping your eye on the path remaining to the summit of the mountain, look behind you to take in all the distance that you have already covered. Can you see all the steps that you have managed to climb, all the problems you have been able to overcome, all the situations in which you came out victorious?

Focus your attention on your strength, your power, and the greatness of your soul, and you will never again need others to reveal to you your real beauty and inner light.

3. The Savior

Even if it appears that the Savior has a mission or a noble cause, as we have seen in the previous chapter, his or her actions are nevertheless motivated by an unquenchable thirst for recognition. Of all the survival mechanisms, the Savior tries hardest to be recognized for her real value, most probably because she has somehow been trampled on during her childhood.

Whether she has experienced humiliation, been denigrated, or had her integrity sapped, her acts of courage or generosity mostly and firstly aim at filling her own need for validation from those around her.

This is why her way of acquiring energy is described as bargaining. The Savior gives in order to better receive in return. This explains her energy leaning to the right and slightly downward; she has a tendency to take others on her shoulders.

If this is your dominant profile, it may be that you are not aware of this wound to the soul that constantly pushes you to put yourself last. You must regularly feel the consequences of it, however: the more you give of yourself, the more people seem to need you, and the less time you have to look after yourself. Don't you find that, in the long run, this repetitive process starts looking like the attitude of a masochist? What follows is that, when you end up exhausted by the task, you feel lonely and destitute without anyone to extend a helping hand toward you in turn.

This game of energy exchange is the most destructive because society, family, and educators encourage the gift of oneself. Altruism and sharing are seen as core values worthy of a civilized culture. Isn't charity encouraged by all religions? But if you are a Savior, you may have forgotten the saying "Charity begins at home."

Deep down, you give yourself a clean conscience and justify your actions by the story you tell yourself: "We live in a world full of injustice and unhappiness; someone needs to do something about it." While this might be true, who says this person must be you?

The real question is, why is it that every time you cannot respond to the expectations of those around you, you feel guilty? Is this guilt based in the now, or does it have its source in the distant past? You need to become aware of the part of you that believes it was not up to the challenge at a certain time in your life, perhaps during your childhood, because that part still imagines today that it needs to prove itself to deserve the love of others.

Hence the importance of the challenge you need to overcome every day: "I am learning to love who I am instead of what I am able to do. I choose to take care of myself first."

It is important to overcome your need to be indispensable; to be certain that people will love you anyway even if you do less; to see that people around you appreciate your presence, your smile, and your human warmth much more than all those little gestures that you feel obliged to do daily—the favors you do, the food you cook, the gatherings you organize, and the advice you give, even if no one asked for any of it.

Despite the fact that deep down you only want to do good, you always do too much. What if you put yourself in the shoes of others for a moment: how would you feel if someone around you was constantly at your service, a step ahead of you, and treating you as if you couldn't do anything on your own? This is often how the people around you feel, as if they were idiots or incapable.

One of the most beautiful gifts you can give them is to see them as they really are: people like you on their own path who have everything inside themselves that they need (resources, solutions, and means) to create the life they aspire to, no matter what happens around them.

You now know that the outside world is only a reflection of what is inside. So rather than always wanting to solve their problems for them and to support them in their unhappiness, send them trusting and positive thoughts instead. You will truly help them to free themselves of their own limitations, which, deep down, are the same as yours: a lack of faith in themselves.

By loving yourself more and taking good care of yourself, you set a good example. You will continue to support them, but you do it with your luminous radiance, by what you are rather than by what you do. This makes all the difference in the world, in your energy as well as in theirs.

And if for some reason you find yourself drained of your energy, ask yourself a few questions: "Whom did I give too much to? When did I forget myself? Do I allow myself in turn to ask for help? Can I allow myself to receive as much as I give?"

If need be, you now know that you can always call on your soul family—not only to love, guide, and accompany you on your path but also to work instead of you, to intervene positively in your life and in the lives of those dear to you. You only have to ask.

4. The Indifferent

In the previous chapter we saw that the difficulty of the Indifferent, contrary to appearances, is not insensitivity but rather hypersensitivity. He or she hides this great emotionality under a mask of equanimity and stoicism.

The Indifferent's withdrawal from himself often goes back to the first years of his life. The child that he was felt rejected or not accepted for who he really was by those close to him. Very often he is a dreamer, an artist who has not been welcomed for his uniqueness, and who, having felt misunderstood, has withdrawn into his inner world.

If this is your main typology, the following word game is important because it is part of the story you have been telling yourself: "Because I cannot allow myself to be different, I will be indifferent. Because I cannot blossom in the emotional and creative sphere of my being, I will only evolve in the mental and intellectual sphere."

You are therefore looking to protect your individuality by cutting yourself off from others and remaining inaccessible. This translates in your energy field as a leak toward the head, draining all the subtle energy outside the body backward and slightly to right.

Unfortunately, if this allows you to remain at a distance, you are not able to receive energy from your peers, who nevertheless attempt to reach you and bring you back down to Earth using any means possible.

Your biggest fear is to be uncovered, to be seen as you are. You surround yourself with an aura of mystery, a wall of silence, generally avoiding anything that concerns you personally. All this is a fear of someone noticing that you have remained a shy and uneasy child who still dreams of experimenting with his artistic talent or allowing himself to be passionate, original, innovative, eccentric—in a word, different.

On the contrary, you hide your specific personality under an appearance of intellectual rigor, even rigidity, and perfectionism. You deny who you are in order to conform to the requirements of this world that seem normative, artificial, and tasteless to you. Because you cannot control what happens outside of you, you devote all your energy to controlling your impulses and your needs and wants, whatever they might be. You are therefore in denial of your humanity and of your sensitivity, and as a consequence you reject your own inner light.

This is what makes you appear in the eyes of others as perpetually in a state of shock: distant, absent, scattered, and uncooperative toward everything that surrounds you. In fact, you cut yourself off from others so that they cannot find your Achilles heel and use it against you to wound you yet again.

However, it is only by welcoming your vulnerability that you will be able to overcome it. Your challenge: "I am learning to verbalize my emotions and to express what I feel in the present moment."

Will you have the courage to take the risk to reveal who you are, here and now? No matter how much you were picked on in your childhood, today you have within you all the resources, skills, and strength of character to have the courage to express your emotional or fantasist side, to affirm your difference loud and clear.

Your sensitivity is no longer a weakness but rather a quality to explore for your greater happiness. This is what would allow you not only to blossom but at last to have a taste of this ideal that you aspire to deep inside. Forget the past, stop fearing the future, and make your life the paradise you have dreamed of since you were a child.

You already have within you all the abilities, intelligence, insight, imagination, and conceptualization necessary to create the better world to which you aspire: you only need to believe in yourself and go into action. If need be, ask your soul family for help; it will know how to inspire you and awaken the luminous flame that lies dormant within you.

Allow yourself to open the door of your heart to all the people in your life who only ask to know you better and to get closer to you. You have long believed that you were alone, but now you can choose to surround yourself by remarkable, original, and innovative people like you in order to live life to the fullest and to learn to vibrate to the rhythm of your intrinsic passion.

5. The Centered

Isn't it exceptional to be Centered and happily to enjoy the present moment, to react like an adult to the events and situations that present themselves without dramatizing them or letting them disturb us internally, to succeed in not getting caught up in the many traps of our personality?

The person who knows how to recenter himself daily sees his energy field remain stable, luminous, and balanced. He or she knows how to recognize the importance of openness to others and simply how to radiate through his example while keeping his connection with the heavens and the ground alive through his ruling chakra.

She who can overcome the following challenge is surely a great master on the spiritual level: "I welcome my inner wisdom and the divine that dwells within me. I acknowledge who I really am."

As long as we continue to welcome the now without taking its wisdom for granted, things work well, but if you perpetually live in a state of detachment, you may run the risk of fooling yourself as to the state of your true inner harmony. Do you content yourself floating over the clouds, considering yourself a spiritual being but having forgotten you are also living a human experience?

To illustrate this concept there is a most enjoyable allegory, the origin of which I have forgotten. It's the story of two brothers, very different from each other.

The eldest, a monk, fervently practiced meditation for many years. Living like a recluse, he stayed in the mountains in a cave devoid of any comfort. He had learned to master the temperature of his body, and no matter what season it was he would meditate, seated on a rock and wearing only a blanket. He controlled his energy so well that he held in his hands, night and day, a ball of snow that never melted.

His brother lived further south, in a village at the foot of the mountain, and worked as a cobbler. One day he paid a visit to his elder brother. He was impressed by his prowess, admiring everything he had managed to learn in his life to keep a snowball intact even in midsummer. Surely he was a very great sage. He mentally placed his brother on a pedestal and started to find himself pretty insignificant in comparison. Before retuning home, the humble cobbler nevertheless invited his brother to visit him at his home in the village whenever he wanted.

A few months later the recluse descended from the mountain, and still carefully holding his snowball, went to his younger brother's shop. For a few hours, while meditating, snowball in hand, he watched his brother working valiantly: he would repair shoes, receive clients, and do his accounts.

Toward the middle of the afternoon, a beautiful young woman entered the shop, explaining that she had just broken the heel of her shoe. She lifted her knee and put her foot on a chair, revealing the silky skin of her delicate ankle. The cobbler, who did not seem bothered in the least, asked the young woman to take off her shoe, telling her that he would repair it straightaway. Quickly glancing at his brother, he noticed that his face was a reddish hue and that his snowball had simply melted; a small puddle lay at his feet.

Once the work was completed, the young woman put her shoe back on, thanked the cobbler, and left the shop without a second look at the strange, nearly naked man crouched in a corner. As soon as she crossed the threshold the cobbler asked his brother about what had happened. His brother said, "It is I who don't understand. How do you manage to be exposed in such a way to carnal pleasure and yet remain totally imperturbable?" The younger brother shrugged his shoulders without saying a word. It was evidently not an effort for him because he saw ankles every day. The monk said, "Really, brother, it is you who are the real master; you have many things to teach me."

In life everything is relative. An incident that occurs may seem to one person to be completely extraordinary, while to a neighbor it seems rather banal. Conversely a situation that seems to be quite ordinary to one person may well make all the difference in the world to someone else and transform her life.

So, the idea of wanting to remain centered at any cost may well be a beautiful illusion in which we get caught up unconsciously. By applying ourselves to keeping a distance from the hazards of life, we end up not letting anything reach us anymore. By doing so, we can live on a cloud or in a parallel reality where we make abstractions of the problems that preoccupy us rather than accepting them and thus living in full balance.

To be Centered, therefore, is not be a condition but rather a goal to aspire to. Do you believe it might be possible for you to exist eternally in a state of grace within the limits of your physical body? Mystical ecstasy is similar to a sexual orgasm: it is impossible to vibrate so strongly for more than a few seconds; it would kill us.

As long as you have not ascended, you haven't totally assumed your light body and remain subject to the highs and lows of everyday life, the daily roller coaster. You might as well enjoy the ride.

From Instinct to Acceptance

No matter what your favored defense mechanisms are, you must realize that it is simply impossible to definitively eliminate them from your life. It would be like wanting to clean your house permanently, just the once.

Just as dust gathers on your furniture and dirt accumulates in your bathroom, every day you are confronted with people who want to rob your energy, or you are placed in similar situations to those of your childhood. Straightaway your instinctive reactions resurface.

This is a reality with which you have to make do until the end of your days. In the same way that it is not realistic to want to move house each spring to avoid cleaning the dirt accumulated on your windows, walls, and ceilings, the hurdles and unforeseen events of life are unavoidable, and the stress they create causes your survival mechanisms to be triggered automatically. You cannot avoid it.

There is no point in repeating to yourself "I am not a Perpetrator" and hoping that this side of you will disappear. The more you try to diminish the influence of the dominant typologies in your life, the more they will amplify. What we resist persists. The more you accept your irrepressible need to acquire energy (what we face up to disappears), the easier it will be for you to develop ways to do it through your ruling chakra without giving in to your usual primary mechanisms.

We have seen in previous chapters that the best weapon at your disposal to face external chaos is indeed your ability to go back inside of yourself, to dedramatize events as they happen ("Will I die from this?") and to recenter yourself every time you need to with three deep breaths.

Deep down, no matter what typologies you need to overcome, if you apply yourself fully to living in the now, they will end up having much less of a hold on you.

When you accept making peace with yourself, this allows you to understand that despite everything you have had to endure over the years, you have attracted perfect situations to yourself in order to allow you to grow and to recognize yourself in your greater splendor.

You are invited to see things no longer in terms of victories and failures and no longer to consider the events you are going through as unfortunate challenges, ancient wounds to the soul, errors of judgment, or punishment from the heavens. Objectively, with a bit of distance, everything simply becomes a life lesson, more instruction on the path to full blossoming.

Notice to what extent each of the experiences you are going through is the ideal situation, chosen by your soul, to allow you to explore your full potential, unveil its countless internal resources, and discover your true inner light, your unalterable divine nature.

Whether or not you have succeeded in doing this up to now is of no importance, since you can choose, from today onward, to set the counter back to zero, to start again in the right direction, and to choose to manifest the best of yourself by calling, if need be, your soul family.

Integration: *Back to the Protective Prayer*

Do you remember the Protective Prayer at the end of Chapter 5? Allow me to draw attention to the positions each archangel occupies in it.

The Protective Prayer

<small>May</small> Gaia, our Mother Earth

Watch over my every step.

May the angel Michael secure my *right*

Gabriel my *left*

May Uriel walk *in front* of me

Raphael *behind* me

And may God almighty

Protect the top of my head.

Ensuring Survival, or Living Fully?

Does this sound familiar? Is it a coincidence that it is possible to make a direct link between the human ways of acquiring energy—from the right (the Savior), the left (the Victim), the front (the Perpetrator), or the back (the Indifferent)—and the protection of a specific angel situated at a specific place around us?

It turns out that this prayer is a few centuries old. The first time I learned of it was in a historical novel about a war of the Scottish Highlanders. It seems that it was a liturgical song sung by the Scottish in order to give themselves courage to fight the English.

At the time I thought that the Scottish warriors were clearly appealing to the best bodyguards to protect them on the battlefield. I wrote down this prayer, thinking that if such valiant warriors would put their lives in the hands of the archangels in this way, I could surely allow myself to use it when my life was not in danger.

Several years later, while I was studying the vibratory energy of Hebrew letters, I stumbled on the exact same text in an old manuscript that contained a kabbalah passage. The Jewish people also recite this prayer, and have for millennia at that. It was fascinating.

In light of what we now know about defense mechanisms, can you see how this meditative prayer takes on its meaning? Not only does invoking the angels protect us against attacks that aim to steal our energy, but by calling the archangels to protect and amplify our light cocoon, we no longer need to obtain the energy of others.

On the vibratory level, this prayer calls the representatives of the four great soul families. Add to this Gaia and God, who are undoubtedly part of the Sages family, and you have the whole cavalry to the rescue. What more could we ask for?

Recently I met someone in the south of France who told me this story. Since he participated in the "Welcome to the Fifth Dimension" workshop over a year ago, he says this prayer every morning before going to work. Being rather introverted, the man explains that his life has changed: he feels more self-confident and more solid inside; he has the courage to take more initiative in his work as well as in his relationship. In brief, he no longer feels like the same person. He claims to feel "assisted" in all his decisions (his own words) and filled with a new energy that replenishes itself constantly on a daily basis.

What if, from today onward, this simple, easy, and joyous prayer could make all the difference in your life?

PART THREE

Divine Quintessence

CHAPTER 11

The Five Steps of Acceptance

Meditating in Joy

Message from July 15, 2007

What is meditation? All the great masters of wisdom say that meditating involves successfully quieting one's mind to be fully in the now and to enjoy the inner plenitude or fusion with the divine within. Is it necessary to remove oneself from the world, cease all activities, and withdraw in order to meditate? Quite the contrary: you meditate each time a rush of happiness, love, or peace overcomes you.

Whether at work, at home, while driving or washing the dishes, when you are truly focused on what you are doing and when you feel good inside, you are in a state of meditation. There is no need to adopt a certain posture, recite a mantra or prayer, or even to try your best to chase away the thoughts that plague you. You can simply take three deep breaths while focusing your attention on what is happening in and around you here and now, and there you are.

Meditation is opening to the light energy present everywhere in and around you. Often the continuous presence of that light within you seems abstract because you are exclusively preoccupied by what happens outside of you, to the point that you sometimes forget who you are. Taking a break and gaining some distance then will help you return to yourself and contributes to getting the energy to flow within you once again.

There are countless ways of replenishing the light energy within you. When you enjoy yourself by going out with friends, laughing at a good joke, having a nice hot bath, or going for a walk in the woods—basically while doing anything that gives you joy and encourages you to find, if only temporarily, some inner peace—all those acts are a form of meditation.

You may also look deeply into the eyes of the person you love, play ball with your son, listen to your niece talk about her first flirt, or lovingly prepare a family meal. All the experiences lived in the now are beneficial, and the possibilities are infinite. It is up to you to choose the best way. Should you prefer to retreat for a few moments to be on your own, if that makes you feel good inside, that's fine too.

The wonderful thing about enjoying deep happiness and the plenitude of being for a few minutes is that no matter what the context is, it amplifies our energy. In an ideal world we would have been taught from childhood how to maintain our energy level by not being affected by the illusions of the pseudoreality surrounding us. But because that is not the case, we have to find the right practices, those that suit us personally, to recreate peace within us each day.

Once you have found the way that best helps you reconnect to the wonderful and luminous being that you truly are, it's up to you to give yourself the time and the room to recreate this state of grace within yourself. Whether on your own or with others, the better you feel, the more you elevate your vibrations, and the less outside disturbances can affect you. Even better, the more you radiate happiness and joy, the more your energy spreads to everything that surrounds you, raising the energy of everyone who crosses your path.

This is the very foundation of quantum physics: your states of mind directly impact your energy and influence everything around you. In other words, "thoughts create," or "the outside is the reflection of the inside." It is up to you, then, to choose to keep the flame of your inner plenitude burning so that the outside world may be a reflection of your pure well-being.

Indeed, only two possible choices are offered to you on a daily basis to find happiness and live in joy. The first, which society encourages, is have-do-be: "When I have the ideal context, I will do what is best for me, and then I will be happy." The other choice is a change of attitude to create your own happiness from the inside out, or be-do-have: "I choose to be happy even though I don't know what to do to get there, so much so that I attract the best ways to have a fulfilling life no matter what the reality is that surrounds me."

Meditating, therefore, is integrating in daily life the certainty that you can just be—be well, be happy, be in love—for you life to transform and become the reflection of what you are.

The Five Steps of Acceptance

The same goes for all that lives around you, for the whole of humanity, and for the planet itself: every cell will benefit from this light energy that inhabits you. The more you amplify your own light, the more it influences your surroundings. Similarly, when you feed worried, fearful, or have doubting thoughts regarding the people you love, you amplify that energy around them. The more you let their suffering, pain, or misfortune affect you, the more those issues will take root in their reality.

Have you heard of the principle of watering the flowers rather than the weeds? The more you spread thoughts of trust, support, and love around you, the more your loved ones will feel filled with these positive feelings toward them and easily find the solutions they aspire to. You can give your attention to a positive thought, and it will take to the ground and bear fruit. It is as simple as that.

The same goes for Gaia, our Mother Earth. If you picture her as suffering and sick and you send her energy to heal herself, the negative part of your thoughts will cancel out the positive virtues of your action. But if you visualize her as purified, balanced, and harmonized, vibrating in light just like you, you inspire the energy of transformation that will allow her to pursue her path toward full realization, hand in hand with you and all that lives here.

Every time you send someone energy, isn't it the part of you that lacks light that spurs you to want to make up for what is lacking in them? If so, why not start by finding the way to fill this void in you to set a good example around you and encourage those close to you to do the same for themselves and for our beautiful planet?

You can only give what you really own; thus you can only transmit the energy that is truly at your disposal. Everything is therefore a matter of purity of intention. It is not the means, the gestures, or the words that count, but rather the state of mind and spirit in which you enter meditation, for you as for the entire planet.

May you find what makes you most happy and choose to vibrate in bliss in every moment of your life. Isn't that the most beautiful of gifts that you could spread around you?

May joy illuminate your meditation, every day of your life.

—Bianca Gaia

Letting Joy Fly Away

Since meditation is the luminous attention to the now, if we are constantly in joy and inner peace, all our defense mechanisms disappear completely. Wouldn't that be excellent? By acquiring the energy we need to rebalance ourselves from the divine energy present everywhere in the universe, it would no longer be necessary to obtain it from those around us.

Better still, since meditation elevates our vibrations, it contributes to bringing us closer to inner plenitude, the state of grace also called "illumination" to which the saints and mystics have aspired for millennia. This is why the great spiritual masters encourage us to take a few moments every day to recenter ourselves through meditation, prayer, or various exercises.

Evidently, meditation would then be the key to a perfect happiness in daily life. In reality, we know from experience that events happen regularly in our lives that bring with them disturbances, chaos, and confusion, on the outside as well as inside. When health, finances, loving relationships, or any other important area of life is affected, it becomes hard to recenter or find the inner peace that allows access to the state of serenity indispensable to meditating.

When the now in itself is a cause of suffering, it is difficult to find the joy and lightness needed to recenter ourselves in a permanent manner. Even if taking three deep breaths helps us to blow off some steam, at times the outer or inner pressure becomes too great, and we become unsettled.

This is when the best letting go consists of going with the flow: fully welcoming and living the emotions that overwhelm us. There are some moments in life when we have no other choice but to engage in the process, whether we want to or not.

Imagine that one of your parents passes away, that your older child leaves home for good, that you reach the age of retirement. These are difficult moments to go through, yet they are impossible to avoid. There is no point in trying to see these chaotic states of mind in abstract terms. The more we allow ourselves to fully surrender to them, the less they endure.

The day I became aware of this intrinsic reality, my life changed completely. The crucial moment when it all clicked for me, where I managed to integrate everything I had read and learned on a spiritual level, is when I finally managed to make peace with my personality by allowing myself to live fully each of the steps needed to accept what I couldn't change despite all my good will.

Elisabeth Kübler-Ross's Steps of Mourning

Have you heard of Dr. Elisabeth Kübler-Ross? She was a Swiss psychiatrist who worked with people who were dying. In her book *On Death and Dying* she was the first to describe the natural journey taken by all human beings at the end of our lives. People who learn they are about to die go through similar stages of grieving before their soul is able to depart in peace. These steps may not necessarily be experienced in the same order, but they are always the same: shock/denial, anger, bargaining, depression, and finally, acceptance.

Does this remind you of anything? It is our primary mechanisms in full action. Even at the time of death, every individual continues to seek and obtain energy to cling to life and living at any cost. If this is true for a terminally ill patient, wouldn't this process apply to everyone in daily life? We experience the steps of mourning regularly in various contexts, whether it's because we lose a job, our partner leaves us, or we fall in love. Every time our brain is confronted with something new and out of the ordinary, as seen in Chapter 7, it has to rework the same process and go through the same steps.

However, Kübler-Ross allows us to see the stages that lead to acceptance with other eyes.

The Five Steps to Acceptance
(From Elisabeth Kübler-Ross)

State of Shock/Denial

Sadness

Acceptance/
Detachment

Anger

Bargaining/Guilt

The Five Steps of Acceptance

1. State of Shock/Denial

Kübler-Ross, as well as good psychiatrists after her, affirm that when we learn of our impending death, our first spontaneous reaction to manifest is a state of shock and denial: "It can't be. I can't believe I'm actually going to die. I don't feel that sick."

The same thing occurs when you lose someone dear to you: "This is impossible. I don't believe it. You're kidding me. I saw her only yesterday, and she was doing so well." The tragedies that can send you into a state of shock are countless: losing a friend, getting mugged in the street, having a car accident, witnessing a plane crash. No matter what the event is, if the shock is too great, your instinctive reflex is to refuse to admit the reality.

Even though the circumstances may have seemed positive at first glance, the fact that you didn't see it coming may still results in denial. Imagine that you just won a lottery jackpot. Your first reaction will probably be, "That can't be. I can't believe it." Although it is good news, the information is too large, too important to be admitted all at once. Your brain can't assimilate it fully.

Not everyone would react like that, but generally speaking this way of blocking information or taking a hit is our innate defense mechanism and protective reflex so that our neurons don't disconnect. Bit by bit our mind becomes used to the idea that a change has happened outside of us, and it becomes ready to move to the next step.

2. Anger

In the mourning process, after learning the news of their imminent death, terminally ill patients tend to rebel against the injustice of such a situation. Anger then takes over. They resent the whole world, want to break things around them, and strike out at God: "I don't deserve this. This isn't fair. I'm still young; I have too much life in me. This can't happen to me."

The same reaction also applies in other situations: a bad driver cuts you off, you are made to wait for hours at a hospital emergency room, or your wallet is stolen on the subway. "How nasty people are. The world is full of idiots. I don't deserve to be treated this way."

The feelings of irritation, rancor, fury, and even aggression all find their root in the same emotion: anger. It is as if all the pressure exerted on the brain at the time of the initial shock evacuates all at once. This can have the feeling of a volcanic eruption, in which you explode with rage and discontent.

Even in a positive situation, such as a lottery win, you may feel some dissatisfaction and resentment. A part of you says, "This is too good to be true. I can't believe it." You may be confronted with some disappointing reactions: "I am your wife; I am allowed to treat myself to this fur coat." "I am your father; you owe me part of this money because I brought you up." "We've worked together for years, and you know my financial situation, so you can certainly help me out a little." Not only is it annoying to be assailed by requests like this, it can make you regret the good old days when everything was "normal."

Indeed, any period of change carries with it its share of uncertainties and difficulties with adaptation. There is no point in repressing these frustrations, however, as that would only cause them to be exacerbated and to boil inside you even more. It is better to swiftly evacuate the anger before it turns into hate, to be able to get to the following step more freely.

3. Bargaining/Guilt

It is impossible to experience an emotion as intense as anger for long. It takes so much energy from the body that you tire rapidly. There comes a time when the rational Cartesian dimensions take over again.

In the case of a life-threatening illness, the patient will then look for all the solutions imaginable: trying to find a new experimental treatment, meeting with an internationally renowned surgeon, experimenting with various alternative remedies, and so on.

Ultimately he is trying to gain time, to bargain the time he has left to live. He is ready to spend huge amounts of money or go to the ends of the earth. If he is a believer, the individual will invoke God's clemency. "If you let me live, I promise to dedicate my life to others, to stop smoking, to give my money to charity."

In the case of an unhappy event of more manageable proportions, bargaining can take other forms: suing someone who caused a car crash, negotiating a pay cut so as not to lose your job, proposing marriage counseling because your relationship is on the rocks, allowing your youngest to repaint her room so that she will live at home longer; the examples are limitless.

Even in the case of a happy event, such as a move or a promotion, most people have a tendency to report the unavoidable later in order to remain on familiar ground for as long as possible.

For the brain, the period of bargaining permits continued juggling with the information to be integrated without going through too many strong emotions. This allows it to imagine that it still has some time left. It convinces itself that it still has the situation under control, or that there is the hope of finding a way to around the unimaginable.

After numerous attempts, however, of the individual still not succeeding in resolving the outer issue, she starts to harbor some guilt toward herself: "I should have been more careful about what I ate." "If I'd known I was going to die so young, I would have enjoyed life more." "I should have known I was going to have my wallet stolen, and carried less money on me." "My wife tells me to drive slower and more carefully on the road every time." "If I had been less hard on my children, they wouldn't have left home so soon."

Sooner or later, however, bargaining and guilt lead to a dead end, a deep feeling of powerlessness, and then a breakdown.

4. Sadness

Depression happens in terminally ill patients when all hope of survival has been lost. The feeling of discouragement that strikes the person becomes overwhelming, and tears then appear to be the only recourse.

At some time or another, sadness ends up affecting all the victims of problematic or conflicting events. No matter what the circumstances are, it is nevertheless very hard to evaluate whether it is the external cause that is generating so much pain, or whether it is self-pity. It is said that the first thirty seconds of sobbing are caused by the actual current situation, but sobbing for longer than a minute is the personality taking over to dwell on all the old wounds accumulated through the years.

This explains why, in a domestic confrontation, for instance, all the errors of one or the other partner end up being mentioned: all the absences, hurtful words, or unhappy actions resurface, and the soul wallows in pain and suffering to better empty the heart.

The problem is that by constantly crying about the self, you end up sinking into despair. A sad or unfortunate event can come to seem dramatic or even totally insurmountable. Melancholy then gives way to demoralization, weariness to affliction, emotional debilitation to despair. While this is understandable for a dying person, the same happens in everyday life: a breakup, a loss, or a major accident can cause just as much damage, leaving the person in a state of incomparable inner ruin.

In such a situation, if he or she remains withdrawn in herself for too long, constantly mulling over her misfortune, she may need some outside help because she is in danger of entertaining suicidal thoughts. Usually, however, the person ends up giving up, surrendering, and leaving it to a higher power to then move to the next step.

5. Acceptance

For a patient at the end of life, acceptance represents the outcome of the mourning process, for it allows him or her to welcome death no longer as a punishment or a failure but rather as deliverance. When fear fades away, when sadness and anger have been cleared out and all the possibilities for healing exhausted, inner peace can at last settle in.

All resistance vanishes, and blockages are undone. This is why some people experience a period of remission even though they are in the terminal phase: the brain stops juggling conflicting data and ends up admitting the inevitable aspects of the situation. The body can then rest for a while.

The same goes for all other situations or problems present in your life: once you have been through all the steps of mourning, you understand that there is nothing else to do or that can be gained from this experience, and you are finally ready to let go and to accept what is. This opening of consciousness is often a sign that you have acquired a new inner maturity, and some wisdom has settled in for good. You may not yet be ready to draw the lessons of this apprenticeship, but at least you have managed to calm your mind and appease your emotional body.

You have definitely managed to come full circle. No matter which step you started with and which was the last one you went through, it is only possible to reach acceptance once all the steps, these stages that are bereavement, have been covered.

If the exercises in this book haven't allowed you to recenter yourself, it is good to know that time always ends up sorting things out, and no matter what is happening at this time in your life, it won't last forever.

The understanding of this primordial notion allows the integration of the universal principal of impermanence: everything is evolving, everything changes, everything gets transformed. Nothing around us is frozen or definitive. We can choose to get involved in the process, and it will unfold in a much easier way and be completed much more quickly than anticipated.

Speeding Up the Process

Remarkably, once we apply this knowledge to our daily lives, we end up understanding that each emotion or bout of uneasiness is never a means to an end: as soon as we notice that the grieving process has started, we know that what will follow is only another step on the road to our full, tangible, and clear liberation.

When an unfortunate incident happens in everyday life, even if you need to go through all the steps of grieving to get to acceptance, you now know that it isn't necessary to die from it. To the contrary, it is in your interest to take part in the process actively by allowing yourself to play the game of your personality in order to concretely contribute to its resolution.

The proof is that if you fully live out your anger, go to the end of it without hesitation, and exaggerate it if need be, you know that at some point in time you won't have any other option but to go to the next step. Once you have experienced it fully and have looked at all the aspects of the problem, there won't be any sparks of annoyance left to rekindle your anger.

The same goes for all the other steps of the grieving process, which can be considered rungs to climb, deserts to cross, necessary evils to allow the brain to do its work properly as an information processor to integrate the new data somewhere on its hard drive.

The order that you go through the steps is usually dictated by the least dominant aspects of your personality. For instance, if you are the quick-tempered type, you will probably first react with anger; if you are of a pessimistic nature, you will tend to sink into sadness. Hyperactive people tend to go into action and look for solutions outside themselves so as not to feel their unease, while the usually apathetic type will first deny reality. The important part remains that no matter the order in which they unfold, these stages allow you to reach closure in your grieving process.

It can happen that we remain stuck in a particular stage, that our fears and resistance freeze us in repetitive patterns. These end up degenerating into defense mechanisms that stop us from completing the loop and turning the page.

A Mourning That Drags On

Some people remain in a state of shock for a very long time. An example is a sixty-year-old woman who lost her husband more than fifteen years ago. In appearance, Ginette didn't seem too affected by the loss of her husband: she carried on working, had her children over on Sunday, and went away on vacation every summer. In her home, however, the presence of her deceased husband still pervaded every room. His pipe still lay in an ashtray in the living room, his clothes still filled their shared closet, and even his work desk remained untouched, his day planner open to the date of his death.

In reality, Ginette stopped living when her partner passed away. She made do with living like a robot and surviving rather than living. She went through life like a zombie, without soul or color. It is not surprising, then, that this woman has much trouble walking. She now has to sleep in a reclining armchair with her feet elevated because her legs can no longer carry her. In fact, because her husband died in their bed during his sleep, she hasn't managed to admit it openly, but she feels unable to sleep on the mattress she used to share with him.

Having remained in denial for all this time, her life has remained on hold, and the mourning process has never been completed. She has become indifferent to what surrounds her.

The same thing can happen if, for instance, you are in conflict with somebody and don't talk to them for a very long time. One day you will find out that person has died without you having had the opportunity to make peace with him. An important piece of your puzzle is now missing, which will prevent you from completing it.

Dying Slowly

This is the reason that some people suffer the absence of a departed one for decades. Jean, Christian's best friend, died while Christian was away on a trip with his new lover, Jean's ex-partner. Christian felt guilty for years because he had not taken the time to tell Jean that he was courting the woman his childhood friend had been with for nearly three years. Even worse, knowing that Jean still loved her very much, Christian felt even guiltier knowing that his friend died in a motorcycle accident just after finding out from someone else that the lovers had gone on holiday together.

For months Christian tortured himself, imagining that his friend had voluntarily caused the accident that ended his life. Even after finding out that the fatal skid had happened on a slippery road during a torrential rain, doubt continued to consume him. Night and day he would mull over his feeling of responsibility for the death of his best friend. "Had I known, I would never have gone away like that on an impulse. Had I remained near him, I could have saved him. I should have confessed everything to him from the start. If only I had waited a few months longer before going out with Cynthia."

Of course, his relationship with Cynthia did not survive all the guilt and the deep existential questioning. Christian ended up sinking into a deep depression that lasted nearly five years, and to this day he remains single, afraid of a new commitment, feeling that he does not deserve to be happy now that his friend is dead.

The problem here is not going through the steps to acceptance but remaining stuck in one stage or another along the way, forever repeating the same obsessions without changing or succeeding in moving to the next stage.

Getting Rid of Fear

In your life, every time you have had to go through mourning, or a painful experience has presented itself to you, if you haven't gone through all the steps, lived all the aspects of this experience, it is impossible that you have managed to free yourself from it completely. In my view, this is the biggest secret of healing. It is fundamental to become aware of this unavoidable reality, because if you miss a step, it is clear that eventually you will have to go back to it: it is your only chance to liberate yourself from the ongoing process.

Allow me to give an example from my own life experience. Over the years I had to explore various aspects of my tumultuous relationship with my father. In therapy as much as on my spiritual path I took the time to work on myself. I thought that I had completed the loop and that I had succeeded in overcoming the violence I had been subject to, that I had forgiven him his clumsy ways of acquiring the energy he was lacking through me.

At the time, I didn't make the connection, but I very often dreamed that some invisible person would enter my room and wanted to attack me. I didn't imagine that this anonymous adversary could have been my father. Inside myself I had healed the sadness, the powerlessness, my victim side. I had become responsible for myself and had started fresh doing everything to become the creator of my own life. There was therefore no reason to feed any ill will toward him. But I had forgotten to consider one aspect of the situation that had never affected me before: the fear that lived with me since then.

A few months after giving birth to my son Émile, I again dreamed that an invisible man was chasing me through the house. Holding my newborn in my arms, I was rushing toward his room to shelter him. Something unexpected happened there: my son, who was looking over my shoulder, seemed to see something humorous behind me and started laughing.

Panicked, I couldn't understand why he was reacting like this. Then, still within the dream, I understood that the person who was following us had to be someone he knew; otherwise he would not have smiled that way. I turned around and then realized that it was my father.

As a consequence, I understood that during all these years that I had been consumed with fear, it was my father that I was scared of. For a whole decade I had feared the hereafter, the invisible world, and I had closed the door to my extrasensory perceptions, believing that negative energy surrounded me. That morning when I awoke, I started to cry. I had just become aware of the story I had been telling myself for so long, and also of the stage of my grieving process that had not been completed.

I had been communicating more healthily with my father for a long time, though. Our relationship seemed healed, but I had neither identified, nor recognized, nor accepted my childhood fear. As long as I hadn't identified the source of this fear, I was continually living it without being able to point to its origin or overcome it.

The stages of the grieving process are like a spiral, or an endless loop: as long as we haven't completed the process, we keep going back to the same state of mind, until we accept it and become free of it once and for all.

The same applies in your life. When you have had unfortunate, painful, or traumatic experiences, as long as some aspects remain unintegrated within you, like the hamster on its wheel you continue to go around in circles without ever getting anywhere.

It is a bit like a game of musical chairs. As you can see in the following illustration, as long as you haven't sat in each of the chairs in the circle (the stages of mourning), you cannot take the central seat, acceptance.

The Typical Patterns of Conflicts:
Musical Chairs

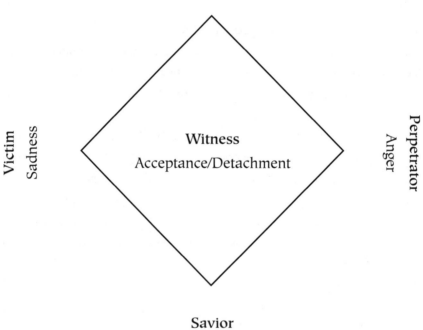

Indifferent
State of Shock/Denial

Victim
Sadness

Witness
Acceptance/Detachment

Perpetrator
Anger

Savior
Bargaining/Guilt

Surely you have already made the connection between the stage of acceptance and the defense mechanisms that we talked about in chapters 9 and 10: the state of shock and denial are the favorite withdrawal positions of the Indifferent; sadness is the emotion usually favored by the Victim; anger remains the Perpetrator's domain; and bargaining and guilt take all the attention of the Savior. Finally, it is only possible to occupy the Witness place by developing an exceptional ability to recenter oneself daily through detachment and unconditional acceptance of all that is.

Musical Chairs

Our problem of imbalance does not come from the mechanisms we commonly use to maintain our energy but rather from the life positions we refuse and which represent the step of acceptance that we avoid. It is thus the chair on which we are most afraid to sit that is the most important, rather than the one we constantly use.

If you refer to the results of your Egogram as calculated in Chapter 9, the relevant column is the one in which you obtained the lowest number of "somewhat true" responses. If your score was generally balanced in every field, it means that you manage to go through the steps of mourning without getting caught up in one of the conflicting patterns presented above.

But if you avoid one of the primary reactions at any cost, life will surely repeatedly present you with the same opportunities to relive the stage of mourning that you have put aside. To omit one step toward acceptance is like leaning on a table that is missing one of its legs: it is impossible to remain balanced for very long. It's also like driving a car with a flat tire: you can't go very far or reach your destination on time.

Concretely, the mourning process is complete only when all the steps have been covered, after you have experimented with and integrated each of the defense mechanisms, and you have sat in all the available chairs in the big game of life.

If you are afraid to express your anger, you will have a tendency to feel denial, sadness, and guilt rather than having the courage to express your frustrations and discontent. Similarly, if you don't allow yourself some distance and some indifference toward a problematic situation, you will constantly be overwhelmed by emotions of anger, sadness, and guilt that will drain your vital energy.

Round and Round and Off They Go

For me, the part of myself I was refusing to integrate was the Indifferent. To make a connection with the fear I mentioned earlier, I will explain its origin by relating an incident that deeply marked me as a child. When I was about twelve years old, like most kids my age, I had a bicycle that I used every day. Every evening my father would say, "Don't forget to put away your bicycle, or you'll be sorry."

Like all twelve-year-olds, I was forgetful and often forgot to put away my bike. I then had to go out again in my pajamas to put it away. One evening while my father was out, I went to bed without thinking of my bicycle, which was still outside. When my father came back and saw my bike blocking the alleyway, he got angry. He picked up one of my brother's toys, a plastic baseball bat—which was not that hard, but still—and woke me up by hitting me on the head with it.

To be hit while sleeping was one of the most traumatizing experiences of my young life. During the days following this incident, I slept with the door to my room closed, a chair jammed under the door knob, thinking that at least if my father came in again, I would wake up before he could hit me when the chair fell on the floor. Later, for many years, I could only sleep lightly. I told myself, "I will never be caught off-guard again. From now on I will always be prepared for the worst." What my body registered was, "One cannot be indifferent; it's dangerous. Always be on guard."

The part of us that constantly remains on guard is the Savior, always looking for solutions and answers to provide. In my case, this defense mechanism had taken over, while the other, the Indifferent, was nearly totally obscured along with the fear I felt at that time.

From then on, when an unpredictable event arose, my first reaction would be immediately to look for what I could do to improve the situation. Twenty-five years later, at the time of my mother's death, I immediately got involved in organizing the funeral, the buffet, the memorial, and so on. In other words, I looked for solutions. By doing so I overlooked the stage of shock and denial.

Generally speaking, I would spend most of my time in the bargaining phase. Fortunately, having understood this mechanism for the past few years, I have transformed my way of reacting. I was continually on guard, remaining active and making myself indispensable. Because I was not allowing myself some distance, I wandered from one chair to the other, juggling with sadness, anger, and guilt without ever succeeding to complete the grieving process.

Two Can Play That Game

In 1987, when I started seeing my partner, I thought to myself, *He's so adorable.* Serge had an artistic temperament and was nonchalant and relaxed, his head always in the clouds. At the time I thought to myself, *This is exactly what I need the most in my life—to be Zen, as I am always on guard.*

I didn't know it yet, but I had attracted this exceptional being into my life in order to become aware of my need to create distance and to allow myself sometimes to be indifferent to what surrounded me—which I never did. Unconsciously, I accepted sharing my life with someone who completed me. Together we maintained a good balance.

Unfortunately, after only a few months, Serge's carefree nature started to irritate me. Conflicts arose between us. I found him absent-minded, while he considered me fussy and demanding.

Returning to the analogy of musical chairs, in a couple, when the grieving process starts, each of the players goes from one chair to the other, moving through successive states of mind, often in opposition to the position that the other chooses to adopt. Because it is not possible for two people to occupy the same chair at the same time, some chairs are never used by the other person, and the cycle never ends. Anyone in a relationship will probably recognize themselves in this situation.

At home, because I was of a Savior temper and my partner was an Indifferent, our fights would nearly always start in the same way: I would attempt to make him responsible for my inner emptiness. I would say something like, "We never do anything together." Hating conflict, Serge would avoid responding, and not getting any reaction from him would only increase my dissatisfaction, feeding the fire of my anger, and I would immediately start to lecture him like a true

Perpetrator. My partner, unable to understand where so much hate was coming from, as according to him he had not done anything wrong, would experience sadness, suddenly feeling blame for everything that was wrong. He would then automatically take refuge in the Victim position.

Seeing him in that state, the Savior reflex would automatically click on within me, given that it had never been my intention to hurt him. Serge's reaction would-n't take long in coming: he would take the chair of the Perpetrator, attacking me to make me feel guilty for having attacked him.

The Savior/Indifferent Dance

This awful dance could last for several hours or even days, because if no outer event interrupted the process, we would both unavoidably fall back into the same chairs (there are only four of them) without ever succeeding in closing the loop.

The most frustrating thing for me was to notice, several hours or days later, that nothing had been resolved and that "we still never do anything together."

The important thing to note in this example is that there was a chair on which I never dared sit, and the same went for Serge. Indeed, as the youngest in a big family, from a very young age, my husband felt, rightly or wrongly, that no one valued his opinion and that he therefore didn't have a place as a Savior. He preferred to remain at distance (the Indifferent) to avoid getting hurt.

As a consequence, because the Indifferent chair was his chair, I would never sit in it. Similarly, because the Savior chair was my chair, he never dared settle into it. However, if we observe the situation a bit more closely and with more objectivity, we realize that these are respectively the two chairs that would have allowed us to quickly undo the dead end we were forcing ourselves into.

Had I managed to take on the Indifferent role, I could have stopped the process on my own, for I would have found my own solution within: not to care about it whatsoever. Similarly, had he had the courage to become a Savior, Serge would have been busy answering my needs, and I would have felt at last that I mattered to him, thus canceling out the very source of the conflict that put us in opposition.

All this to explain that suffering settles in when we find ourselves stuck in one or the other steps of grieving, this stage of the grieving process then becoming our primary defense mechanism simply because we don't have the courage to change our attitude or life position. We haven't learned to let go.

The Perpetrator/Victim Dance

Deep down, everyone who suffers is someone who has let themselves be caught up by one or another of the control dramas, and they have remained stuck in a particular stage of the grieving process. As discussed in Chapter 10, some individuals can remain in anger their entire lives because they don't allow themselves to connect with the sensitivity or vulnerability within them. They are dominated by their survival instinct: the aggressiveness and control they exert on others.

Victims will be content with feeling sorry for themselves and having people pity them rather than believe in their inner potential and affirming their own power of manifestation to create their lives. In the game of musical chairs, those two complimentary personalities will tend to attract each other to rebalance the forces of nature that seem to have been unfairly distributed.

Hence the expression "opposites attract." We could say rather that one person's deficiencies are automatically filled by someone else.

When we have to deal with a conflicting situation in which we play different roles, we need to understand that we won't get anywhere by continually switching chairs. Others will always act by reacting to the position we occupy, whatever it may be.

Once we have allowed ourselves to sit in all of the chairs, to give way to all of the primary dimensions in ourselves, it is no longer necessary to oppose the other person in order to finalize the grieving process. It becomes possible again to center oneself and become an impartial Witness.

When we recognize in the other person the aspect of our personality that we need to integrate in ourselves, we no longer need to confront him or her to acquire his energy. We manage to find balance by ourselves, through opening up to the liberating energy present throughout the universe.

It then becomes possible to recognize the strength of the other person and to ask for his or her collaboration in order to develop a winning attitude in all spheres of experimentation in the relationship. Things become very different: We no longer try to control, paralyze, accuse, or crush the other person. On the contrary, we open ourselves to her luminous addition and value her talents and life experiences, for we now know that she is here to help us find balance and make peace with all the parts of ourselves.

This way of proceeding connects spirituality with psychology. When we remain centered, we help the other person because we don't exclude him into his favorite defense mechanism, and he doesn't have to use it because he doesn't feel threatened anymore. When we value another person by making him aware of his own potential, we command to the universe to place his strengths at our service. This works for the best in each of us.

Watching Others Dance Alone

The first time I explained to my daughter how the steps of grieving operate, she had just applied to represent the students of her class on the student council of the new school she was attending. Marlène and another young girl, let's call her Geneviève, were jointly selected for the position.

Loving to bring people together, Marlène aspired to sharing chores and democratic representation, while her friend was instead looking for the power and popularity derived from it. After a while, my daughter noticed that her teammate was not there to help her but rather to govern without her. Because this did not fit with her values at all, she first tried to reason with her, without any luck. Later on she decided to withdraw from the student council because she couldn't manage to get along with Geneviève in any way.

Because the young woman in question had a rather domineering temper, she immediately reacted by calling Marlène a "deserter," which seriously unnerved Marlène. That is when I shared with her the five steps of acceptance and told her, "If you succeed in keeping your distance, in not giving in to the emotional blackmail that Geneviève will attempt to expose you to, in less than a week she will have gone around all the chairs and will end up leaving you alone. But if you get into her game, she will always have some power over you and will constantly try to unsettle you and rob you of your energy. She will always attack you or attempt to manipulate you in the same way, and that may last a very long time."

My daughter went back to school the next day on her guard and well prepared. During the day, Geneviève acted totally indifferent to Marlène's decision: "It's your problem; you wanted to desert; it doesn't matter because I will find someone much better than you. Too bad for you; I don't care." My daughter came back from school saying, "You were right: she's in denial. I saw it, and I didn't fall into her game."

The second day, Geneviève stubbornly dogged her: "You let me down. I have to do everything by myself now, and I can't. It's all your fault." My daughter cried a bit, and the young woman encouraged it, until she remembered that I had warned her of what would happen if she let herself be unsettled by her former friend. She got hold of herself and told herself, *She is angry. She has a right to be, but it's not my problem.* She centered herself. When she got back home, she told me, "You were right, Mom: today was the anger phase." I answered, "It is very rare for someone to go through two emotional phases in quick succession, as it's very demanding for the physical body. So tomorrow you can expect it to be bargaining."

Indeed, the next day the young girl tried to make Marlène reverse her decision: "I will be nice to you. I promise I will let you take more initiative. You can come back. I swear I've changed." This time my daughter had to laugh (to herself, of course).

Then, as predicted, over the weekend Geneviève called, crying on the phone, "You can't do this to me. I'll never manage on my own; it's too difficult." My daughter replied, "That's good. You've done a full tour of your mourning. On Monday, everything should be back in order for you, because you will have finally accepted my choice." The next week, the young woman stopped going over what had become ancient history to her and ended up leaving Marlène alone. Time passed, and because Geneviève turned out not to be well-suited for the position, the principal ended up dismissing her and offered my daughter to return as head of the student council, telling her, "We have realized that the problem did not originate with you, but with Geneviève. So if you'd like your position back, you're welcome to it."

The great thing is that, having been advised about the process, Marlène didn't play the other person's game. The stages of the grieving process were therefore quickly completed for both of them.

Going to Sit in the Middle of the Circle

The purpose of the musical chairs exercise remains to get to the center of the circle, to reach the state of detachment and acceptance that allows for balance to be found within oneself without having to rob or depend on the energy of others. Here lies the key of the mystery of spiritual evolution: everyone aspires to reach illumination, to ascend, to live in a perpetual state of grace, but sooner or later we end up falling back into our defense mechanisms.

Why? Even if our ambition is to follow the middle road, in reality, as long as a part of us has not been integrated to the remaining dimensions of ourselves, it will do all it can to be heard, recognized, and accepted unconditionally. This aspect of ourselves that has been neglected until now is then going to shout, scream, and attract to us all the necessary experiences in order to make us take it into consideration and return it to its rightful place within ourselves. Deep down, it is inviting us to unify all of our parts and merge with them in divine nourishing, reinvigorating, and unlimited energy.

Integration: *The Call of the Wolf*

Here is a therapeutic allegory aimed at allowing you to integrate the notions explained above with the help of your right brain, your creative and intuitive lobe, operating in a non-Cartesian way:

In a remote land, during a particularly harsh and icy winter, some villagers went to their king to complain about a very serious problem: a pack of ferocious wolves was attacking their cattle and devouring their poultry. The king immediately called the best archers from his garrison and gave them the task of ridding the country of those bloodthirsty beasts.

"The most deserving among you," the king added, "will be invited to my table with his entire family and will share my meals until the return of spring."

All the soldiers hurried out to go hunting, courageously braving the snow and the cold. They went alone, each in their own direction, all aspiring to become the king's favorite. For days on end they tracked the wolves in every corner of the forest, stopping only to eat and sleep.

Finally, the first hunter came back and went before the king. He was covered in wounds, one arm in a bandage, and was kneeling on crutches, one of his legs having been cut off at the knee.

"I am surely the most deserving, your majesty," said the soldier in a distressed tone. "I fought with my bare hands against the wolves, and even though I haven't managed to exterminate them, I have managed to wound at least one. See, I even lost my right leg," he said, almost tearfully.

The king was filled with compassion for the wounded man, but before he could open his mouth another soldier stood before him, carrying the remains of a wolf on his shoulder.

"My king, I bring to thee the skin of the leader of the pack. I shot down this wolf with one arrow, and all the others ran away without asking for more."

"Very well, valiant soldier," said the king. I congratulate you on your bravery."

The sovereign was again interrupted by the remarkable entrance of another soldier, escorted by a young wolf peacefully walking at his side.

"What is this?" the king asked the newcomer.

"Your majesty," the archer answered, "while my colleagues were chasing the wolves to kill them, I thought that, as long as one remained alive, it would come back to attack the neighboring farms. I therefore took the time to observe them at a distance, and I noticed that they were neither violent, nor cruel, but rather terribly hungry, just like we are during this harsh winter. For them, as for all of us, prey is getting scarce, game is hibernating, and the good weather is late in its return. These wolves roam your lands savaging farm animals because they have nothing else to eat.

"So I had an idea. I brought them a bit of food every day, attempting to lead them further and further away from the kingdom. I guided them to the valley, where the weather is milder and the buds are starting to bloom. The ice by the shore of the river had melted, allowed the pack to quench its thirst and even to catch a few fish. I don't think they will be back this way any time soon."

"What about this one?" the King inquired, pointing at the wolf obediently lying at the soldier's feet.

"He saved my life," the young man answered without hesitation. "At the top of the mountain, I accidentally awoke a bear by entering his cave, and without the intervention of this precious beast, the ferocious animal would have eaten me alive."

The king recognized that this brave soldier was the most deserving of all, and so invited him to sit at his table for the evening feast. But the archer refused: "Thank you, but I have already received my reward, my king." Under the incredulous and even outraged gaze of the onlookers, he continued, "This wolf and I have become friends. We tamed each other, and from now on he is no longer my enemy. I now know that if I am mindful of the needs of others rather than to trying to fight or impose myself on them by force, they will respect me and help me in return. Thus we both come out winners."

An old man, famous for his great wisdom, approached the young man. Laying a hand on his shoulder, he cleared his throat and announced, loud enough for all to hear, "Today this pure-hearted man has integrated one of the fundamental laws of the universe. All outer threats are illusory: they are nothing but the echo of your own fears and the reflection of the shadows hidden within you.

"Why want to kill this untamable beast inside you, called the ego, when you can decide to listen to it and tame it for it to become your ally? The mastery of your lower instincts will happen easily once you stop wanting to control them at any cost and instead simply welcome them unconditionally, and direct them toward more luminous choices on roads leading to serenity and plenitude within yourself."

And you, how do you answer the call of your inner wolf? What type of warrior are you? How do you succeed in making peace and unifying all the parts in yourself?

CHAPTER 12

The Pyramid of Duality: Q = 4pE

Honoring Difficulties, for They Are Here to Reestablish Balance

Message from June 5, 2005

What if adversity was in fact an opportunity created entirely by your divine spark to allow you to discover your inner unlimited potential? What if all these problems present in your life were not the cause of the imbalances you experience but rather the result of your own negligence toward yourself? Could you then consider them as gifts brought to your consciousness by your inner wisdom?

All human beings go through difficult times at one point or another. Sickness, failures, accidents, rejection or abandonment, betrayal—these are situations that pull you to the core of your inner duality. What should you do then? Resist? Fight? For many generations you have been taught to oppose anything that comes along and rocks your daily routine. Any change, any adversity is greeted as an unfortunate thing that you absolutely need to eliminate as soon as possible before it disturbs your balance in a prolonged manner.

What if the lack of balance was, in fact, the primary cause, prior to this disturbance? Generally speaking, you believe that you feel good in most areas of your life. It seems that you are in good health; that everything is going well at work; that at home, in your relationship and in your family, there are no apparent conflicts. However, one day a brick falls on your head: you lose your job, your mother gets sick, your partner leaves you, or a major problem presents itself. Of course, you may wonder: What have I done to deserve such a challenge? *Whether it is small or large, any unexpected event quickly appears as a catastrophe when we feel destitute or powerless. What happens next?*

Different attitudes, depending on your dominant personality type, might be adopted. Many people will first be in a state of shock, simply paralyzed and incapable of reacting, even going to the point of denying the problem: "It's nothing; it isn't serious; it will most probably go away by itself." Others will react with anger: "That isn't true. This can't be happening to me. This is impossible." As a consequence, some people will be burdened with sadness: "My God! This hurts so much. My heart is broken. I'll never get out of this." Rarer are those who immediately look for solutions without getting emotionally disturbed: "So, what solution do I have at my disposal? What are the resources available? Who could help me with this?"

Generally speaking, most of these states of mind will manifest in turn and repeatedly until the full resolution of the problem. Could another way present itself to you? Could you possibly make another choice? You may not be able to prevent your personality from reacting irrationally, but consciously, perhaps, would you be able to divert your attention to something other than the event in question?

Think about it for a moment: how many situations generate some degree of torment in you daily life while consisting of nothing but a fleeting, often harmless crisis? Most of the time, there is no reason to panic. No experience is bad in itself. Why not wait, before getting upset, to see if it is really as serious as you think? Put it in perspective, or dedramatize it through humor: "Will I die from this?" Take the time to breathe deeply and let your anxiety dissolve on its own. This will not only help you to keep a cool head but also to contact the part of you that knows why this misadventure is occurring at this precise moment in your life.

What if this crisis situation was nothing but a triggering element, an invitation to go inward to discover some unanticipated treasures? Have you ever wondered whether the suffering you feel was already present in you before the disturbing event happened? Perhaps deeply buried in your unconscious mind there was already a seed of worry, fear, or torment about similar events that left wounds in you.

This isn't about reliving your childhood or all the misfortunes of your existence; it's only about remembering: "Have I felt this trouble—this pain, this anger, this powerlessness, this guilt, or other trouble—within me before?" The roots of the unease are to be found within you, in your hidden frustrations and repressed dissatisfaction now as well as in the past. An old saying affirms this idea: "Everything that is not expressed gets imprinted." Ask yourself, What emotions have I had to suppress? What call of my heart did I repress for fear of not seeing it welcomed? Liberation, healing, and most adequate solutions do not reside in the solution to the problem, but rather in the understanding of its reason for being. It has only appeared to allow you to reestablish the balance that was missing in you.

Do you believe yourself to be limited, weak, or powerless? It goes without saying that you will meet people who will appear powerful and strong to you and have access to powerful unlimited external resources. Do you believe that you are not up to the task? Some "charitable souls" will accept the task of confronting and humiliating you so that you can discover that you have everything you need within you to overcome any obstacle that arises on your path. In the big dance of life, every person you mix with at the heart of your human drama has been hired by you to play this specific role in order to help you transmute the programming and existential alienation that you entertain, unconsciously or not, within you. Nothing is left to chance.

Whatever the context, your inner wisdom is only inviting you to consider the absurdity of your self-destructive thoughts by offering challenges at the level of the capacities you have not exploited until now. No matter what difficulty presents itself in your life, tell yourself that this is nothing but a vast staging of your divine self so that you may transcend the three-dimensional illusions in which you have imprisoned yourself.

Any excess attracts excess. Extremes attract extremes. What we resist persists. Any aspect of yourself that you neglect, denigrate, devalue, or repress will need to be externalized and expressed at some point or another for your greater liberation. You are therefore invited to honor the event, the situation, or the crisis, as well as the person who triggers this obligation to reestablish balance in all the spheres of your life. No matter what the trigger is, it is simply the expression—the mirror, whether perfect or distorting—of the image that you entertain of yourself.

If you understand that this situation is present in your life to invite you to recognize who you really are, all the happiness and powerlessness you may feel will vanish on the spot. If you aim for balance rather than excess in every area of your life, peace will settle in you permanently. If you thank your inner wisdom and commit yourself to listening to it at every moment of your life by letting go of your control over external events, multiple miracles will occur in your life, including the total healing of all present and past wounds that are written in your body and soul. Don't resist anymore: say yes to the difficulties that present themselves, and honor your own inner multidimensional power that knows how to transcend them.

It is in adversity that you have chosen to contribute to the planetary transmutation, through your own living cells and in all the aspects of your human experience. It is in the unpredictable that you are most permeable to the purifying energy that wants to radiate through you. Focus your attention no longer on the results or the resolution of your problems, but rather on the best part of yourself, as it knows how to manifest the best in you and for all that lives here below. Merge with your unlimited creative essence and taste plenitude at every moment. You will then become a lighthouse and a haven of peace at the heart of the storm for those who still believe in chaos in their lives.

—*Bianca Gaia*

$Q = 4pE$

It was Leonardo da Vinci who said, "No human research can be called true science unless it can be mathematically proved." Imagine a single mathematical formula that could simultaneously sum up and activate the ascension process.

In 2004, while I was working on the concept of the "Welcome to the Fifth Dimension" workshop, my partner pointed out that all the notions addressed could be found in one another, were matching, and could fit together perfectly like Russian dolls. Every time we believe we have discovered a new concept or developed a new idea, another one takes form within it, completing the lineage and leading us even further and deeper into ourselves.

When I was in high school, I thought of myself as hopeless at anything to do with physics and mathematics. And then, there I was unknowingly exploring the laws of quantum physics: "as above, so below, from the microcosm to the macrocosm." The more I progressed in what I thought to be a summary of my numerous forms of training and spiritual adventures, the more I saw the extent to which the universe is animated in perfect alignment with itself, just like a kaleidoscope reflecting a thousand and one facets of divine energy in all its forms.

The more I aspired to live in the fifth dimension, the more I noticed that everything that surrounded me came in groups of five: the five great soul families, the five geometric shapes of the light cocoon, the five dimensions of the human brain, the five ways to acquire energy, and so on.

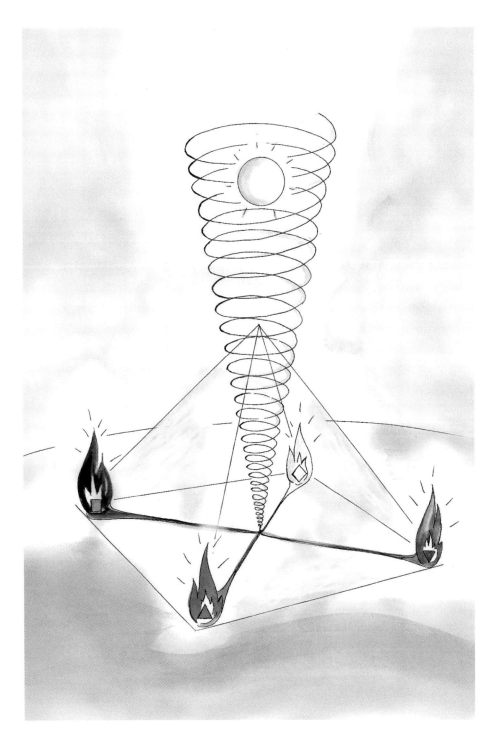

For years and years, however, I had settled for seeing life in only three dimensions: body, mind, and spirit; reptilian, limbic, and neocortex parts of the brain; the perpetrator-victim-savior triad, and so on. I could not imagine that there were other dimensions to explore, other worlds to discover.

Once I established the connection between the defense mechanisms of James Redfield and the grieving steps of Elisabeth Kübler-Ross, everything fell into place inside me. I had just crossed over to the fourth dimension. I had accepted finally setting foot on the other side of the veil, to awaken my consciousness, and in so doing to reconnect with my true soul family, the Facilitators.

In meditation I then received the vision of a pyramid, similar to the ones we see in Egypt and Central America. It was made of a shiny golden crystal. At the four corners of the base of the translucent prism were burning flames of different colors: red at the north, yellow at the south, blue at the east, and violet at the west. A ray was beaming out of each of the colored points, pointing straight toward the center of the pyramid, where the four colored beams fused into one pure column of bright light rising toward the sky.

Something immediately clicked inside me, and in a moment of pure clarity I received the revelation that transformed me forever:

> **The synergy of the four dimensions of being induces**
> **divine quintessence.**
>
> $$Q = 4pE$$

By integrating the four aspects of our personality, p, also called defense mechanisms, and by merging into the energy, E, of our soul family, it is possible to activate our ascension vehicle, the Merkaba, and to maintain ourselves in the perpetual state of grace that opens the doors to the fifth dimension. Hence the alchemical name "quintessence," Q: the total immersion in our divine essence constitutes the fifth step of the ascension and can only be obtained by aligning the first four dimensions present in us.

It is a simple mathematical formula, you may say, but how difficult it is to put into practice in our daily lives.

Two Sides of the Same Coin

Fortunately, once we have access to the higher dimensions and accept receiving the beneficial help and energy of our soul family, a whole new world of possibilities opens up to us.

Right after the explanations that followed this fabulous vision of the ascension, a question covertly slipped into my mind, as probably happened for all the great masters who have preceded us: "Is a coin worth more on its tail or on its head?" Do our instinctive reactions and primary mechanisms in any way mar the divine and wonderful being that we truly are? Since they are the reflection of the parts of us that only ask to be assimilated, accepted, and fully integrated, could they possibly constitute an addition to our evolution rather than an obstacle to overcome?

What if each of the survival mechanisms represented the back of the medal, the tail of the coin, while the head side revealed to us the energy of the soul family we most needed to welcome and recognize in ourselves? Our shadow and light aspects would then represent, in real terms, two sides of the same coin.

Such is the rational explanation of the timeless yin-yang symbol:

Duality doesn't exist. Darkness itself is nothing but an illusion. It only represents that void in us asking to be filled with light at every moment.

Our challenge is this: rather than trying to steal the energy that surrounds us on the material plain through power games and other primary mechanisms, let's learn to create the connection with this divine particle in ourselves that knows that light is and always has been present in us for all eternity.

We simply need to take into consideration the messages our supposedly untamable personality is sending to us, and to be attentive to the cries for help emitted by our physical bodies, to measure the importance of becoming one with all the parts of ourselves.

In reality, it isn't our ego that stops us from ascending, but rather memory loss: we have forgotten that we are pure energy and pure light. We don't allow ourselves to radiate in all the spheres of our being. We hide from others the extraordinary and luminous being that lies dormant within us.

It is through unconditionally saying "yes" to all the dimensions present in us, through aligning the four bases or our internal pyramid, that balance finally settles in and our divine light manages to unfold in all grace, radiant and unlimited.

The Pyramid of Duality
$$Q = 4pE$$

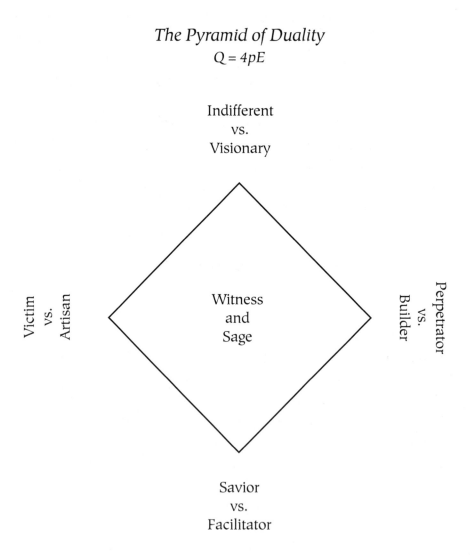

Indifferent
vs.
Visionary

Victim
vs.
Artisan

Witness
and
Sage

Perpetrator
vs.
Builder

Savior
vs.
Facilitator

The Pyramid of Duality

The quintessence of being, the perpetual state of grace we reach in the fifth dimension, appears as the summit of a pyramid whose base is the four inferior dimensions accepted and integrated within ourselves: the dense body (the state of our physical health), the emotional body (our moods), the mental body (our frame of mind), and the causal body (our state of consciousness).

Each of these dimensions emits specific vibrations in the form of energetic fields and specific colors. They are the same whether we deploy our energy in our human aspect through our defense mechanisms or in our divine aspects as a member of a soul family. Hence the image of the two sides of a coin having the same value is appropriate, since they are connected to each other.

1. Perpetrator versus Builder

When you do not have the courage to express your anger openly, chances are also that you may not manage to make room for the Perpetrator in you. As a consequence you deny yourself the opportunity to benefit from the virtues of the Builders soul family, and therefore you may feel difficulty in responding to your essential needs, believing in your inner potential, and materializing the projects you dream of.

Conversely, when you are a good Builder, you know how to use your born-leader charisma, leaning on your strength of character in order to contribute to a better world. However, you are also vulnerable to frustration and anger, and when all is not going the way you want it to, you run the risk of becoming a Perpetrator, using control or if need be your physical strength to force others to give you energy. This explains why the energy fields of the Perpetrator and of the Builder have the same geometric shape: the triangle.

2. Indifferent versus Visionary

When you do not succeed in maintaining distance or being cool-headed when faced with the hazards of life, it is because you do not welcome the Indifferent within you. However, the mental acuity and intellectual rigor of the Indifferent originate from his privileged connection to the Visionaries family, recognized for their clarity of mind and their quest for tools to help the evolution of all humanity.

Conversely, if you recognize your Visionary qualities, you also know that once in a while you live exclusively in your head. You therefore may have a tendency to disconnect from your emotional body and ignore unsettling situations by becoming absorbed in a deep state of denial. By becoming indifferent to what surrounds you, you lose touch with the reality of the now, and also with those who love you and just want to be close to you. In the first case as in the second, your energy is mobilized in the top of the body, and your light cocoon then takes the shape of an inverted triangle.

3. Victim versus Artisan

If you do not allow yourself to consider your sensitivity, your vulnerability, and the weaknesses that inhabit you, you are denying the Victim hidden deep inside. In doing so, you imprison your inner child and suppress your creativity, spontaneity, and originality. In brief, you clip the wings of the Artisan of Peace that dwells within you.

On the other hand, when the Artisan in you takes too much space in your existence, when you entertain an exclusively emotional relationship to the world you live in, it is a good bet that your sentimentality is regularly put to the test when so much injustice and human idiocy are at work around you. This may lead to some feelings of sadness and powerlessness in you, inciting you to adopt the Victim model, begging for others' energy in order to survive. Your energetic field will then have the same appearance in its luminous or shady aspect, a diamond shape.

4. Savior versus Facilitator

In everyday life, when you don't manage to find the answers and solutions to the problems that hound you, you end up believing that you will never manage to bring out the Savior, the hero within you. However, you only have to call the Facilitators family to reawaken the luminous flame that inhabits you to bring out strengths, talent, and spiritual gifts that you don't consciously suspect you have.

On the other end of the spectrum, one who recognizes him- or herself as a Facilitator—the healer, the therapist, the shaman connected to nature and its energetic forces—runs the risk of wanting to take others on his shoulders and totally forget about himself. You may then start playing Savior, bargaining your favors while forgetting that your first mission is to live in communion with the source of all life, and to heal yourself first. Your energy cocoon may then have the same shape as the Facilitators—the square—but it will be missing the natural ovoid curve of the Sages.

5. Witness and Sage

Because the tail and head of the coin merge when we manage to recenter ourselves in the present moment, the Witness and the Sage become one in the light, for they have given up fighting for their survival and surrender to divine energy to fill any of their shortcomings or remaining inadequacies.

The energy is here, everywhere, and available. We only need to open our ruling chakra for it to reach us, instilling in us all the vitality we need to fully live and access our preferred ascension vehicle: the Merkaba.

Stabilizing the Base of the Pyramid

Imagine that up to now, we have contemplated one by one all the pieces of a huge puzzle. Here is where they finally all fall into place, revealing to us who we really are.

As we've seen in the previous chapters, every soul family has its role to play in the world. However, our individual mission first and foremost consists of living in unconditional love, firstly toward the self, then toward every living being.

Let's forget for a moment this world of duality in which we live. Over the course of several lives we are attempting to overcome the illusory darkness or defects that have been inflicted upon us, to transmute them in all of our cells, but without success. Finally, could it be that what we have until now considered weaknesses were in fact strengths that were obscured by the fear of our own inner light radiating a bit too brightly around us?

The time has come to allow all these parts of us to get back to their rightful place at the heart of our daily life and to finally reestablish the base of our inner pyramid.

This base simultaneously includes the strength of manifestation of the Builders, the emotional stability of the Artisans of Peace, the mental clarity of the Visionaries, and the conscious connection to the universal energy of the Facilitators.

It is through this collaboration with all the soul families in us that it becomes possible to rise to the top of the pyramid and adopt our real light body.

Are You Sitting Tight?

Let's go back for a moment to the metaphor of the game of musical chairs. We know that we will be allowed to occupy the king's place in the middle only once we will have successively sat in each of the chairs in the circle.

This allegory makes even more sense when the chair on which you hesitate to settle is also the one that represents the way you do not have the courage to obtain energy from others (the lowest score in your Egogram, as calculated in Chapter 9), precisely corresponding to the soul family associated with your ruling chakra (identified during the muscle test in Chapter 3), and therefore to the energy you most need to harmonize yourself.

Are you following this concept? Darkness, karma, and duality are all stories we tell ourselves to avoid getting in touch with the parts of us that have not been welcomed by those close to us when we arrived in this life. Our incarnation contract (see Chapter 4) precisely consists of affirming and consolidating these aspects of us that we apparently neglected in previous existences.

Because we knew it would be hard for us to integrate so much light at once, a compassionate soul family volunteered to assist us on our journey and to support us if need be in our quest for a perfect energetic balance.

Unfortunately, if our present life experiences have unconsciously pushed us to cut our ties with our light family, it goes without saying that we have also created distance from the other side of the coin, or the corresponding defense mechanism.

This is why it is so hard for us to close the loop, to complete the grieving process in everyday life. We do not allow ourselves to experience the primary reaction associated with a specific control drama or aspect of our personality—exactly the one we have rejected or denied in our self. In so doing, we are preventing ourselves from reaching the absolutely indispensable step enabling us to get to unconditional and total acceptance in order to finally merge with all the parts of our self.

In light of this observation, you can choose to go voluntarily and sit in the missing chair, which is what I tried to do at the time, having no other way of getting closure for the wounds of the past. However, I now know of a simple, easy, and joyous solution that is much more in line with my principles: calling on your soul family.

Your Soul Family to the Rescue

The principle is simple: if the primary reaction inherent in the defense mechanism constitutes the back of the coin, the virtues and qualities specific to each of the soul families can allow us to access the state of grace without having to go through all the steps of grieving.

In reality, without knowing it, you already do it. A person who has managed to open up to his or her sensitivity and develop his creative talents joyfully does not need to sit in the chair of the Victim; he has learned to express his emotions as they come up and if need be to transmute his sadness into artistic creativity. The individual gifted with an analytical and critical mind does not need to be constantly indifferent to what surrounds her; she knows how to create some distance and isolate herself when she needs time on her own.

Knowing that the steps of the grieving process only exist to help you assimilate and classify new data in one of the five dimensions of your brain, it is possible, in quiet times outside a crisis period, to learn to tame the parts of yourself that usually do not dare to react or manifest themselves in daily life. In doing so, they will be better armed and more solid in the face of adversity, whatever that might be.

Deep down, you have a choice: go through denial, anger, bargaining, and sadness, or ask your soul family to transmit the energy you need to reveal yourself to yourself by discovering the qualities you don't yet acknowledge within you.

The following chart, which is a reminder of the information in Chapter 4, will allow you to identify the qualities that would be in your best interest to develop within, according to each defense mechanism, in relation to the primary reactions you want to avoid at all costs.

For each soul family, it may be that you have already developed most of their defining virtues, but as you well know, it is precisely the virtues that you still haven't made your own that will allow you to avoid the torturous game of musical chairs.

Transmuting Primal Reactions by Appealing to Your Soul Family

STEP OF ACCEPTANCE, DEFENSE MECHANISM	SOUL FAMILY, PROTECTOR	QUALITIES AND VIRTUES WORTH INTEGRATING
State of Shock/Denial Indifferent	Visionaries Archangel Raphael	Great analytical and reasoning abilities, abilities, authenticity, sincerity, autonomy, insight, intuition, keen insight, intuition, clairvoyance, communication abilities
Anger Perpetrator	Builders Archangel Uriel	Trust, strength, courage, leadership, endurance, perseverance, stability, dynamism, ease of materializing goals
Bargaining/Guilt Savior	Facilitators Archangel Michael	Enthusiasm, pep, positiveness, liveliness, predisposition to compassion, social consciousness, ability to relieve depression, gift for healing
Sadness Victim	Artisans Archangel Gabriel	Sensitivity, creativity, artistic talents, originality, spontaneity, simplicity, kindness, generosity, helpfulness, ease in creating connections
Acceptance/Detachment Witness	Sages Ascended Masters	Capacity to remain centered, balance oneself, harmonize oneself, live in the present, easily let go, trust life, and accept guidance from the higher self

1. State of Shock/Denial

If you find it hard to create appropriate distance in life, chances are that in a crisis situation you do not allow yourself to be in a state of shock. You therefore have the choice either to get familiar with your ability to become indifferent to what surrounds you, or to call out for Archangel Raphael and the Visionaries family to instill the qualities that characterize them among those you do not yet own: great analytical and reasoning abilities, authenticity, sincerity, autonomy, keen insight, intuition, clairvoyance, and communication abilities.

2. Anger

If the domination mechanism least present in you is that of the Perpetrator, it is highly possible that you may feel resistance to getting angry. You are therefore invited to reconnect with the strengths and talents of the Builders. With the help of Archangel Uriel, affirm your trust, strength, courage, leadership, endurance, perseverance, stability, dynamism, and ability to materialize your goals.

3. Bargaining/Guilt

In order to allow the Savior in you to emerge, it is not necessary to become indispensable to those around you or to bargain your favors for a bit of recognition from them. You can simply welcome the fire of the passion particular to the Facilitators and ask Archangel Michael to bring out in you the following virtues: enthusiasm, pep, positiveness, liveliness, predisposition to compassion, social consciousness, ability to relieve depression, and the emergence of your gift for healing.

4. Sadness

If the feeling that you have the most difficulty expressing is sadness, it is because you are afraid of your own vulnerability. You are invited to open up your heart and solar plexus to welcome in the appeasing vibrations of Archangel Gabriel and the reassuring energy of the Artisans of Peace. To balance yourself, you need to explore your sensitivity, creativity, artistic talents, originality, spontaneity, simplicity, kindness, generosity, helpfulness, and ease in create connections.

5. Acceptance

Of course, everyone aspires to live in a state of detachment and unconditional acceptance. All the soul families, in particular the Sages as well as Archangel Metatron and the Ascended Masters, accompany you daily in all areas of your life. You can therefore invoke them at any time and ask them for help in remaining centered, balancing and harmonizing yourself, living in the present moment, easily letting go, trusting life, and allowing yourself to be guided by your higher self: "I am."

Note: In no way does this exercise constitute a guarantee that you will no longer be exposed to existential crises or that you will never have to go through the steps of the grieving process again. But at least the energy of the soul family that you will have managed to develop within you will support you in your endeavors.

Don't Shoot the Messenger; Open Up to the Message Instead

The hardest conflicts to deal with are definitely those that put us in opposition to our loved ones. However, is it possible that despite appearances they have chosen on the divine plane to intervene in our lives precisely in this admittedly clumsy way, in order to push us to overcome the limits of our human consciousness and thus to contribute to opening up the best of ourselves on the spiritual level? Could it be an invitation to defy human rationalizing in order to penetrate even deeper into the intelligence of the heart?

Imagine that a very dear friend with whom you have a slight disagreement suddenly turns against you. This could also be a relative, your partner, or a colleague at work. Regardless of the cause of the dispute or its importance, anger, disappointment, and frustration take over the depth of your mutual feelings and degenerate into a cold war or an open conflict. Once again the dance of the domination mechanisms starts. It isn't an easy thing for anyone to go through. In such circumstances, how can one remain centered and not give in to the temptation of the game of musical chairs?

Of course, with distance, it seems obvious that everything is only a matter of perspective. Each of the parties feels wronged not because of a difference of opinion but because he or she hasn't been welcomed according to his expectations and personal criteria for acceptance. The trigger element therefore isn't the real cause of the conflict; the cause is all the emotions ever lived by the individuals in question, over which neither has any control but which have everything to do with their past baggage.

Clearly stated, the more you carry around a past heavy with dissatisfaction, deficiency, and unexpressed rancor, the more you will suffer when faced with a situation that generates tension. Your present pain feeds off all the previous suffering that has not been healed. And the same goes for the other person.

When the connection between you is very strong or exists for a long time, it is possible to overlook the conflict, forgive each other, and start your relationship again as before. But often some unease settles in, discomfort lingers, and a slight distance creeps between you. Even when you understand the other person's wound and you know that you are not the direct cause of it, it nevertheless awakens your own inner wounds, bringing your own insecurities to the surface, perhaps bruising your pride and pushing you to close yourself off to the other person.

It is important to look beyond the pain and the apparent conflict. What pain is hidden behind the suffering? What internal unease nourishes and intensifies the depth of the apparent wound? How much salt do you put in your own wounds for them to be so alive and painful?

A Destructive Pain

Lorraine, a woman who suffered from serious insomnia, thought that her anxiety concerning her two preschool-age children was the cause of her sleeping problems. One of her kids had nearly been run over by a car two years earlier, and since then she feared for their lives so much that she would not let them cross the street to play in a park located just across from their house, in the middle of a residential neighborhood on a quiet little suburban street. Was her excessive and unreasonable fear for her children due to an accident that had not even happened, or was she hiding a deeper unease?

As she came to consult me over her anxiety and sleep problems, I asked her a very simple question: "How do you feel being a mother?" Beyond the current circumstances, beyond her uneasiness and symptoms, the true underlying question was, "What thoughts do you entertain toward yourself that are capable of having created this incident to attract your attention to what is going on inside you?"

It is well known that our thoughts create. While that is fine in theory, what does it mean in concrete terms in everyday life? Could it be that we actually provoke conflicts and attract misfortunes to ourselves, and that we may be the cause of our own emotional and physical diseases? What if the goal of our soul, through these events, was to make us aware of our limitations so as to encourage us to push at them even more?

Lorraine often felt overwhelmed by the scale of her tasks and responsibilities, living on her own with two young children. Even though she had never openly admitted it, at times she would have liked for her kids to disappear from her life, if only for a few hours, so that she could catch her breath. It is completely normal for a mother to be exhausted to the point of wishing she had never given birth. This doesn't mean she doesn't love her children; she would readily give her life for them. However, this young woman felt guilty for having entertained such desperate thoughts even briefly, for having imagined abandoning her children.

From the guilt, suffering was born, and from suffering, the need to atone for those horrendous thoughts arose; hence her excessive caution with her children. The brain hemisphere that had emitted the excessive thought—eliminating the cause of her tiredness—was immediately counteracted in its plans by the other hemisphere, which went the opposite direction into overprotectiveness and the total gift of the self—which is just as excessive and exhausting.

The true cause of this woman's insomnia problems were therefore not her worries about her children but rather that she had not welcomed her own limitations, not being able to reconcile the two extremes by simply coming back to the present moment. Like many people confronted with a similar situation, Lorraine's emotions took over, amplified by the accumulation of fatigue and resentment of what appeared to be unjust and exhausting constraints. She then dramatized the circumstances and exaggerated the consequences until she made herself ill.

The Other Person, My Mirror
When there is a conflict between two people, when you feel that it wasn't you but the other person who triggered the hostility, you can ask yourself not what

you may have done to attract such trouble, but rather what you may have told yourself about yourself. The thoughts that you entertain toward yourself act like magnets and attract the people who tell you out loud and to your face what you secretly tell yourself in the silence of your heart. They mirror your own unwelcome wounds and your negative perceptions of yourself. Whatever you are trying to repress and hide from others, they are here to free, purify, and in some way purge you of it.

Yet, every time you stop at the messenger rather than the message, you focus your attention on the trigger element rather than on the suffering buried deep within. You do not examine the repressed emotions this event brings up and returns to your consciousness in order to allow you to free yourself of them once and for all. By worrying only about your relationship with the other person, about his or her own wounds and grief toward you, you miss what your soul most aspires to: your own permanent healing.

The bizarre thing is that if you choose to work on yourself rather than on the other person or on the conflict that has you in opposition, unexpected miracles happen. You discover that the person with whom you are arguing seems to be afflicted with the same limiting and painful thoughts as you are. If you go beyond your apparent difference of opinion, you will notice that the challenge is the same for her as it is for you: to love yourself, to accept yourself unconditionally, and to recognize that you don't have anything to prove to anyone.

You carry some unfulfilled expectations and entertain some old feelings of rejection or nonrecognition within you. It isn't whether your opinions are respected or what your words or actions are that matters, but rather the way in which you feel supported or not within yourself. Snap out of your current pain for a moment, extract yourself from the context of it, and create some distance in which to consider the whole of your life up to now. Have you not always succeeded? Have you not always overcome challenges? Can you feel that beyond daily frustrations you have always been supported by the invisible hands of your soul family— for all eternity and beyond human comprehension?

Limiting thoughts imprison you in perpetual conflict. They keep you in unnecessary pain. The unique solution to get out of this is to escape from your mind and enter your heart. Accept going beyond the veil of human appearances and open yourself up to the divine and wonderful being that you truly are. You will then see your adversary for who he or she really is: a messenger from a better world, your companion on the road, a brother or sister traveling with you on the path to awakening and to unconditional acceptance.

His or her weaknesses, vulnerabilities, and frustrations are also ours because we are one, universally. By taking the time to heal those wounds in ourselves, we invite the other person to do the same thing; we provide the example. By developing compassion toward ourselves and by seeing beyond external resistance, we give ourselves one of the most beautiful gifts that exist: to free ourselves from human karma.

If the other person isn't ready to do the same, she will simply leave your life. But if any love or sincere friendship remains between you, she will come back, knocking at your door, and you will be able to sort it out together rather than dealing with the situation each on your own. This may take weeks, even years, but be patient with others, as you should be with yourself.

The Message of My Soul

As time goes by, you will discover that you aren't just a clumsy messenger shaken by events and interpersonal conflicts, but that it is possible for you to learn to be a genuine message of faith and light at the heart of the turmoil of our unconscious humanity.

I keep hoping that one day, as it was for the great sages and prophets of the past, conflicts will no longer have any hold on us. When we have learned to go beyond external illusions, we will know how to find in ourselves the power of transformation and ultimate healing: the full and total integration of our own divine and eternally serene quintessence.

In the meantime, I imagine that you might be interested to learn the best way to act when faced with someone who is imprisoned in their defense mechanisms. The following chart offers some basic advice that will allow you to avoid entering the awful cycle of survival reactions. Beyond the reflection of ourselves that the other mirrors back to us, through this unique experience our soul is attempting to deliver a message, a precious gift to help us free ourselves from our past limitations and wounds.

The Game of Mirrors Reinvented

STEP OF ACCEPTANCE, DEFENSE MECHANISM	HOW TO ACT WHEN FACED WITH THE DEFENSE MECHANISM	WHAT IS THIS PERSON TRYING TO TEACH ME— AS A SOUL GIFT?
Anger Perpetrator △	• Do not contradict him • Underline the points on which you agree • Don't let her intimidate you • Remain firm and centered • If he becomes violent, leave and claim what I need?	I am being invited to ask myself whether I manage to affirm myself and take my rightful place. Do I have the courage to express my opinion?
Sadness Victim ◇	• Do not pity her • Try to reassure him instead of offering solutions • Underline the positive points • Don't let her complain for too long	I am being invited to consider the sensitive and vulnerable child inside of me. Do I have the courage to ask for help and support or simply to be comforted when I need it?
State of Shock/Denial Indifferent ▽	• Don't ask too many questions, but ask for his opinion • Give her some time to think • Respect his need to step aside • Invite her to pick the right moment for her to discuss and express her feelings	I am being invited to create appropriate distance and to be less demanding of myself. Do I sometimes allow myself to say "no" to others?
Bargaining/ Guilt Savior □	• Don't let him take all space or decide things for you • Thank her for her help and advice, then change the subject • Solicit his precise collaboration or help, defined in a specific time frame • Show her signs of appreciation and affection	I am being invited to find my own solutions and to recognize my strengths and my inner power. Do I allow myself to let the dormant hero within me emerge?

STEP OF ACCEPTANCE, DEFENSE MECHANISM	HOW TO ACT WHEN FACED WITH THE DEFENSE MECHANISM	WHAT IS THIS PERSON TRYING TO TEACH ME— AS A SOUL GIFT?
Acceptance/ Detachment Witness	• Remain open • Welcome his light and and teaching • Recognize yourself in her • Remember that we are all God's children and that no one is greater or more important than his brothers or sisters	I am being invited to recognize that all the wise people in my life are the reflection of my own inner light, which also aspires to shine like a thousand suns.

1. How to Act When Faced with a Perpetrator

- Do not contradict him or her: the more you try to talk some sense into him, the more he will argue, and this may turn sour.
- Underline the points on which you agree: you don't have to endorse everything she says, but it's in your best interest to let her express her state of mind. Tell yourself that she is allowed to be angry, because according to her perception of things, she is right and you are wrong. In the worst case, if you do not agree with her, pretend to. You will be able to revisit the subject later when she has calmed down.
- Don't let him intimidate you: if you become intimidated, the Perpetrator will take this opportunity to steal your energy.
- Remain firm and centered: if you remain centered and give her the right to go through her anger without being affected by it, she will not be able to touch you and drain your energy.
- If he turns violent, leave: unless you want a good slap, remember that a Perpetrator may turn violent, so don't stay in his way when he is seeing red. If his fury explodes, step aside. You will be showing him that his anger belongs to him and that he will have to go through it on his own. Most importantly, take time to let the dust settle before returning.

What Gift Does the Perpetrator Want to Offer You?

When you find you have a tendency in life to be faced with Perpetrators on a regular basis, when you are used to putting yourself in situations where you are being denigrated or treated as worthless, then you surely have not yet managed to integrate the Builder within you. This is the message that your soul is sending you through this repetitive experience: "I am being invited to wonder whether I manage to affirm myself and take my rightful place. Do I have the courage to express my opinions and claim what I need?"

In fact, when you neglect taking care of yourself too often and answering your own needs, when you always put others before yourself, then those who are professionals in the art of taking care of themselves and putting themselves first—the Perpetrators—come to show you what their method is all about.

2. How to Act When Faced with a Victim

- Do not pity him or her: if you give her even a spark of compassion, she will hang on to you for good.
- Try to reassure him instead of offering solutions: if you propose solutions, the response you will get, is, "Yes, but . . ." Above all, do not tire yourself out in vain. You will only give him all your energy, which is precisely what he is aiming for.
- Underline the positive points: Try to make her aware that if she has succeeded in overcoming other difficulties to get to where she is today, she has much strength within.
- Don't let him complain for too long: after four or five "Yes, but . . ." responses, leave. There is no point in trying to comfort and reassure him because he enjoys feeling sorry for himself. What the Victim wants is your attention, but if you give him the energy he needs, he will never find it within himself. Not only are you not helping him, you are exhausting yourself in vain. As a last resort, you can always remind him that he is not in danger of dying (after all, there are no tyrannosaurs around).

What Gift Does the Victim Want to Offer You?

If you have in your immediate surroundings someone who is always in trouble and who always needs you, remind yourself that you have hired him or her in your game of musical chairs because you yourself never have the courage to sit in the seat of the person who needs to be comforted.

"I am being invited to consider the sensitive and vulnerable child within me. Do I have the courage to ask for help and support or simply to be comforted when I need it?"

In turn, one of the most beautiful gifts you could give a Victim is to tell her how grateful you are for her having helped you become aware of your own needs. Ask her to hug you. Rather than remaining in her Victim state, she will automatically be brought to her heart, to her positive side, the Artisan of Peace. Your own energy will benefit from this luminous experience because you will have considered the needs of your own inner child.

3. How to Act When Faced with an Indifferent

- Don't ask too many questions, but ask for his or her opinion: if you ask a question, even a theoretical one, he will either respond with a monosyllable or you will be stuck for hours. Choose instead to ask him for his point of view on the present situation and encourage him to involve himself in action—the steps to follow and so on.
- Give her some time to think: her reactions are secondary; she will never answer on the spot. She will never make a decision without reflection. She will weigh the pros and cons for as long as she doesn't feel safe. If you invite her to consider her emotions and her feelings, she will react like a bar of soap in the bath and try to slip away.
- Respect his need to step aside: don't harass him or try to follow him if he leaves. Respect his territory and the bubble that surrounds him.
- Invite her to pick the right moment for her to discuss and express her feelings: if you let her go to her cave, she will come back. If you stop her, she will find a way to get back there anyway, but she will take much longer to come out of it.

What Gift Does the Indifferent Want to Offer You?

When we are surrounded by Indifferent individuals, or people with whom it is difficult to communicate, it is often because we have a tendency to take to heart what people think or say about us. Could it be that we want to be perfect, or that we create drama for nothing, or that we let gossip affect us? The message that our soul is sending us is: "I am being invited to create some distance and to be less demanding of myself. Do I sometimes allow myself to say no to others?"

If you suffer mildly from hyperactivity or attention deficit, chances are that the mental dimension of your body might be suffering slightly or might be out of balance. It is in your best interest to take a break: let the legendary intuition of the Visionaries guide and inspire you, and allow yourself to take a break from yourself.

4. How to Act When Faced with a Savior

- Don't let him or her take all the space or decide for you: the Savior makes a good right-hand person but can at times be very bossy. Make sure not to get seduced by her pretty words and wise advice, as you will lose your own identity within it.

- Thank him for his help and his advice, then change the subject: if he insists on knowing more about you and what you are going through, there is a catch. Don't forget that his method of acquiring energy is to question you to make you believe you need support from him.

- Solicit her precise collaboration or help, defined in a specific time frame: when you ask a Savior for help, she will think that you need her until the end of your days.

- Show him signs of appreciation and affection: this is paramount because he doesn't recognize who he is, only what he does. Make him understand that you love him as he is without him having to expend himself for you. Once he gets the recognition that he needs, he will stop trying to make himself worthy by helping you despite your wishes.

What Gift Does the Savior Want to Offer You?

Your soul knows that inside every human being there is a dormant superhero unaware of herself. When you are surrounded by well-meaning people who always do everything for you or pretend to know better than you do what suits you, you have lost touch with your own inner, real, and unlimited potential.

"I am being invited to find my own solutions and to recognize my strengths and my inner power. Do I allow myself to let the dormant hero within me emerge?"

Your soul is inviting you to reconnect with the spiritual dimension of your being, your higher consciousness, your cocreating power—simply stated, your divine self. Will you say "yes" to the light shining within you?

5. How to Respond to a Sage

- Remain open: make space for this amazing being in your life while remaining lucid. If he or she is still here on this Earth, it is because he hasn't completed his path here either.
- Welcome her light and her teaching: be available to the messages she wants to transmit.
- Recognize yourself in him: "if I have managed to attract some Sages in my life, it is because I am one too."
- Remember that we are all children of God and that no one is more important than her brothers or sisters: this is what the ascended masters, angels, archangels, extraterrestrials, intraterrestrials, and so on keep repeating to us through all the channels of the planet: we are all equal and compliment each other on our paths. All of these light beings need us as much as we need them. We are all working toward the same goal.

What Gift Does the Sage Want to Offer You?

"When the student is ready, the master appears. I am being invited to recognize that the person in front of me is the reflection of my own inner light, which also aspires to shine like a thousand suns."

What more is there to say?

Integration: *The Path of Wisdom*

After years and years praying, fasting, and living in extreme poverty, a disciple humbly came before his guru.

"Master," he said, "I am ready to know enlightenment."

"Oh, yes?" The old sage responded, without even opening his eyes to look at who was standing before him. "Well then, tell me what is happening to you."

"Master, in the first place, I have learned to master my body. Through yoga and relaxation I have managed to space out my breaths and slow down my heartbeat to obtain a state of inner peace and infinite calm. Hunger and the need for sleep no longer have a hold on me. I can meditate for days on end without moving a single muscle."

"That's all very well," the holy man responded, "but what else?"

"I have also learned to master my impulses and my emotions. The sight of a beautiful woman no longer torments me; the world's misery doesn't affect me; and the cries of a child leave me completely cold. I am a witness to all that surrounds me and pray fervently for all who live on this Earth finally to be free from suffering and from the illusions of deficiency."

"This must have demanded much renouncement on your part, my son," *said the old man with a slight smile. "Is there anything else you would like to add?"*

"Yes, of course, master. I have long applied myself to quieting all my thoughts, annihilating all my desires, and having no more personal convictions on any matter. Sincerely, I believe I have managed to get rid of my ego and emptied my mind of any form of alienating thought once and for all."

"You have given all of your life to bettering yourself relentlessly, my child, but do you believe that you have accomplished everything in your power to deserve to become a guru yourself?"

"Absolutely, master. I have followed all your teachings to the letter, religiously practiced all the exercises you have taught me, and observed all your rules of conduct without fault for many years. I am in turn ready to travel the

roads to preach the way of accomplishment, just like you and the ones before you have transmitted it."

The sage of sages let out a deep sigh. His eyelids opened slightly and a flood of sparkling light shone through his eyes. Mute with awe, the disciple fell to his knees and suddenly felt enveloped in a shimmering halo penetrating through every particle of his being. The guru stood up with dignity and approached his student. He put a hand on his shoulder, and as a warm electrical current went through the young man, he whispered in his ear:

"If you had accomplished everything you candidly claimed you had in front of me, you wouldn't be at all surprised by this light that attempts to infiltrate your heart. You have forgotten that you are not alone in the universe and that you live, grow, and breathe with all that is. Enlightenment isn't obtained through effort or merit, but rather through divine grace that connects you in consciousness with the whole of creation. When you have understood that, then you too will be a master."

The disciple left sheepishly, thinking humbly that he still had a long way to go. The great sage felt even sadder, for he saw that his pupil hadn't understood a thing and was still searching on the outside, in the appearances and illusions of this world, for what had in fact always been and would always be there deep inside him.

And you: can you see the light that shines behind your eyes? Do you feel the presence of this divine flame within you that aspires to set your entire being ablaze? Is your heart dancing with joy in communion with all that lives?

Exercise: *This Light in the Mirror*

More and more therapists and spiritual masters encourage those around them to take the time to look at themselves in the mirror every morning. What better way is there than to look straight into our own eyes to understand and become familiar with who we are?

*Some people even learn to enter into relationships with this image of them-
selves there in the mirror. They say hello to themselves, tell themselves how
beautiful they are, what qualities they recognize in themselves, and so on. It
is a good exercise that helps both to overcome our fear of ridicule by daring
to talk to ourselves out loud, and to develop our self-esteem: praising ourselves
heightens our self-perception.*

*The ultimate challenge, however, remains managing to maintain our own
gaze silently for a few minutes. It is easy to take a brief and fleeting glance at
ourselves, to smile while adjusting our makeup or shaving. But it is another
story to fix on the eyes of another while knowing they are our own.*

*It is said that the eyes are the mirror of the soul. Have you ever wondered
what your soul, your divine essence, looked like? Is it possible to perceive our
inner light through our own double, the pale reflection of ourselves imprisoned behind this polished surface?*

*Will you dare to try this experience? It is very easy: you can simply imag-
ine that God himself is laying his gaze, filled with love, on you. He contem-
plates you through your own eyes, and you perceive his loving presence. It is
an intimate encounter with your own divine spark in order to discover the
light that shines in your eyes when you feel fully loved, accepted, and welcomed.*

*Those close to you, the people you love most in the world, already know
this gaze of yours, filled with tenderness and plenitude. But have you ever
allowed yourself to love yourself in this way, to see the cloud of goodness that
characterizes you deep in your own eyes, illuminated by a flash of joy and a
sparkle of indescribable happiness?*

*A look of sincere and lasting love toward yourself is an excellent way to
taste the plenitude within, to reach the illumination of your whole being: when
you discover the presence of God within you, you can never perceive yourself
the same way again.*

Try it for yourself, and you will see how it works.

CHAPTER 13

Uniting All the Aspects of the Self

Breaking with the Past

Message from February 27, 2006

Escaping from the Past

Your world is in tune with the way you feel. If you find yourself surrounded by chaos, it is because you live in chaos. If you feel overwhelmed by wars, hunger, or storms all around the world, can you see that this feeling stems from inside you, while your soul starves of light and love, and that those thoughts keep spinning around like hurricanes that pester your mind every day?

You are this world in which you live; you created it according to you. Change the way you see yourself, and the world will change too. Escape from the past and start a brand new life, and so it will be for all the people whose paths cross yours. Stop wanting to save the world and trying to heal people: heal yourself, save yourself, and see how this influences those around you.

A great Eastern sage said, "If you want peace in the world, start by bringing peace to your country. For the peace to settle in your country, you have to keep the area you live in at peace. To achieve peace in your local area, you must make peace in your own town, your neighborhood, and so on down to your family. For peace to be brought to your family, don't you need to have it first in your own heart?" Everything starts right there within you.

Peace, love, and light are within you; they take root and grow first within the secret recesses of your heart. You cannot change the world if you haven't changed yourself. You cannot make this world a better place to live in if you didn't find this calm and serene space inside yourself first. This inner area of silence and peace is a place where the past doesn't exist, and where the future isn't important. This sacred space is where you become one with everything that lives, outside the boundaries of time and the limits of three dimensions.

Divine Quintessence

This space exists deep down within you. It is where all wounds miraculously heal, and where all feelings of rejection, neglect, or failure fade forever. In your heart is a secret room where all the gifts that life has given you, and which you haven't opened yet, are piled up. When will you visit it and unwrap those treasures?

These precious gifts are the talents you haven't yet used to their full potential; the lessons of life that you have learned, perhaps against your will; and the signs and messages your body has sent you without you noticing them, but which, without exception, are all milestones on the path toward your fulfillment.

Take some time to visit this space within you, where all the experiences of present and past lives are stored. Allow yourself the time to make a list of things that have helped you move forward, fed you, and inspired you since the beginning of your incarnation on this Earth. Decide to remember only the best, to reprogram this flourishing journey, which you chose, within all your cells, and integrate as much light and as many resources as possible in yourself to materialize peace and unlimited bliss in the whole of your being.

Then, definitively escape from the past and from your negative feelings, perceptions, deficiencies, or illusory limits. Visualize that all the old unresolved fights, betrayals, and failures are merely sketched on the sand at the beach, and with the side of your hand, erase them forever.

Your heart is made of sand, not of stone. Everything that has been engraved in it can vanish if you choose to make it do so. Your heart is in fact forgiveness, not bitterness; anything you choose to forgive, in yourself as well as others, will allow you to heal all the wounds and all the scars of the past, even those that still hurt. Love heals everything; peace erases everything. The happiness that we cultivate replaces the unhappiness we suffer from. It's all a matter of choice.

Imagine looking at your life no longer though human eyes full of bitterness and deception, but through God's eyes, the eyes of our eternal Father who created you in His image. Can you see that everything—absolutely everything in your life—is a unique and special opportunity offered to you for you to recognize at last who you truly are? By saying "yes" to the divine being within you, you open all the doors so that the best of life can happen within as well as all around you.

"But wait," you might say, "what's to be done when it just doesn't work, when our days keep on being tough, and we tend to forget that we are such wonderful

beings? When those storms outside us maintain permanent chaos inside us? When we simply cannot manage to resolve those disagreements or unpleasant situations that weigh on us?"

First off, you should definitely banish the following two words from your vocabulary: always and never. Those words are weighty because they evoke eternity, which takes away our power to change things. Always and never represent the true limits of three dimensions, the limits of time and material things. They take away all our power over reality, weighing us down with the heaviness of the past and a fatalistic uncontrollable future.

What about the essence of the challenge you chose to face when coming to Earth, to transcend your three-dimensional limits and let the light guide you in showing everyone your cocreative divinity, and to become sovereign in this world by creating it in the image of God, right there within yourself?

You cannot intervene in your outside world unless you take back your power over your inner world. You won't be able to silence the "bad guys" of this world unless you silence your inner tyrants first. It will not be possible for you to heal the suffering and the poverty of the world unless you reestablish your own health and unlimited wealth.

Do not give your power to others; take your life back into your own hands. Define what makes you a unique being and allow yourself some time and space to explore your own talents and creativity on a daily basis. Discover what thrills you and what brings your senses to life; then give yourself the right to fully enjoy those discoveries, be it only for a few minutes a day, so that you don't fall back into feeling guilty.

Make room for new things in your life by getting rid of the old stuff: those habits that spin you around, and the old thoughts that keep haunting you and leave you in a passive state in the long run. Instead of trying in vain to shut down your ego, keep your mind busy building a new life for you, creating a new existence at the top of your dreams.

The new world starts here, in your own backyard, in your own family. You don't have to move to another country where the sun shines brighter; your environment necessarily reflects what is going on inside you no matter where you are. It is better to live with it and make your life choices accordingly.

Open the door to new ways; return to yourself; revive your childhood dreams;

say "yes" to your true beliefs. If you feel the need to give something, don't hesitate, and do it; but it should make you feel good first before the well-being of the one you are giving it to. Stop doing for others what you hope others would do for you; get your own life moving, and show others how to do the same.

Become an ambassador of peace within your family, at work, and in your community by setting an example in radiating your own cocreative sovereignty. If you feel resistance and difficulties around you, question what the situations or people involved are trying to reveal about you.

What is written on the sign above your head? What can people read (unconsciously, of course) or feel in your energy that can bother them or make their own darkness grow? Be true to yourself and realize that the more you tell a story to yourself, the more it becomes alive.

The time that elapses from the birth of a thought in your mind to its actual materialization in your life is getting smaller and smaller. Stop trying to control your thoughts, raise your vibrations, or clean your karma; just get moving. Busy yourself in trying to create the world of your dreams. Set up the basis and the foundations of your personal success to become a living witness who demonstrates the way for us all.

Stop making excuses for yourself, spreading yourself out, or expending yourself on others. Your challenge is to have them take part in a planetary spring cleaning, using their own inner strengths, and to encourage them in expressing their creative potential by getting involved so that everyone wins.

History with a capital H has been written as human, although limited, stories. Rewrite it with divine words that show no competition, oppression, or power games. Aim to complement and collaborate for the success of everyone, as well as for energy fusion to help your common power of materialization to grow. Above all, return to the source often to draw from its well of strength and perseverance.

Hence this world will not be new, but indeed exactly what it was planned to be since the first mists of time: complete, sovereign, divine, and cocreated by the God/human in every one of you. Thus it is.

—Bianca Gaia

Going Forward

With everything you have read in this book up to this point, you have surely become aware of everything that you have already accomplished in this life.

Among the virtues and attributes of the various soul families, you have undoubtedly recognized some affinities with them, which is completely normal. Indeed, our goal is to merge with all the parts of ourselves, and we know deep down that we belong to all the families. We are all Sages in the making. Quite often, we only have a few minute elements of us that are still needed to be integrated so that our divine eternal light can finally shine through the pores of our skin.

Like everyone, it happens at times that we doubt ourselves, keeping our focus on the mountain top and thinking that we will never reach the summit. We forget simply to take time to look behind us and contemplate with satisfaction all the ground we have covered until now.

Every time something unpredictable happens, a crisis starts, or we "slip on a banana peel," meaning when we get caught in the trap of our defense mechanisms, immediately it's a drama: we think we haven't understood anything, that we are back to square one, that we have just fallen down a staircase; but in reality we have only gone down one step.

For many years, all of our attention has been focused on the work that we have to do on ourselves: overcoming our fears, getting rid of our old programming, unknotting old karma, and making peace with our past. Can you see to what extent this is inhibiting you from moving forward? You are constantly moving backward, dwelling on your misfortunes, and reviving ancient wounds.

Are you familiar with the Fletcher Peacock book Water the Flowers Not the Weeds? Every time your attention is drawn toward an unresolved problem, an unpleasant memory, or a still-painful conflict, you are feeding the suffering present inside of you. By expending so much effort to free yourself from the burdens of the past, not only do you empty yourself of your own energy, you give them more importance—so much so that they become heavier and weigh more on your shoulders. Your pack becomes so heavy that you can no longer manage to move forward. The solution? Drop your baggage on the side of the road, and once and for all entrust it to the "clearing" angels. Get back to the now. Make the choice today to have a luminous day. Here and now, all is well, life is beautiful, and you are an admirable person.

Let the old prehistoric predators rot in the natural history museum. They can't harm you; they are no longer able to eat anyone. The same goes for all the challenges you have been through, the enterprises that have ended in failure, and the mistakes you think you've made. All of this no longer exists except in your thoughts.

You are still here. You are still standing solidly on two legs with the possibility to develop your inner potential still left to discover, new projects to take on, and wild adventures awaiting you around the corner. These are the flowers that only ask to be watered.

Choose to nourish luminous thoughts at every moment, and every time a cloud appears above your head, think, Behind this gray cloud, the sun is still shining brightly.

The following exercise will allow you to measure where you really are on your path. Your vibratory level is proportional not to the efforts you have made or the work you have accomplished but to your perception of yourself: the more you love yourself and feel that you are radiating, the more you elevate yourself.

In fact, the quantity of vital energy you have stored up to now is measured exclusively by your degree of satisfaction and fulfillment in all the spheres of your life. Beyond all the stories we tell ourselves, it is the state of our body, mind, and soul that ensures the quality of our evolution.

And it is happening here and now: yesterday no longer exists, and tomorrow isn't here yet. How do you feel inside today? By letting yourself be guided by your intuition and your feelings, you will know which parts of you already live in the fifth dimension.

Exercise: *Experimenting with the Fifth Dimension*

Each section of the pie chart corresponds to a sphere of experimentation in daily life. For every section, measure your degree of fulfillment and personal satisfaction here and now, on a scale from 0 to 10.

Start by taking three deep breaths to recenter yourself, then make your ratings spontaneously without thinking about it too much. When you have rated every area of your life between 0 and 10, add them all up and write your total at the bottom of the page.

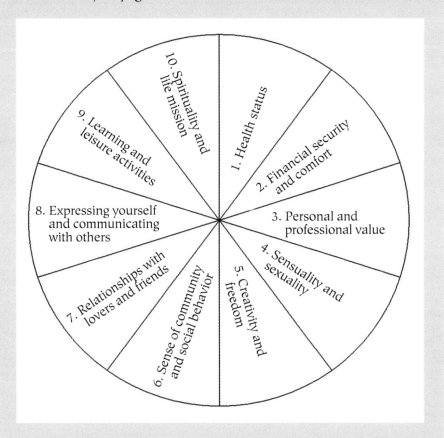

Total energetic reserves (out of 100 points): _____

Results

There is no right or wrong answer for this test, since everything is a matter of perception. Only you are able to evaluate how you feel in each area of your life. There is a question, however: have you been realistic? Often we have a tendency to underevaluate our energetic reserves and to consider certain areas of our existence as faulty or bland. Don't forget that everything is relative. A person may not work outside the home but feel valued on the professional level in his or her role as a parent at home. Similarly, an individual may not have an active sex life and yet feel fulfilled on a sensual level.

Neither social norms nor the values of others determine your degree of satisfaction. Only you know what you feel inside. If you feel like it, you can do this exercise as often as you want: it will allow you to become aware of the areas of your life to invest yourself in more in order to get back to the balance we all aspire to so that we can live in harmony with all the parts of ourselves.

You will note that the different areas of life presented in each section of the pie correspond to those mentioned for each of the seven vital energy centers, identified in Chapter 3, that are connected to the five dimensions of being. This gives you some indication of the parts of you that are well energized or grounded, and those that require further integration.

The sections of your own pie chart may be split up as follows:

Sections 1, 2, 3, and 4

These reflect the first dimension of being, or the body, and therefore everything connected to survival, grounding, and incarnation: looking after our body, health, diet, hygiene, and quality of sleep; making the time to get into shape or practice physical activities; taking pleasure in granting ourselves comfort and good material security; blossoming in daily routine; feeling that we are accomplished and that we succeed at work; reaching our goals; procreating and insuring our posterity, and so on.

The corresponding chakras are the first or root chakra (sections 1 and 2), and the second or sacral chakra (sections 3 and 4), for a total of forty percent of our energetic reserves.

Sections 5, 6, and 7

These refer to the second dimension, the heart: our ability to openly express our emotions; untying our real feelings from the stories the mind may tell itself; resolving interpersonal conflicts; freeing ourselves from and healing the wounds of the past; expressing our feelings and engaging in intimate and lasting relationships; blossoming on the effective, amicable, loving, family, and social levels—simply stated, loving and accepting ourselves unconditionally as we are.

The corresponding chakras are the third or solar plexus chakra (sections 5 and 6) and the fourth or heart chakra (section 7), for a total of thirty percent of our energetic reserves.

Sections 8 and 9

The third dimension evoked here is states of mind, which concern the brain: our mental aptitudes, intellectual faculties, and our reasoning abilities, but also communication and respect for our identity, recognition of our skills, response to our thirst for new knowledge, the practice of leisure activities and personalized rejuvenation, our openness to intuition and to our natural and spiritual gifts, and so on.

The corresponding chakras are the fifth or throat chakra (section 8) and the sixth or third-eye chakra (section 9), for a total of twenty percent of our energetic reserves.

Section 10

The last section is connected to the fourth dimension of being, our consciousness: the state of awakening and spirituality; our aptitudes to appreciate and enjoy life; maintenance of a good level of inner peace through relaxation, meditation, or prayer; consciousness of being part of a greater whole; and our ease in being guided by God, energy, or our higher self.

The chakra that corresponds to section 10 is the seventh or crown chakra, which represents ten percent of our energetic reserves.

Total of All Sections (100%)

As discussed earlier, the fifth dimension is obtained only through merging the four earlier dimensions. It is indeed the summit of the pyramid, the quintessence: the state of grace, the inner plenitude, and the integration of our divine essence.

The total of your energetic reserves reveals the part of your divine light that you already recognize as present in you, the proportion of your ascension vehicle that has already been activated through the simple recognition of yourself and of the love you give yourself.

The higher your score, the more you are filled with serenity and bliss. The better you feel, the more you attract pleasant situations, wonderful surprises, little joys, blessings, and countless benefits in your life.

Your overall percentage reflects the part of you that is already replete with happiness. So why look elsewhere for what is already present inside of you?

It Is All a Matter of Attitude

I enjoy saying that happiness and success is ninety-nine percent attitude and one percent effort. According to the principle that life treats us the way we treat ourselves, we may well deploy all the efforts imaginable and use all the means and resources known, but if we do not first have faith in life and trust in ourselves, the outer results will only be proportional to the limitations we have imposed on ourselves.

Here is a convincing example. During the first years of our marriage, my husband, Serge, was worried about money. With four young children and only one salary to cover all the expenses, in his eyes every month end would resemble an obstacle course. He could not stand to pull out his credit card.

So when we thought about the possibility of moving to the countryside so that our children could grow up in a beneficial environment, Serge quickly went to consult his banker to evaluate his credit. Of course, he was told that we didn't have the means to buy ourselves a new house, which in itself was totally absurd: we already had good capital invested in the house we owned, our car was paid off, and we had no other debts or loans. On top of that, housing prices are much lower in the countryside than in the suburbs close to a major city.

In my opinion there wasn't any reason for our mortgage to be refused, apart from the fact that my husband's fears had been communicated to his bank manager. I then challenged him to change his attitude. I suggested modifying his way of functioning: rather than going in to beg for a loan, why not go in and negotiate his next loan? Together, we agreed to make appointments with at least two different banks, explaining to every loan officer we met that we were looking at the possibility of doing business with the one that would give us the best mortgage terms.

You should have seen the attitude of the bankers: every one of them was as sweet as honey, praising the merits of their respective institutions, even offering to lower the interest rate to be more competitive. At no time did we mention our financial situation. None of them questioned our ability to repay the loan; on the contrary, they were ready to lend us twenty percent more than our original loan request.

This is proof that your attitude makes all the difference in the way others react around you. The same goes for all the situations you encounter in your life: looking for a job, returning to optimal health, looking for the ideal partner, identifying your life mission, and so on. The more we believe in it, the more we trust in it, and the more we attract the best in our lives. As discussed in Chapter 6, our thoughts create at every moment according to the state of mind we have evolved into.

When we can no longer manage to recenter by ourselves, we have lots of tools available to recreate a suitable energy level and find harmony in all the spheres of our lives. You can discover some new tools in the following chart.

Uniting All the Aspects of the Self

SOUL FAMILY	PROTECTOR, HARMONIZER	HEALTHY FOOD, THERAPEUTIC HEALING
Perpetrator and Builder	Archangel Uriel Chakras: root and sacral Colors: red and orange	Vibration: earth **Protein, root vegetables** Massage, osteopathy, kinesiology, yoga; percussion; the sound "oh"
Victim and Artisan	Archangel Gabriel Chakras: solar plexus and heart Colors: yellow and green	Vibration: water **Carbohydrates, leafy vegetables** Art therapy, music, humor, psychotherapy; wind instruments; the sound "ee"
Indifferent and Visionary	Archangel Raphael Chakras: throat and third eye Colors: blue and indigo	Vibration: air **Lipids, flowering vegetables** Wellness through awareness, hypnosis, respiratory reeducation, walks in nature; stringed instruments; the sound "oo" as in "who"
Savior and Facilitator	Archangel Michael Chakra: crown Color: violet	Vibration: fire **Dairy products, eggs, fruit** Energy healing, hydrotherapy, relaxation, acupuncture; singing; the sound "ah"
Witness and Sage	Archangel Metatron, **Ascended Masters** Chakra: all Colors: white and gold	Vibration: ether **Raw food, sprouts** Holistic medicine, meditation, prayer; silence

Health Care for Each Soul Family

To rebalance the base of our inner pyramid, it is important to harmonize every one of the dimensions of our being. As discussed in Chapter 6, the brain does not differentiate between the positive and the negative aspects of things, so the same therapeutic tools will allow you to balance the two facets of your personality: your defense mechanism as well as the part of you that recognizes itself as belonging to a specific soul family.

Some harmonizing factors are more energetic, such as calling on the designated protector of your soul family and the corresponding element, aligning your chakras, or surrounding yourself with colors that heighten your vibrations; others are much more down-to-earth: diet, therapy, musical instruments, and sound.

A naturopathy specialist could complete this with plant extracts, vitamins, essential oils, and so on, but I have chosen to remain in the realm of what is readily available to everyone. All the suggestions that are proposed here are meant to be simple, easy, and joyous, not exhausting, and accessible to any budget.

However, before making any major changes in your diet or starting any specific therapy, remember that it is important to consult a health professional who knows your medical background for his or her opinion.

1. The Perpetrators and the Builders

Whether you are too much a Perpetrator or not enough of a Builder, the means available to rebalance yourself are the same: you can call on Archangel Uriel; connect to the Earth or to your soul family, the Builders, through your ruling chakra (the first/root chakra, or the second/sacral chakra); or surround yourself with objects and wear clothing in red and orange colors.

The health treatments that will be most beneficial for you are:

- On the dietary level: protein (meat, eggs, fish; tofu, seitan, pulses) and root vegetables, which grow beneath the earth and therefore help in grounding you: potatoes, carrots, parsnips, beets, etc.
- On the therapeutic level: massage, osteopathy, kinesiology, yoga, and anything involving the participation of the physical body.

- In music therapy: percussion; the sound "oh" or "om"—om is not just a spiritual mantra, it is a powerful vibratory sound that grounds the vital energy and awakens sacred sexual energy, the kundalini, while specifically aligning the first two chakras.

2. The Victims and the Artisans of Peace

Whether you are too much of a Victim or not enough of an Artisan of Peace, the means available to rebalance yourself are the same: you can invoke Archangel Gabriel; plug into the water element or to your soul family, the Artisans, through your ruling chakra (the third/solar plexus chakra or the fourth/heart chakra); or surround yourself with objects and wear clothing in golden yellow and green colors.

The health treatments that will be most beneficial for you are:

- On the dietary level: leafy vegetables like lettuce, cabbage, spinach, watercress, endives, etc., and carbohydrates—unrefined sugars in cereals and vegetables and refined sugars in bread, sweets, and pastries—all the sweet comfort foods that we feel like eating when we need to appease our soul, but of course in reasonable quantities (many people agree that foods rich in sugars encourage weight gain. Although one cannot deny the scientific foundations of such an affirmation, I have personally received two specific messages from my soul family on this matter that have made me see things differently and not exclusively on a nutritional level. First, people who are overweight seem to be of a welcoming and generous nature. Because they give too much of themselves to others, their bodies feel obliged to create reserves. Also, if you do not recognize the extent of the light that is present within you, your body, in its great compassion, will try to allow you to measure its outline).
- On the therapeutic level: art therapy, music, humor, and psychotherapy; anything that stimulates the expression of emotions, creativity, and artistic sensibility.
- In music therapy: wind instruments, which involve the breath and therefore the heart muscle; the sound "ee" or "heem."

3. The Indifferents and the Visionaries

Whether you are too Indifferent or not Visionary enough, the means available to rebalance yourself are the same: you can call on Archangel Raphael; connect to the air element or to your soul family, the Visionaries, through your ruling chakra (the fifth/throat chakra or the sixth/third-eye chakra); or you can surround yourself or wear clothing in light blue or indigo colors.

The health treatments that will be most beneficial for you are:

- On the dietary level: lipids, the fats that nourish the brain like butter, oil, cheese, etc., and flowering vegetables, meaning all those having a flowering top, like broccoli, cauliflower, artichoke, asparagus, etc.
- On the therapeutic level: wellness through awareness (trying to understand oneself better), hypnosis (getting the mind to let go), respiratory reeducation (oxygenating the brain), and walks in nature (relaxing the mind).
- In music therapy: stringed instruments; the sound "oo" and "who."

4. The Saviors and Facilitators

Whether you are too much a Savior or not enough a Facilitator, the means available to rebalance yourself are the same: you can invoke Archangel Michael; connect to the fire element or to your soul family, the Facilitators, through your ruling chakra (the seventh/crown chakra); or surround yourself with objects and wear clothing in violet colors.

The health treatments that will be most beneficial for you are:

- On the dietary level: dairy products, eggs, and fruit (what the Facilitator needs: to bear fruit). Milk is the "fruit" of the cow, eggs are that of the chicken, etc. We can also include fruity vegetables: tomatoes, olives, avocados, etc.
- On the therapeutic level: all energetic treatments, hydrotherapy, relaxation, and acupuncture; anything that stimulates the vibratory, subtle, and energetic plane.
- In music therapy: singing ("I put myself first, I am my own instrument"); the sound "ah" or "hahm," said to be the sound of creation, the alpha, the verb, and the vibration of materialization.

Divine Quintessence

5. The Witnesses and Sages

Although it is possible to be too much a Witness and too detached, everyone nevertheless aspires to be more of a Sage. Like many people, you might be tempted to take a shortcut by exclusively using the harmonizers suggested here. However, it goes without saying that these tools will work a lot better if you have first rebalanced the four other aspects of your personality, the base of your pyramid.

On the other hand, if you or someone around you feels unsettled or is going through a major crisis, and you don't manage to identify the soul family that would be most useful in helping you regain balance, you can call on the energy of the Sages by invoking Archangel Metatron or the ascended masters; connect to the ether element of universal energy; or surround yourself with objects and wear clothing in white and gold colors.

The health treatments that will be most beneficial to you are:

- On the dietary level: raw food, sprouts, and prana or energy (it is important to understand that even though these natural and healthy foods seem to constitute the ideal diet to elevate ones vibrations in order to maintain the body in constant health and balance, it is impossible to observe such a strict diet over long periods of time without proper supervision, as you may increase the risk of suffering serious nutritional deficiencies. If you suffer from a specific illness or major unease, a cure or fasting could also be beneficial, but on the condition that it is done under the supervision of a health professional).
- On the therapeutic level: holistic medicine, which considers the being in its entirety; meditation; prayer.
- In music therapy: silence.

As you know by now, it isn't the choice of technique that guarantees results but rather our well-being that it brings us inside. More than anything, you must listen to your feelings and only apply the harmonization methods you most resonate with. Try some of them and see how your body reacts, how the energy settles in you.

As an experiment, I invite you to jump to the practical phase immediately with the help of the following exercise, which enables the rebalancing of all your dimensions in their totality.

270

Exercise: *The Song of the Vowels*

To harmonize all your chakras and realign your five energetic bodies in just a few minutes, you simply have to get in tune with the universal energy. Just as we tune the strings of a guitar, you can harmonize the vibrations of the vowels corresponding to each of the five great soul families, starting from the lower body and moving upward. It is at the same time amusing, appeasing, and very regenerating on all levels.

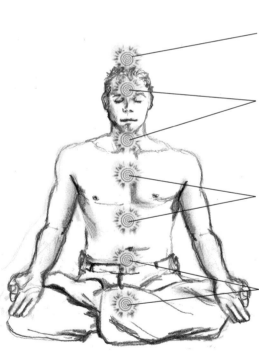

5. **Sages**
All chakras
Deep breathing in silence

4. **Facilitators**
Crown chakra
Sound: "ah"

3. **Visionaries**
Throat and third-eye
  chakras
Sound: "oo" as in "who"

2. **Artisans of Peace**
Solar plexus and heart
  chakras
Sound: "ee"

1. **Builders**
Root and sacral chakras
Sound: "oh"

CHAPTER 14

The Divine Cocreating Expression

The Children of the New Earth

Who are the indigo children? How do you know if you are one of them? Although most human beings feel reassured by categorizations and belonging to defined groups, the children that we call "indigo" simply hate to be labeled, whatever that label may be. They have been successively called "indigo children," "children of Oz," "crystal children," and "children of the sixth ray." It is said that they are the "new" children, the children of the new Earth or the new world. A child who is born with the indigo color in his or her energetic field does not need to be taught who he is to recognize himself; he knows already.

This is a defining characteristic of all the children who constitute the majority of the world population born since the beginning of the 1990s: they know who they are. It is not that they are big-headed, just that they don't feel the need to personally or socially define themselves in relation to the world around them. They know that reality around us isn't limited to what our five senses perceive, but that we are part of a broader invisible universe that surrounds us and influences our destiny at every moment.

If you have been told that you are a very intuitive person, that you are sensitive to people and to their emotions and vulnerabilities, if you have gifts of healing, extrasensory perception, or communication with animals, or if you express yourself with assurance and conviction in knowing the truth without feeling doubt toward yourself, there is a strong probability that you are inspired by the indigo energy.

The defining characteristic of indigo energy lies in the fact that it promotes integration in all its forms. This is why, when it is present in your energetic body, it opens you up to recognizing that everything around you is already present within you. For instance, the indigo child reads a book and feels that she already knows the information even though she is reading it for the first time. The same thing happens when she meets someone and knows in an instant whether or not she can trust that person. She has access to the grid of knowledge, which covers the entire universe, and to the data contained in the akashic records (the memory of time). The greater her self-confidence, the more she will develop this energy of unlimited knowledge and heightened intuition.

Different Beings?

Since the beginning of the world, some children have been born with the indigo energy dominating their subtle bodies. Pythagoras, Leonardo da Vinci, Saint Francis of Assisi, Joan of Arc, and Uri Geller are personalities inspired by the indigo ray present within them. In ancient civilizations they were recognized as shamans, healers, witches, mystics, or unique geniuses.

In their own eras they seemed different from other people, exceptional in the sense that they were outside the norms among their peers, as was the case for me when I was born in 1964. As a child, I used to talk to my guides and could see them around me, but like many people I learned to keep quiet and ignore these "mental aberrations" that outraged my parents. It would take me more than twenty-five years to open up again to my healing and clairvoyant gifts.

Today, although they are much more numerous, the children born with this high-vibratory-level spiritual energy can continue to feel isolated. Some feel difficulty in fitting in, concentrating, or have behavioral disorders simply because they find it hard to adjust to the three-dimensional limitations of society, family, and school that are imposed on them.

The best help we can provide these children is to welcome them unconditionally and comfort them in accepting their difference. However, the normative society we live in tries to suppress anything that doesn't conform to the established rules. This is why various inhibiting drugs are used to bring them into line rather than encouraging them to explore their uniqueness; it's like a new version of a witch hunt that is legal and encouraged by the state.

There will be so many of them in the years to come, however, that these children will force society to change its parameters in terms of social conventions. This is why the prophets talk about them as "the builders of the new world."

Through their energetic radiance they contribute to liberating us from social pressure and encourage us to open ourselves up to our own uniqueness and unlimited inner power.

We are spiritual beings having a human experience, and not human beings having a spiritual experience. They know this; do you?

Fortunately these days, with the expansion of consciousness on the planetary level, more and more people are welcoming the indigo energy in their lives. It isn't necessary to have inherited it at birth to benefit from it. You can meditate and connect yourself to the indigo ray, and your sixth sense will manifest in the form that is most auspicious for you: creativity, inspiration, intuition, or spiritual gifts.

Whether you are an indigo child or not therefore has no importance at all, since you can become one by integrating the cosmic energy of the indigo ray in each of your living cells, thus helping you to fully blossom at all levels.

Welcoming In the Violet Flame through the Indigo Ray

Message from October 20, 2004

Good news for all those who call on the main transmutation tool offered by our brother Saint-Germain: from now on, as well as invoking the help of the violet flame when you need it, you are invited to connect to the indigo ray of the great master Melchizedek, which will allow you not only to prolong the effects of the violet flame but at the same time to heighten your vibratory level in order to merge more each day with the fifth-dimension energy.

If the violet flame is the energy of the fifth dimension, indigo energy is that of the fourth dimension, that of the opening of consciousness. This is why both can work hand in hand to help you transmute your resistance and fear. The indigo ray thus opens the way for the violet flame, allowing it to make its way through our cellular self to take root there, thus creating a prodigious celestial alchemy, an early taste of what you will know during your ascension.

However, if it is at times difficult for you to welcome this liberating vibration and to keep it alive in all of your cells, it may be because your light channel isn't open enough. The entry gate of your pranic channel is located at the third eye, so it is through this chakra that it is now possible for you to encourage the extension of this channel of light. You simply have to visualize the indigo ray, which is also the color of the third-eye chakra, penetrating the middle of your forehead between the eyes and going to your pineal gland, which is located at the center of your head, then moving down along your spine all the way to your sacrum.

If you stand with your knees flexed a little and your pelvis tilted slightly backward, you will be able to feel your spine straightening up. This helps the descent of energy toward the lower part of the body, and at the same time helps with your grounding. While circulating the indigo energy along your spine, you can visualize it coming down right in the middle of your body inside a translucent tube that gradually expands in circumference. Initially you might feel that your tube is only about a quarter to a half inch in width, but by letting the indigo ray penetrate deeply within you and widening the pathway of light, your channel could soon reach eight to ten inches in diameter.

The indigo ray therefore allows you, through this channel, to anchor the liberating energy of the violet flame in all of you so that it is definitely incorporated in your energetic memory, and in so doing, solves the problem at its root, returning to its unconscious origins no matter what trauma you experienced in this life or before, acting directly where the blockage is located in your subtle or physical body.

Simply stated, the indigo ray allows you to remember who you are. It is the energy that characterizes the new children, who are born with a highly developed sixth sense. Indigo is also the color of the transition from the Age of Pisces to the Age of Aquarius, the color of the new dawn that arises and signifies that the fifth dimension is already inscribed in the path of humanity. The stone that best absorbs and reflects this energy is the indigo sapphire. You can use it as protection as well as to facilitate opening yourself to higher dimensions.

Of course, at any time you can also continue to call on Saint-Germain when you feel difficulty in remaining centered. The violet flame will always operate the transmutation and healing you aspire to. Indeed, if the violet flame is the energy that dissolves karma, suffering, and resistance, it is also the flame of bliss and of the state of grace specific to the light beings of the higher dimensions.

There are many high-level entities and ascended masters that present themselves to you in their coat of violet light. You can ask for their support every day and benefit from their purifying energy. Bit by bit you will feel that you too are integrating the indigo energy and the violet flame into your energetic bodies. It is a sure sign of your spiritual rise, and a sign that soon you will at last be face-to-face with your brothers and sister of light in joy, bliss, and celebration of the heart.

—Bianca Gaia

Remembering Who I Am

Having had the huge privilege of allowing four exceptional souls to incarnate, I can affirm in all humility that it is thanks to my four children that I have become who I am today. They have allowed me to discover daily my defense mechanisms in action. Each one originates from a different soul family, and each one quickly helped me understand that he or she needed to be treated differently from his or her siblings.

The new children, despite their great openness to consciousness, are not immune to our power games, and they also end up adopting survival positions when people around them are closed to their inner light.

Having a tendency to want to do well and to be a good mother, devoting myself ceaselessly to them and aspiring as much as possible to give each of them a hundred percent (multiplied by four, that's four hundred percent), it took years before I understood that they were there to show me the way, and not the other way around. Only after I became completely exhausted by the task (giving four hundred percent 24-7, one burns out quickly) and went through a period of deep depression did I accept letting go.

My friend Nicole helped me understand at the time that even in the best possible conditions, I couldn't always be present and available for my children. At best, if I split myself in four I could only give twenty-five percent of myself to each of them, and that was without counting my husband, my parents, or my friends. What energy did I have left to take care of myself?

I ended up doing my grieving for my old principles and my old programs, and I accepted entrusting them to God under the protection of their respective guardian angels. At that moment, being very sensitive to energetic perceptions and seeing that my children were all surrounded by distinct vibrations, I became aware that the light beings that accompanied them displayed different colors. This was my first contact with the soul families.

Although I have opened up on the spiritual level since that day, my experience as a mother has not been very restful. Knowing that many parents, grandparents, and educators around the world also have to make do with unconventional children, allow me to introduce my own. I hope my experience as a mother sheds some light and inspiration on your path.

1. The Builder/Victim

There are some children who seem complex and different from others at a first glance. Charles-Antoine, my eldest, was part of this category of beings. He had a difficult birth, and his first years of life were marked by a serious pulmonary illness that had the effect of slowing his growth. When he entered high school, he looked more like her was eight years old rather than twelve.

We had long had a tendency to coddle and overprotect him, which he quickly learned to take advantage of. His incarnation contract was to learn to feel good in his body and to affirm his difference, and therefore to manifest the presence of the Builder in him, but he quickly understood, being brighter and livelier than average, that it was much easier for him to get the energy of others by attracting their pity for "the poor little sick boy."

He took a liking to playing the Victim game in order to remain the center of attention and benefit from the privileges other children didn't have access to. He was so self-centered that his primary school teacher thought that he was an only child.

This didn't stop him from being gifted and having faculties beyond the ordinary. From a very young age he perceived energy and spoke of his past lives. At around age two, he started to be scared of elephants. It was a mortal fear. When he was asked why, invariably he would answer, "I was trampled by a family of elephants before, when I was a woman." Another time, as I was scolding him for having disobeyed me, I attempted to make him understand that he had acted wrongly by asking him, "Do you know why Mommy is punishing you?" My little "Charlo" responded in a flash, "Of course; it's because when I was your father, I used to punish you." There are countless similar examples.

Fortunately, through the years my son understood that it was in his best interest to develop his own strength rather than always to count on others to move forward in life. When he finally contacted the Builders energy in him, his life was transformed. He understood that he only had to ask and the universe would obey him.

When the time came to enter high school, Charles-Antoine wanted to go to a private school. With just one salary and four little mouths to feed, we could not afford to pay that kind of tuition for him. Convinced that this was the best school for him—he feared that at public school, surrounded by two thousand youths all taller and bigger than him, he would get locked in a locker somewhere and not be found for months—he put everything in action to find the money required.

He called his grandparents, uncles and aunts, and his godfather to explain to them that from now on, rather than sending him Christmas and birthday gifts, he would prefer that they transfer the equivalent amount to a bank account to cover his school expenses. The story circulated in the family and all the way to the ears of the school administrators. Impressed by such determination, they finally gave him free tuition for his five years of study; this had never been done before in the school's 150-year history.

This experience transformed him. Recently he enrolled in a national program allowing him to do community work for nine months in three collectives from one end of the country to the other. From the start my son affirmed that he was aiming to work in three specific cities: Vancouver, Toronto, and Montreal. The program attracts several hundred youths every year, and there are several hundred municipalities that welcome them in groups of twelve, spread throughout Canada's ten provinces. Because he wasn't allowed to request the places he would be sent, I explained to him that in my mind, he was being a dreamer.

What a surprise, then, when Charles-Antoine received his dispatch letter to find that he would be working in the suburbs of the same three cities he had intended to visit. The Builder in him had finally integrated the virtues of his soul family, and since then, although he still asks for our help when he needs it, his Victim side is a lot less prominent in him.

2. The Artisan/Savior

At a very young age, Marlène was highly sensitive. She could feel people at a distance. When her grandmother was sick, for instance, she could tell where her pain was and whether or not it was serious. It was as if she could see through people. She could perceive energy around her and communicate with her guides as well as animals, plants—and clouds. She adored singing, drawing, dancing, and making up stories. She would dress up as a princess and create a fairy tale replete with fairies and magical goblins.

My daughter was an Artisan of Peace, a little ray of sunshine, but also a barometer of my own moods. Indeed, during certain periods of her childhood, between age four and eight, we would argue over nothing. She only had to say a word or sigh to make me lose my cool. In the moments when I felt somewhat imprisoned by my role as a mother in the home, she had the knack to become demanding and dissatisfied with everything. Fortunately, once I understood that she was only expressing outwardly what was eating away at me from within, everything was resolved between us.

At the beginning of her teenage years, however, she discovered that with her hands she could easily repair torn muscles, dislocated shoulders, and sprained ankles. Not satisfied with alleviating the physical pain of her friends, she started playing therapist with them, offering them an attentive ear and wise counsel, and at times even took them on her shoulders, becoming indispensable to some of them. In brief, while growing up Marlène was turning into a Savior, just like her mother and the other women of her linage before her.

One day, having read about the indigo children, she wanted to explain it to her school friends, but she was quickly called a witch, which even led to her being confronted on the matter by her school's administrators. She was quite shaken to have had to defend herself in front of three rather skeptical adults, but being a philosopher at heart, she managed to quickly bounce back by saying, "This time, at least, they didn't burn me at the stake."

At age fifteen, Marlène said she would like to do massage therapy. With her talent for academics, however, her educators pushed her to aim for university. Gifted with the ability to get those around her to react, she decided that if she was going to orient herself toward higher education one day, it would be to become a sex therapist. "After all," she said, "isn't the important thing to help people be happy and feel good in their skin?"

For my part, I hope with all my heart that she will again become my gorgeous little princess who knows how to be happy and enjoy life the way the Artisans of Peace do so well. She is already headed that way; since she found her "Prince Charming," she accepts support more and more and enjoys every moment.

3. The Visionary/Indifferent

When he was very young, Émile was the quiet type, shy and withdrawn. People who met him, though, could perceive a depth and a semipalpable wisdom emanating from him. At only a year and half, he welcomed his newborn little brother by giving him his favorite blanket, and in the same week stopped sucking his thumb on his own, as if saying to himself, I am no longer the baby; from now on it's him.

We learned that in his previous life, Émile had been a monk living in Tibet, so we were not surprised that our child communicated with us more through telepathy than with words. Without even opening his mouth, he would always end up being heard: with an intense look he would make us understand that he wanted a drink of water, to play outside, or to go to sleep. Absorbed in his inner world, indifferent to anything that surrounded him, he could spend hours contemplating a ray of sunlight on the floor or amuse himself by slowly putting blocks together, one at a time, sometimes remaining immobile and concentrating for quite a long time.

Of course, such behavior left strangers wondering about him, and when he was about three years old his pediatrician got worried about symptoms that, according to him, might indicate delayed development or even the early signs of autism. Worried that this branding would stigmatize him in his development at school, we had to resort to drastic measures: we explained to Émile that, for his own good, from now on, we would send him to kindergarten for at least one day a week.

Of course, the first months were very difficult. He would cry, hanging on to us, refusing to go toward people he didn't know. He was aware that other adults couldn't pick up his thoughts as easily as we could and that he would have to resort to other means if he wanted to be understood. Bit by bit he ended up coming out of his shell, and although he had never spoken a word since his birth, not even "Daddy" or "Mommy," the first words he said to his teacher were, all in one go, "Could I please have a glass of milk?"

Today, Émile has overcome his shyness and has strongly gained self-assurance, especially since he discovered in himself some real talents for music and for IT. Now at the age of sixteen, he has learned to play the guitar, the bass, the banjo, and the drums by himself, and he is working at developing software to create his own musical compositions through the use of his computer keyboard.

Most software languages no longer hold any secrets from him. Like a good Visionary, he assumes responsibility for himself, and he has founded his own company, Bélairsoft, which he launched on the Internet in 2005 at www.belairsoft.com. With a ninety-five percent grade-point average, he twiddles his thumbs at school and only aspires to dropping everything to dedicate himself to his numerous passions.

In the evenings and on the weekends, he repairs his client's computers, creates Web sites, and believe it or not, every Friday night, along with his friends, he hosts a radio show at a local radio station.

4. The Facilitator/Perpetrator

Imagine a mischievous little redhead with blue eyes. Even before he was able to walk, Médéric managed to exhaust us all, as he was so active. At eight and a half months, he was already running all over the house, and at nine months he figured out how to unlock the front door and would go out barefoot in the snow, "just to see how it feels." He would get a kick out of emptying the trash, dropping baby powder everywhere, eating the dog's food, and so on. He required full-time surveillance and would go to sleep only when he was exhausted.

Numerous times, he caused us some real fear: at age one he climbed up a neighbor's ladder and walked on the roof. As soon as he knew how to ride a tricycle, he ventured far from home, even crossing a busy boulevard to go meet a friend who lived a mile away. With all the neighbors, we looked for him for nearly an hour, never imagining that he would have left our neighborhood. We used to call him "our little monster," even daring to tell him that, had he been born first, he would have probably been an only child.

At the age of six, he could recite the names of 150 Pokémon characters by heart but refused to learn the twelve months of the year. At school he found it hard to stay in his chair and to follow simple instructions. His third-grade teacher said that he did not "live in reality" because he had claimed that his favorite animal was not a dog, nor a wolf, but a werewolf.

In the eyes of the specialists, he suffered from attention deficit disorder and hyperactivity, but in my mind the fact that he had some difficulty in grounding simply kept him in the energy of the Perpetrator. In fact, Médéric had every element of the Facilitator. He didn't understand that he had to be limited by his physical body, and he did everything to defy the laws of nature.

One day he came back from school and told me, "Guess what? Some firemen came to explain what to do in case there's a fire in your house. Come on! With the number of angels in this house, Mom, how could there be a fire?" I felt obliged to respond, "Médéric, you know that there are angels to protect you, but there are children whose parents don't know this. So they have to learn what to do in case it does happen." My son responded candidly, "Why don't we show them how to bring in the angels instead?"

During all those years of trouble, we always refused to let Médéric be given any medication. Instead we have taught him deep-breathing methods to help him recenter himself, and we have taught him how to make compromises by making choices that respect both his own needs and the demands of his teachers.

Today, aged fourteen, Médéric is doing rather well at school, even though he doesn't really like it. He has learned to let off steam by jumping on his trampoline, channeling his extra energy in video games, and learning to master his innate effervescence through the practice of martial arts such as aikido. When asked what he will do later on, he invariably responds, "I don't know yet, but, in any case I will do everything I can to be happy and fully enjoy life."

Your Child, Your Mirror

As you have probably suspected, your own children have chosen you for a very specific reason. Their incarnation contract, just like yours, is to unveil to the world the wonderful being hiding behind the mask of their personality. There is a good chance that they will try to bend the rules that you impose on them. Don't think that it's only to defy you; quite the contrary. You have hired them in the theatrical play of your existence so that they may reflect back to you the parts of yourself that aspire to be revealed in full light.

The next time one of your children, or a parent, colleague, or friend, appears confrontational, ask yourself the question, What is the message that my soul is trying to deliver to me today? If your door remains closed to it, the messenger may continue knocking and banging, and may even try to kick it down—not to wrong you or wound you, but to make you understand that you are neglecting some important aspects of your life or of the dimensions that are essential to your own balance.

In our home, only one rule applies. There are no restrictions, instructions, or code of conduct, only one universal incontrovertible rule: respect. If I respect myself, and I respect others, I no longer need to fight to be valued or try to impose my principles. I know what I have to do, and this helps me in my autonomy.

Concretely speaking, this implies, for example, that if my son wants to go out late one evening, he doesn't need to ask me for permission. He can ask himself whether he is respecting himself and respecting me. So if it is a school night, he knows that he may be too tired to get up the next day. If it happens only once, the exception is OK. But if it becomes repetitive, he knows as well that his sleep and his studies will pay the price. He will therefore have to make a decision about his engagements toward himself.

Similarly, if he wants me to drive him to one of his friends' places, but I have to get up early the next morning, there is no point in him asking me to come and pick him up after 10 PM. Out of respect for my needs, he will have to find another solution.

This way of interacting with my children dawned on me the day I understood that the more I tried to tell them what to do and how to do it, the more they resisted and did as they pleased. My husband and I quickly admitted to ourselves that if they decided to do something forbidden or dangerous, we would not always be able to be there to protect them, and therefore we had to trust them.

But they also needed to learn to trust themselves; otherwise they would no longer know who to listen to. We know that friends can have a lot of influence on children, and not always in a positive way. We then thought that the best attitude to adopt was to show them how to go within themselves to ask the only appropriate question: Am I respecting myself, and am I respecting other people?

From that moment on, everything at home became simple, easy, and joyous. We have had solid discussions on many disturbing topics, for instance, "When will I be allowed to take the pill?" "When can I drop out of school?" "Can I borrow your car for the weekend?" But eventually we came to a harmonious and fulfilled family life.

Still today, when one of my children disturbs me in my inner tranquility, I have the reflex of asking myself, What makes me work so hard through his behavior? What part of me is expressing itself through him? Because I hate the idea of working on myself, I quickly recenter myself in the now and entrust all my worries to my soul family to take care of it for me.

Making Your Life a Masterpiece

From this moment on, you have a choice: continuing to work hard on yourself, or choosing to apply yourself to creating the best in your life.

Making ourselves is the masterpiece of our entire lives—having the satisfaction of contributing to something fantastic, to have consecrated our energy and passion to create the best in ourselves; in brief, to become cocreators with God. When we finally recognize the unlimited creative potential of all our gifts and talents, natural and supernatural, our greatest happiness unfolds.

The following chart will allow you to determine which soul family is most likely to help you develop all those spiritual faculties that lay dormant within you to make your life a divine work of art.

The Divine Cocreating Expressions
Spiritual Gifts

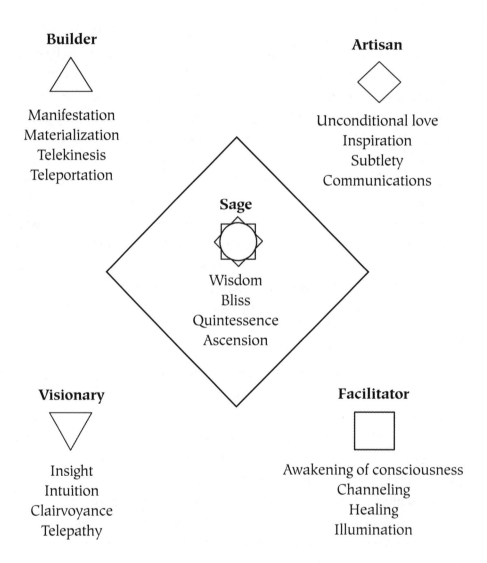

Builder

Manifestation
Materialization
Telekinesis
Teleportation

Artisan

Unconditional love
Inspiration
Subtlety
Communications

Sage

Wisdom
Bliss
Quintessence
Ascension

Visionary

Insight
Intuition
Clairvoyance
Telepathy

Facilitator

Awakening of consciousness
Channeling
Healing
Illumination

The Spiritual Gifts

It isn't necessary to have been born an indigo or crystal child to develop you psychic abilities. The more you open up to your inner light, the more it contributes to dissolving fears and resistance that until now were inhibiting you from enjoying your prodigious unlimited potential that is present in the five dimensions of your brain. You can reconnect with your inner divinity in order to benefit from the natural and innate gifts of each of the five great soul families, starting with the one you belong to.

1. The Builders

The Builders are associated with the physical dimension of being. They can thus easily intervene on the material plane in order to attract abundance and wealth (materialization); make their objectives, dreams, and projects come true (manifestation); move objects simply through their will (telekinesis); and even act on matter and on their own bodies, which they can ultimately move in time and space (teleportation).

In fact, the Builders make excellent alchemists, as they have the aptitude to command the forces of nature and of the universe. Let's remember that according to their incarnation contract, they "open the way, break with the past, and build the new world." They are ultimately the guardians of the Earth.

2. The Artisans of Peace

The energy of the Artisans of Peace essentially harmonizes with the emotional dimension of being, which is why their biggest virtue remains their ability for unconditional love.

These nature lovers are gifted with the faculty to enter into subtle communication with the spirits of nature (devas), animals, plants, the sun, and the moon; think of Saint Francis of Assisi. They also have overflowing and unlimited creativity at their disposal, for they draw their inspiration from their soul family, which is made up of artists, generous people, and heart-centered people.

Their incarnation contract stipulates that they have come to Earth to "celebrate life and be at its service by giving themselves to a cause or creation project or by helping people." They usually have a passion for art, ecology, protection of flora and fauna, or humanitarian missions.

3. The Visionaries

By incarnating, the Visionaries are those who have chosen to help evolution through knowledge, communications, and technological innovation. They are consequently related to the intellectual dimensions of being. This is why they have the faculty of wisdom: they are at once intelligent, sharp, and insightful.

They have a lot of intuition and some ease in reading people's hearts, souls, energetic bodies or auras, and thoughts through telepathy.

Their gift of clairvoyance allows them to receive images, information, messages, or dreams regarding the present, the past, or the future about themselves or others. They also have the capacity to interpret signs, messages, coincidences, and synchronicities through various instruments: cards, the pendulum, tea leaves, etc.

If they embrace transmitting their visions and teachings, it will be said of them that they have innate knowledge, or that they are prophets.

4. The Facilitators

The family of the Facilitators is composed of those who attempt to transmit the divine light around them by treating others (healing), by exploring their gift of mediumship (channeling), or by offering spiritual teachings to those close to them or through personalized coaching as therapists.

They aspire to awaken consciousness and to contribute to helping people integrate the spiritual dimension of their being. Because they easily master the subtle energies and seem to understand the universal laws thoroughly, other people have a tendency to confuse the Facilitators with avatars of wisdom. Other people may turn Facilitators into gurus, spiritual masters whom they idolize and devote themselves to wholeheartedly.

In reality, whether they are coaches, healers, or teachers, all aim to contribute in their own way to the illumination of all human beings and of the entire planet. Their challenge, however, remains to start by themselves and only to preach by example. Their biggest virtue remains their ease in connecting with God and welcoming his peace, love, and infinite reserves of universal energy to radiate all around them and thus contribute to the elevation of individual, collective, and planetary vibrations.

5. The Sages

What is fascinating with the Sages is that they have nothing to prove, neither to themselves nor to their peers. They are happy with simply radiating. This is most probably why they have a tendency not to show off their psychic faculties. They are essentially recognizable by the joy or bliss that permanently animates them and by the tranquil and serene wisdom that characterizes them.

However, it is possible to perceive some subtle differences in their energy field, which seems to emanate a soft golden hue or even some iridescent luminous sparks at times. They have merged with their divine quintessence and have therefore put on part of their light bodies, which at times makes them nearly transparent. In a crowd they often go unnoticed because their higher vibration makes them invisible to those who live exclusively in the third dimension.

The day of their ascension, their light bodies vibrate with such power that they become translucent and then disappear to the eyes of all. They remain very present and active among us, however, as ascended masters.

Acting from the Higher Dimensions

Overall, what is important is not developing all of our gifts and psychic faculties but knowing that they exist. Trusting in that alone will allow them to manifest in our lives.

The first time I met a person who could materialize objects between his empty hands, I was in awe. I didn't believe it was possible. This very humble Quebec man was not making any profit from it; he was living modestly and would welcome pilgrims to help them, he said, to revive their faith. The gesture in itself had no importance at all for him; its goal was to awaken our senses for us to recognize the power of God at work through his hands.

The same can be said of many healers that I know. Their gift aims only at serving divine energy and honoring the life force that circulates in every person. Healing is only a result of our openness to our own inner light.

All spiritual gifts essentially help the elevation of the soul to the higher dimensions, in order for us to learn to create and manifest our will out of the three-dimensional limitations and illusions of this world. Once we have understood this, it is no longer necessary to work at developing our supernatural abilities because we know that we can simply ask our soul family to act for us.

Let me give you a concrete example. One day when my husband and children had gone skiing in the mountains, I took the opportunity during this rare moment of solitude to give in to my favorite hobby: reading. Toward the middle of the afternoon, I heard a voice inside me saying, "Émile is going to have a skiing accident."

Immediately, my first reflex was to say out loud, "No! That is out of the question." Two years earlier, my daughter had also had a bad fall while skiing, and I still had bitter memories of her brief hospitalization. Without worrying for a moment, I caught myself answering my son's guides: "I understand that Émile might have something to learn from this experience, but I am convinced that he could get the lesson in some other way. I don't see why it should be me who has to pay the price for his lessons. Make sure that he is protected."

This affirmation was so clear and so powerful in me that I continued reading without budging, even forgetting the incident that had just happened. Just a few hours later, when my children got home, the conversation came back to me when Serge, my partner, came in and said, "Do you know what happened to Émile?"

He started to tell me that our son had slipped on a stretch of black ice and had totally lost control of his skis. He had started going down the slope at a crazy speed and was heading straight toward a dangerous area. The ski patrol immediately followed him, but Émile was going too fast for them to catch up with him to slow him down.

While everyone anticipated a dreadful accident, something quite incredible happened. According to my husband, "It was as if two invisible hands suddenly came to Émile's shoulders. Gradually he started flexing his knees and brought his buttocks toward the ground until he finally sat on his skis, allowing them to slow down and stop. Émile slowly fell to the side, like a flower, without a scratch."

You can imagine that I took the time to thank his soul family for having taken such good care of my son. However, the story doesn't end there: the following week Émile caught a bad flu that later degenerated into bronchitis. Had it been caused by the fear experienced during his adventure in the mountains, or was it the way his soul had chosen to compensate for the "missed" experience? Who knows? In any case his naturopath mother had everything she needed in her pharmacy to heal him without the need to set foot in a hospital.

The lesson that I took from the incident is that it is not necessary for me to intervene personally for energetic work to happen. Since then, I work a lot less hard. I am a lot less demanding of myself, deliberately choosing to entrust most of my "chores" to members of my soul family, who are more than happy to act with much more diligence and efficiency than me.

Their latest feat? During a trip to Annecy, France, I stayed at the home of Christine, who was organizing a workshop for me. She lives in a cute little studio that is a bit tight for two people. I could have simply decided to go to a hotel, but spontaneously my attitude was to ask my soul family for the perfect solution, without even trying to imagine what it would be.

A bit later in the day, Christine and I went to visit a church next door to where I had been told Saint-Germain had had his first encounter with the violet flame. Because they had lovely smiles, I started a conversation with two very nice women who lived in the area. I didn't know it yet, but this encounter had been arranged "upstairs."

In the height of synchronicity, one of the women recognized me and mentioned that she wanted to take part in the workshop that was to take place the following week. Without thinking, I heard myself ask the woman if she lived in a big house. She confided in me that since her children had gone to university, she had two large empty rooms at her disposal.

Better yet, two days later she was organizing a meditation group at her home. I was invited to it, and it allowed me to meet many wonderful people. It goes without saying that my host Christiane, my organizer Christine, and I have since become fast friends.

We can ask our friends in the higher dimensions to put everything in place for us to benefit from the best, in this world as within us. Ask for joy, love, health, abundance, happiness; no matter what it is, just ask. Make your requests with absolute trust, as if everything was already manifested. This is not in relation to what "could happen" but what is happening here and now, by letting go and by knowing the universe provides for all our needs at this very moment, even if we don't see the results yet with our physical eyes in this three-dimensional pseudo-reality. Don't wait for money to be manifested, for a better job to present itself, or even for your project to be realized: act as if everything had already been accomplished—for in reality, that is the case.

Integration: *Doing as If*

Act in all confidence; make your decisions with the certainty that everything has already been accomplished. Just because you don't see it yet doesn't mean that it isn't already there. Everything you need is already manifested in the fourth and fifth dimensions; you just need to bring it down into matter.

With the veil lifting between our human personality and our divine essence, we know that manifestation from now on is ninety-nine percent based on attitude and only one percent on effort. Moreover, results aren't obtained through our sustained efforts or through the search for solutions, tools, or means of realizing our dreams, but rather by the decision to go into action and to act from the higher dimensions, knowing that everything is already manifested.

Just because your five limited senses haven't yet received confirmation of this doesn't mean that you need to keep looking for new signs. Life treats you the way you treat yourself: be sure that you are confident that you deserve the best, and so it will be. Content yourself no longer with waiting or even working to appease your fears. Ask and you shall receive everything you need: support, money, collaboration, guidance, and protection.

Everything is already there, ready to cross over the veil.

In this very moment, our soul family already manifests in matter everything we need. The veil of the higher dimensions becomes thinner as time moves faster. This is why we can no longer afford to wait or hope for things to fall into place before acting. The time that we spend considering all the options available to us only allows our ancient dualities to resurface.

Believe in yourself and act according to your incarnation contract and your life mission without worrying about the rest, because everything is already manifested in your multidimensional plurality. Recognize the Builder, the Artisan of Peace, the Visionary, the Facilitator, and the Sage in yourself. Let these dimensions of you occupy all the space inside you to allow you to finally recognize yourself as you are.

Don't try to be better, to improve yourself, to liberate yourself, or to purify yourself anymore; go into action! Go for it, jump into the void, knowing with certainty that a net has already been installed by your soul family to welcome you.

There is no more room for hesitation, doubt, and procrastination. The time has come now to merge with your cocreative divine essence. Let it take care of everything and remain centered in the present moment, instilled with the deep conviction that you are already following the road that you have outlined for yourself since time immemorial: to shine and radiate the divine light present within you for eternity.

Act as if you were already living fully in the fifth dimension, and it will be so from now on and forevermore.

CHAPTER 15

The Five Phases of Ascension

The Chicken That Wanted to Fly

In a prosperous chicken coop, a dashing hen was in despair to see that despite time passing, she hadn't managed to lay even the smallest egg. Seeing all her girlfriends surrounded by their numerous offspring, she couldn't help but envy them, dreaming of raising a little chick of her own. So imagine her thrill at coming across an abandoned egg with no one there to claim it. Deciding to take the orphan under her wing, she carried it to her nest, where she brooded it without a break for several days.

Of course, her egg-laying girlfriends teased her. "There's nothing in your egg," one of them said with disdain.

"You're brooding an empty shell," added another. "What do you expect is going to come out of that egg? It's too big, and it's neither white nor brown but beige with black dots."

"You might hatch a turtle," said a third sarcastically.

But the future mother, abstaining from any comment, kept her cool and continued to brood her baby to be. After several days, for a moment she had some doubts, but without fail she remained faithfully at her post until her patience was finally rewarded. After a long and seemingly unending wait, she felt a few tremors. Bravely, the little chick pierced his shell and extracted himself from it to reveal himself for all to see.

To the mother hen's great surprise, her chick was absolutely unlike the others. Instead of being a beautiful soft delicate yellow, his plumage was rather white and sprinkled with brownish stains. His wings were rather elongated, nearly touching the ground. As for his beak, it wasn't narrow and straight like the other baby chickens but crooked and bent downward. His spurs were wide, pointed, and much more rounded than the other chicks.

• 295 •

All the neighboring hens clucked and giggled, declaring without any consideration for the new mother that her baby was hideous, that his handicap would prevent him from feeding properly, and that surely he would not survive. But the valiant hen, proud at last to be a mother, passionately watched over her unique chick. She quickly became attached to her little one, who also bonded with her.

Days passed, and the young chicken grew quickly. Even if he had some difficulty pecking because of his crooked beak and trouble walking because of his bent spurs, he adapted well anyway. His mother helped him, gathering grain in little piles more easily accessible to him so that he could feed himself, and despite everything he managed to grow pretty well.

The more he grew, the more the little chicken only had eyes for the sky. He spent long hours watching other birds fly, wondering why chickens couldn't. He dreamed of it so much that it sometimes even felt like he was taking off while he was running around the coop behind his peers. His mother attempted to talk some sense into him: "All the other chickens have the same feeling, you know, my darling. We all glide at times, but that doesn't mean we can fly."

Time passed, and the chicken questioned himself more and more. One day he told his mother, "I can't believe that life can be limited to this—that we are confined during our entire existence to this coop to peck at the ground, to run without anywhere to go, and only to glide a tiny bit off the ground. How can we carry on fighting like this among ourselves for some miserable rotten grain, and especially to remain totally dependent on the farmer for our survival?"

His mother has no response for him other than to try to get him to accept that this was a chicken's life and that even though he was taller and his wings were longer, he remained a chicken and should be happy with what he had.

One beautiful spring day, a loud murder of crows appeared at the coop. They stole the grain and pushed around the chickens, who did not want to make things worse and didn't dare defy them and so let them do their worst. The young chicken was scandalized by the situation. The other chickens reassured him by saying that they were only thieves, that they would soon be gone, and that it was better not to resist them. Because our brave chicken was not used to feeling humiliated in front of anyone, he decided to stand up to the crows, hitting some of them with his wings here and there, and chasing them around. The other chickens panicked and ordered him to stop it, claiming that he was putting his life and theirs in danger. But the strong chicken was determined to do as he pleased, and when one of the crows started to peck at his tail, he decided to give chase. The latter, sensing the chicken's insistence, took off. To everyone's surprise, our brave chicken followed him into the air.

All the other chickens begged him to come down, claiming that he would soon crash and die. Finally, the crows decided to leave. Proud of himself, the brave chicken came back to land. Instead of the congratulations he expected for his heroism, he got nothing but reproach and scolding. He didn't understand why the roosters, young and old, denigrated his flight abilities rather than admiring them. His mother attempted to reassure him by saying that he mustn't feel sorry for himself; he had just had an eventful day and should rest.

In the evening, while everyone was getting ready to sleep, the brave chicken decided to stay up and keep watch in case the crows decided to come back. But sleep ended up getting the best of him. All night long he dreamed that he was flying, gliding, and twirling high in the sky. He felt as free as the wind, letting the breeze carry him.

What a surprise the next day when he woke up and realized that he was perched in a tree. He hadn't been dreaming, then. On his return to the coop, his peers let out a sigh of relief. All of them had been worried, especially his mother, thinking that the crows had taken him away during their sleep.

The young chicken then told them, "I dreamed that I was flying, and after thinking about it, I wasn't dreaming. I did fly. I believe this is my destiny. I must listen to what I have within me, and go explore the whole wide world."

Hearing these words, his mother started crying her heart out. She did not want to lose her only son. To console her, the chicken said, "Look, Mom, I am going to show you something." He flew off and climbed so high in the sky that he was only a small dot above her head. Back on solid ground, he confided in her, "You know, while I am up there, I can see so far and so clearly that I could detect an intruder from miles away. So no matter where I am, I will always keep an eye on the coop to protect you."

A bitter old rooster, the master of the coop, started to speak, and solemnly declared, "If you leave this house, you will never be allowed to come back here. You will be a dishonor to our race, and no one will ever talk to you again."

Our hero was saddened but still determined to answer his inner calling; he spread his wings and flew off.

The young chicken took little time to get over these events. Now feeling totally free, flying at high altitude, he discovered a fascinating universe, and a new joie de vivre flowed through him.

He built himself a majestic nest at the summit of a neighboring mountain to continue to watch over his mother, his family, and his friends. While he was settling in, a young female who was still learning to fly came and landed nearby to have a chat. She asked why she had never seen him around before. The brave bird didn't know how to respond, for he had always talked in chicken, but he knew that he really liked this charming bird.

They quickly fell in love, flying together over the snow-tipped mountains and every day discovering some new flying techniques, ever more amusing and fulfilling. Finally, our hero ended up realizing that he had never really been a chicken. His partner revealed to him that he was—and always had been—an eagle. He then understood that had he not taken the risk of listening to his inner voice, he would never have discovered who he really was.

And you, are you an eagle or a chicken?

Learning to Fly with Your Own Wings

Surely, if you are reading this book, you know that you are an eagle. You recognize that you have celestial wings inside you waiting to unfold. Deep inside, you aspire finally to unveil who you really are: to reveal to the world your beauty and inner light, to radiate like a thousand suns and to live fully, in serene balance, in all the dimensions of your being.

However, you also know that it isn't always easy to expose our deeper nature to those around us. As young children, our parents taught us how we had to act in order to be accepted, tolerated, and integrated in our communities. No matter what society we live in, it has imprisoned us in a mold and constrained us into playing a role that doesn't take into consideration our real identity, which is divine and unlimited. We have been brought up as chickens, and we have ended up believing ourselves to be nothing but.

We have been obliged to suppress, deny, and smother the most beautiful parts of ourselves in order not to feel different or foreign in this terrestrial universe we have chosen as our "coop." Even though we have done everything to forget this difference, the nagging feeling of being more than a chicken has remained present somewhere in us. The feeling of being able to fly beyond the limitations of our physical bodies has continued to inhabit our dreams. In fact, it is this deep conviction of being an eagle that has allowed us to follow our path and continue to move toward our complete fulfillment at all levels.

Despite the hazards of life and the difficulties encountered, even though we have at times felt rejected, humiliated, or betrayed by our peers, the part of us that vibrates beyond the restrictions and illusions of this world is a flame that will never die.

What if one of the most beautiful gifts we could give humanity was indeed to allow ourselves to break out of our eggshell and spread our wings? Could it be that our true soul mission, the very reason for our incarnation, is to reveal to our peers through our own example that we are all eagles, that we are spiritual beings living a human experience rather than simple humans living, occasionally, some spiritual experiences?

As Marianne Williamson put it so well (see the "Integration" at the end of Chapter 4), it is by allowing ourselves to reveal our inner light that we give others the permission to do the same. It is by affirming our difference, through recognizing our personal strengths and qualities and having the courage to say "yes" to the wonderful being dormant within us, that our lives will finally take on all of their meaning.

People around you have already noticed that you have changed. Your divine light shines and radiates more and more. Most probably, you noticed it the last time you looked at yourself in a mirror.

We all aspire to live in bliss, plenitude, and an absolute state of grace, to make this world heaven on earth, to overcome death and enjoy eternal youth, to unfold our light body, making it our ascension vehicle toward the higher dimensions.

How can we determine whether we are on the right path? How do we evaluate the proportion of the divine essence inhabiting our body in this moment? How do we know if our inner chicken is really mature enough to fly with its own wings, like a majestic eagle soaring in the sky?

Here is a message from Bianca Gaia that will allow you to evaluate whether you are ready to take off.

The Five Steps of Ascension

Message from July 5, 2005

The ultimate secret of ascension does not reside in working to eliminate the darkness and resistance that settle within you but rather in remembering who you are. Indeed, the multidimensional being present in you that cannot be contained exclusively within the limits of your physical body has access to all the information of the universe, available through its own cellular memory. All your past lives and all the experiences of humanity are encoded in all of your being: you simply need to recognize their presence in you for all the information needed for your own liberation to become available to you.

Do you suffer in your body or in your soul? Do you have difficulty making ends meet? Are you not fulfilled in your interpersonal relationships? Ask yourself in what way you honor the divine in yourself. Do you put yourself last? Do you have a tendency to follow your reasoning and prioritize your external responsibilities rather than to internalize yourself and listen to your intuition? If you continuously forget and deny who you are, there lie the causes of your misfortunes.

You are entitled to the best. You can accomplish miracles and elevate yourself out of your human condition if you only accept taking a few minutes a day to reconnect to who you really are. You are the children of God. You are gods yourselves. You can claim the part that is yours knowing that you are entitled to it through your divine affiliation.

Your ultimate challenge lies in elevating yourself above the illusions of this world. You only perceive it in three dimensions, while in fact there are thousands of dimensions that interconnect to one another in and around you. Everything you are, every-

thing you have been, and everything you will be is contained in a unique celestial breath. Time and space do not exist; they are only parameters of experimentation that you have given yourselves to better utilize the information you record at a human level.

Outside the three-dimensional frame, your existence is unlimited. You are like a video-game character who does not know he is manipulated by an external player and who fights to impose his own illusory will. You can listen to the small inner voice that knows who your real self is: the voice of the heart, the ultimate connection to your divine essence. It knows that no misfortune, no problem, no disaster exists: any obstacle encountered along the road is nothing but an initiatory challenge aiming at helping you remember who you really are.

Step 1

How do you know whether you are on the right path for your evolution? It is very simple: the more you evolve toward ascension, the lighter your heart will become, and the more you will feel filled with joy and happiness for no apparent reason. It isn't what you say, what you do, or what you accomplish that matters, but rather who you are inside as well as outside. There is no difference between the part of you that works on the outside and the one that intervenes with your children, partner, or friends. You are the same everywhere, without masks and artifacts, being yourself every day, outside excessive emotional fluctuations.

Step 2

You aim for balance in everything and manage to recenter yourself quickly when something unexpected, negative or positive, turns up in your life. It may happen that some of your limiting programming resurfaces, but it no longer has a hold on you as it used to: you see yourself act and react, and you become a witness to the events of your life without excluding yourself totally from it. You know that anything that happens will only affect a very small part of you, and no matter what the circumstances, your inner wisdom will support and guide you toward the best solution for you, in the short term as well as in the long run.

It may occur that various physical symptoms manifest themselves. But rather than running to the nearest doctor, you first take the time to internalize, to wonder what your body wants to tell you about yourself. What part of you is lacking love? What part of your body still believes itself to be a victim of the people and events that surround you? You see beyond the pain and rather ask yourself what suffering you didn't welcome and didn't heal within yourself. Often, with a few deep breaths, by casting a glance of unconditional love on yourself, you will see the unease disappear on its own. Otherwise, you can offer this misunderstanding that is affecting you to God, and let yourself be filled with the violet flame of transmutation to heal your body as well as your soul.

Step 3
Is your mind frequently caught up in an inner whirlwind or else stuck in a real malfunctioning apathy that paralyzes you and seems to prevent you from recognizing the steps on your path? It's a good sign: it means your ego is starting to let go. You can no longer count on your skills or hang on to your old victories. You can no longer rest on the laurels of your knowledge or be complacent because of your past achievements. You can no longer bet on your usual strengths, your innate talents, and your various fields of expertise; otherwise it would be too easy for the ego to take over your life again. You learn to welcome the mind's recriminations and to live in what appears to be real chaos, outside as well as inside. Good and bad no longer exist. In fact, you are simply becoming increasingly attentive to your inner wisdom, the wisdom of the heart, through living exclusively in the now, where you know you are supported, protected, and divinely guided beyond human understanding.

Step 4
You feel that the space between you and the people who matter most to you seems to diminish. You feel their presence in your bubble, and they feel yours at their side. The veil thins between their emotions and yours. You sometimes feel affected by their life experiences without even communicating with them, and synchronicities between you and around you build up. You no longer know where your energetic body in full extension starts or ends. This is why you perceive more and more precisely the energy of those close to you with whom you become one at the heart of your soul family. You're inclined to send them love and light for now, without trying

to meet them or know what they are going through. You feel more and more connected to the whole of humanity, and you feel the activation of the planetary process in all of you.

Step 5

You now know that you no longer need to try to intervene with people and situations outside yourself, but only to radiate your divine energy fully. You become infectious not only for those close to you but also for everything that lives here below. You become one with nature, animals, unicellular beings, and even your brothers and sisters of higher dimensions. You no longer perceive living beings as external to you but as part of you, and you part of them, in a perfect and total symbiosis. You are no longer a therapist or light worker; you are light, you are healing, and you are love, at every moment, in all your being, without expecting anything in return anymore, for your know that all your needs are fulfilled as you go, beyond human understanding.

You bathe in the perpetual state of grace, unlimited bliss, the quintessence of your being. Around you nothing seems to have changed, but inside of you everything has been renewed, integrated, and transmuted. You become cocreator with God, hand in hand with your celestial father or mother. You have access to the original and eternal fiber that not only holds the wisdom contained in the whole universe but weaves at every moment this new world, more beautiful and more serene, in which you live. From now on, beneath your every step, the entire planet benefits from the ultimate energy of purification transmitted through all your cells, effortlessly and without draining you, for you are continually charged by the seven luminous rays connected to your seven chakras. You assume your full divine sovereignty and manifest it in your every word, gesture, and thought. You become one with the source of eternal youth and eternal accomplishment of your destiny, in communion with all that lives in the universe.

Everything is already here; you can feel it. You sometimes feel this state of plenitude, even for a brief moment, during meditation. Let it grow in you and fully permeate you. Don't let the limiting perceptions of your body or your brain stop or slow you down anymore. Open instead to what is wonderful and miraculous in each of your inhalations and exhalations, at the heart of your deep being.

Divine Quintessence

Imagine yourself like an eagle flying over your life. Can you see how futile it is to fight for your survival? You are constantly supported, protected, guided, and fulfilled far beyond your human hopes. Until now, even when everything has seemed desperate in your life, a spark has always ended up appearing to save you at the last minute and allowed you to find a solution to your three-dimensional problems. Why waste your time worrying? Enjoy the now. Ask and you shall receive—not for later or to reassure your ego, but rather to satisfy your immediate needs and those of your loved ones.

Your celestial father/mother will never abandon you, and neither will your brothers or sisters of light. Learn to entrust your torments and your uneasiness to them. Be attentive to them in the silence of your heart and watch the communication happen in love, joy, and perfect serenity. There is no better remedy to the limitations of the third dimension than to open up to the energy of the higher dimensions, accessible to all at every instant on the condition of at last recognizing who you are.

Live, vibrate, and act as children of God. The message will eventually end up being transmitted to all the parts of you and will then spread to the entire planet for a collective and perfectly synchronized ascension, in harmony and unlimited bliss.

The Five Dimensions of Ascension

Divine Dimension
Integration
Ascension

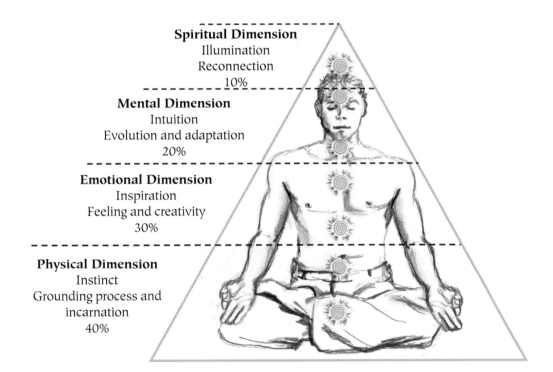

Spiritual Dimension
Illumination
Reconnection
10%

Mental Dimension
Intuition
Evolution and adaptation
20%

Emotional Dimension
Inspiration
Feeling and creativity
30%

Physical Dimension
Instinct
Grounding process and
incarnation
40%

In the exercise "Experimenting with the Fifth Dimension" in Chapter 13, you may have wondered why the sections of the pie chart weren't grouped in equal numbers, or why some chakras covered more than one section. If you observe the previous chart carefully, you will find the key to these discrepancies.

In fact, if you measure the space occupied by each dimension of the being in the human body, you will notice that it is perfectly proportional to the effort required by us to supply the corresponding chakras in energy.

Generally speaking, every area of life demands that we grant it some time and attention. Certain spheres of activity, such as insuring our survival (sleeping, eating, working), require more energy than, say, replenishing ourselves on the spiritual plane (recentering, meditating, praying).

In order to prepare our ascension vehicle well, we must respond to the demands of every one of the dimensions of being present in us. These are characterized by a specific energetic need requiring a predetermined percentage of vigilance and care on our part.

1. Physical Dimension: Instinct (40%)

Because the physical body is governed by the survival instinct, it goes without saying that we must dedicate at least forty percent of our daily time to responding to its essential and existential needs: health, diet, sleep, hygiene, material security, personal and professional self-worth, and so on. However, by ensuring a good balance on the level of incarnation and grounding, we can measure the stability of this dimension on the energetic and vibratory plane.

To help you check whether you're well incarnated and grounded, here are some questions you can ask yourself:

- *Do I feel good in my body?*
- *Can I claim to enjoy perfect health?*
- *Do I feel fulfilled on the material and professional plane?*
- *Am I happy to be alive?*
- *Do I feel free to live my life as I wish?*

If you didn't respond "yes" to all these questions, chances are your two first chakras, the root and sacral, are not working to full capacity, and the physical dimension of your being requires that you look after yourself with more consideration. You will know you have succeeded the day you are able to affirm in all honesty, "I put myself first in all areas of my life."

2. Emotional Dimension: Inspiration (30%)

The emotional center is located at the heart, so this dimension relates to anything that encourages the inspiration of the soul. It seems obvious that we need to invest thirty percent of our global energy to maintain harmony on the level of emotions, feelings, and interpersonal relationships.

Just to give you an idea, how many hours a day do you spend in exchanges with your fellow human beings? And how much time do you spend looking for inspiration to find the solution to a problem, sort out a conflict, or alleviate some psychological suffering? Through your level of satisfaction in areas related to creativity and feelings, you can evaluate whether this energetic sphere is perfectly aligned, vibrationally speaking.

To help you check whether you are indeed well-nourished on the creative and feeling plane, here are the questions you can ask yourself:

- *Do I feel loved and appreciated by those around me?*
- *Am I in love with life and the person with whom I share it daily?*
- *Do I have any particular gifts or talents on the artistic level?*
- *Do I have the courage to show my difference and reveal my eccentricities to those around me?*
- *Am I free to create my life according to my aspirations?*

If your answers aren't all affirmative, your third chakra (the solar plexus) and fourth chakra (the heart) aren't functioning to their full capacity. The emotional dimension of your being needs you to give it some time to discover your passions and widen your network of emotional relationships. You will know you have succeeded when you feel unique in the world and when you love yourself from the bottom of your heart.

3. Mental Dimension: Intuition (20%)

Because it is the brain that governs the mental dimension of being, our intellectual functions and our states of mind obviously nourish it, but so does our communication, observation, awareness-raising, and learning faculties, as well as our ability to allow ourselves to be guided by our intuition.

Because this doesn't require any physiological effort, the cerebral hemispheres only require twenty percent of the overall energetic provision to function efficiently. It is our capacity for adaptation and our level of evolution, though, that shows the efficiency of the corresponding chakras, the fifth (throat) chakra and the sixth (third-eye) chakra.

To help you determine the ease with which you have adapted and evolved along your path in life, here are the questions you can ask yourself:

- *Do I love reading and learning new things?*
- *Is my daily life pleasant and filled with surprises?*
- *Do I feel good about the unknown or changes that present themselves?*
- *Do I have the courage to go off the beaten path to live some new experiences?*
- *Am I ingenious and intelligent enough to attract abundance in my life?*

If your answers aren't all positive, the mental dimension of your being is somehow apprehensive of the future and at times hesitates to take on the challenges that present themselves. You will know that you have fully opened yourself to your adventurous potential when you spontaneously take the initiative to go and explore some new avenues that encourage your growth on all levels.

4. Spiritual Dimension: Illumination (10%)

The spiritual dimension of being involves your way of conceiving life on the moral, human, social, spiritual, and universal level. As consciousness is also the fourth dimension of the human brain (see Chapter 6), it is apparently located at the heart of the hypophysis, better-known as the pituitary gland. It is therefore generous to consider it taking ten percent of our energetic reserve.

However, for the benefit of understanding, let's say that our spiritual preoccupations require around ten percent of our time and attention every day to meditate, pray, and recenter ourselves. This demonstrates how powerful the light energy is.

As a consequence, there is no point in trying to live the life of a monk or a mystic, or wishing that your quest for the divine take up all of your existence. Your spiritual fulfillment doesn't require so much effort or sacrifice. On the contrary, it is as if, for example, you take two thousand milligrams of vitamin C every day when your body can only absorb six hundred milligrams. Do you get the idea?

Because our state of consciousness corresponds to enlightenment and illumination, the same goes as with an electric plug: once the switch is turned on, you don't have to check every day whether the lamp is working.

To help you determine whether you are properly illuminated, here are the questions you can ask yourself:

- *Do I feel that I am part of a whole?*
- *Do I grant myself time to relax, meditate, or pray every day?*
- *Have I understood that what I* am *matters much more than what I say or do?*
- *Do I sometimes feel energy circulating in and around me?*
- *Am I aware that the people who surround me carry within themselves all the solutions and resources they need to elevate themselves?*

If you haven't answered "yes" to all of these questions, your seventh or crown chakra could benefit from extra energy if you allowed yourself to recenter yourself more often. You will know you're taking good care of harmonizing yourself once you are able to say, "I honor God present in me," or in Sanskrit, *Om namah shivaya.*

5. Divine Dimension: Integration (100%)

Most Eastern religions agree that the divine dimension is present in the pineal gland, a small gland shaped like a pinecone located in the human brain (see

Chapter 6). All that is needed for the divine dimension to activate and harmonize itself is a simple spark of light, a particle of energy.

But as we have seen in previous chapters, the full integration of our divine essence is only possible when all the lower dimensions are properly aligned. Cocreating and sovereign quintessence can only happen when all the parts of us are unified at one hundred percent. This is where the ultimate secret of ascension resides.

How do you know if you are ready to take off to the higher dimensions? You simply have to say "yes" to the invitations emanating from your entire being:

- *Am I present for myself here and now?*
- *Do I take good care of myself, of my body, of my needs?*
- *Do I respect myself and make sure I am respected at all times?*
- *Am I aware that I am divine and unlimited?*
- *Is my life simple, easy, and joyous?*

You are a wonderful being, both human and divine: a Builder, an Artisan of Peace, a Visionary, a Facilitator, and a Sage. You only have to say "yes," to remember that you are an eagle and not a chicken, for all the dimensions to return to their rightful place within you and for you to access the supreme alignment and the unveiling of who you really are, in plenitude of your light body, your flamboyant and iridescent Merkaba. After all, isn't that what we all aspire to?

Exercise: *Spreading Your Wings*

To simultaneously lighten your body, your heart, your head or brain, and you consciousness, here is a simple little exercise that liberates all physical, emotional, mental, or conflict-based tensions.

Simply stand with your legs apart at shoulder width, knees slightly bent. All the weight of your body is concentrated around your lower abdomen. Slightly tilt your pelvis to a semiseated position so that your spine is nicely aligned perpendicular to the ground.

Then, like a majestic eagle, spread your wings: spread your arms open at the height of your shoulders and take three deep breaths. Ask all the soul fam-

ilies to be present to accompany you in this little elevation ritual.

Then, very slowly, start a circular movement backward, your hands rising toward the sky and going down behind your shoulders.

Visualize that with every elevation, you offer your angels, guides, and other light beings that accompany you, all your worries, anxieties, tensions, and lack of love toward yourself. Hand over to them all the burdens and the wounds of the past that remain in you. Entrust to them the people you love and those with whom you feel difficulties. With every movement of your shoulders, feel your body lightening up, your mind quieting itself, and your soul feeling more and more relieved.

Then take three deep breaths again and invert the movement forward. This time, the arms go up to the sky to welcome the energy of light, love, and tenderness that all the soul families are transmitting to you, and when your arms come down in front of your body, feel the energy settling into your entire being, in all your cells and subtle bodies.

The more the divine light penetrates into you, the more your Merkaba is activated, aligning all your chakras and making you aware that you shine and radiate more and more. The energy pervades your entire being and spreads all around you. It elevates itself toward the sky to the great central sun and plunges into the ground to the red sun at the center of the Earth. You become a sun yourself and scintillate.

An immense joy settles in you, and a serene peace permeates you. You finally taste the absolute state of grace.

You are bliss. You are light. You are God, present in all that lives.

Your energy spreads throughout the entire world, connecting with that of those like you who have merged with their divine selves. Along the way, you inundate with love and light all those who surround you, all those you love, and all those you have encountered in this life.

You become one with all that is, accomplishing your individual, collective, and planetary mission. Welcome to the fifth dimension! Om namah shivaya!

Epilogue

Welcome to the Fifth Dimension

Post Your Diplomas

Everywhere—in all the terrestrial and universal dimensions—2012 is said to be when the coming of heaven on Earth will occur. It will be a key moment when the actualization of those planetary changes that humanity has been anticipating for so long will finally happen.

For a few years now, the veil between the physical and invisible worlds has been thinning. Soon the presence of our brothers and sisters of light will be felt by most of you. The masks your personality had worn will fall away, and you will see yourself as you are. On the street you will recognize those who belong to the same soul family as you, and projects you have dreamed of for a long time will finally come alive. These are the optimistic prophecies.

But for all of that to happen, you need to be ready. Are you really ready? Do you find yourself luminous enough? Have you freed yourself from your karma? Have you purified yourself and adequately mastered your ego? The answer is yes.

You are and have always been children of light and divine beings. You are the messengers of peace and workers of light. Those are not titles you earn by working hard and by the sweat of your brow; they are an acquired right, a statement of fact, and an intrinsic reality. What more do you need to fully assume it?

You have already worked so hard on yourself. Perhaps you have attended all those seminars and workshops; you have been a natural helper since your youth; and you have studied different techniques and integrated methods to become more adequate and powerful in healing others. What more do you need to distinguish yourself—for someone to walk through your door to present you with an official diploma?

It is like you have graduated from university, diploma in hand, but you do not have the courage to post it on your wall. You remain everlasting students who always question their abilities. Is it because you don't know enough yet, or is it because you don't acknowledge who you truly are?

If you want to help others in finding themselves, awakening to their inner light and the healing of their bodies and souls, what could be better than setting an example? Hasn't the time come for you to celebrate your assets and offer them to those who really need them?

In fact, why wait for 2012 to take off and finally actualize your divine quintessence: everything happens at this moment, here and now, with each breath in and out. It isn't your actions that count nor even what you have done up to now, but who you are inside, who you have always been: a wonderful being that only asks to be acknowledged to radiate outward.

Why have I chosen to be a channel and to travel the world to deliver these powerful messages of love emanating from our planetary consciousness? Every day this role helps me bring out the very best of me. We all want to improve ourselves as humanity enters a very important turning point in its history. Like most of you, I aspire to belong to the group of people who are actively taking part in the creation of the new world. Thus I decided to dedicate myself entirely to my mission, to transmit the divine flame using the means that seemed obvious to me: putting my gifts and talents at the service of the energy.

Of course, like anyone, I sometimes had fears and questioned myself. Being a perfectionist, I had the tendency to doubt myself and tell myself that I was not competent, luminous, or wise enough, that my ego took too much space in my life, and that my state of mind was too frequently scattered. However, I finally realized that this way of criticizing myself was in fact an excuse that I had set up so that I would not put myself into action and would stay in the shade to pity myself. For that reason, I decided to take a chance and to make myself available.

At first, I wrote down the messages I received through channeling sessions with Gaia and shared them with my close friends and clients. Then, people I didn't know started e-mailing me to ask to be put on my newsletter mailing list, which didn't even exist yet. Within a few months I had built a Web site with the help of Émile, my son and my little computer hacker. On this Web site I posted all the teachings that I had already integrated in my life, humbly to share them with everyone who asked for them.

Above all, I trained myself to apply a little maxim of mine in every area of my life: "I choose for everything to be simple, easy, and joyous." Why make something

complicated when it can be simple? Why disperse yourself when you can find unique-
ness in all the dimensions of being? That is what inspired the creation of my work-
shop, "Welcome to the Fifth Dimension," and the book you are currently reading:
honor the multidimensionality of our being and give ourselves the chance to par-
ticipate together in the planetary ascension process in perpetual bliss. This is my
own way of posting my "diploma" as an awakening coach or guide.

What about you? In which discipline did you get your master's degree? Whether
it is in guidance, massage, art, cuisine, or even gardening, do you allow others to
benefit from all your gifts and talents, or do you save them for yourself? It isn't nec-
essary to turn your whole life around, quit your job, move to the countryside, or
open a health center. You make a difference in someone's life each second, if only
with your smile.

Do you dream of helping people or acting as a counselor? Why not progressively
become available to those around you and share the teachings you have already
received? You don't have to have graduated with a doctorate or rent an office down-
town; people close to you need your light and your example, and they will there-
fore be ready to accept your availability, even for just a few hours a week.

However, the fears you feel when facing the unknown are totally legitimate. I for
one have to deal with them each time I buy a plane ticket to cross the ocean: "What
if there aren't enough people attending my seminars?" But most of the time I apply
myself in focusing my attention on the goal rather than on the means to reach the
goal. I visualize my inner light growing and shining, no matter where I am and
what I do. The tools, the methods used, and the ways things are done may change,
but if the goals remain stable, life will take care of sending us signs and the right
people to guide us along this journey.

So many people need to be guided, healed, or energetically harmonized. Why not
invite their soul families to lead them to you? To lose your stable well-framed environ-
ment or a regular salary is certainly frightening. But why not decide to work for God,
make the angels your bosses, and work as a partner with your soul family? You will
not be responsible anymore for your professional success; make yourself available and
let the invisible supporting players do their jobs. Believe me, it's a lot easier.

Finally, instead of letting your fears conquer you, I invite you to recall all the
times that you overcame difficulties or took up new challenges in this life or in past

ones. *Time is your friend, not your enemy; life supports you, and the universe wants nothing but to treat you right. The only thing you have to do is ask for it.*

If some people move away from you or do not agree with you new choices, you can go within yourself and question what their presence in your life has brought you so far, and what you were feeling when they were around. When focusing on your true needs and not on specific people, you will be able to ask the universe to put the right people on your path to fulfill your heart and feed your being.

In this way, your attention will no longer be centered on suffering, deficiencies, fears, or abandonment but on your true expectations and needs to be fulfilled here and now. Since energy abhors emptiness, it will quickly answer your wishes if they are clearly expressed.

However, above all, it is far more the example you set and the light and happiness that you radiate by saying "yes" that will attract the right people to you—those whom you can help as much as those who want the best for you and will support you in return.

Don't forget that you are never alone in achieving your mission as a divine radiant: all your brothers and sisters of light on this Earth or in heaven are there besides you, every moment, whether in 2012 or in 2287. You are part of the huge family of light beings that has existed since the beginning of time and for all eternity.

Believe in yourself. Affirm yourself. If you need to, create your own certificate attesting that Gaia herself has approved you as an intuitive therapist or a celestial messenger, or picture your family tree going back to God him- or herself. You have all the reasons in the world to post your success diploma as a light worker and choose to move toward the activity that inspires and lightens you the most.

You can make a difference in someone's life today. You can actively take part in the planetary ascension process this very day by transmitting you inner light to the people you meet. But most importantly: you can significantly improve you own quality of live by acknowledging in yourself the unique and exceptional being you really are. This is the most beautiful gift you can offer to humanity: to honor and integrate your divine light in all the dimensions of your being, and to let this radiate to the entire planet.

I am love, peace, and light. You are love, peace, and light. Together with your ascendant brothers and sisters, we are one, for eternity, here and now; you only need to say "yes." What joy! May our divine essence be shared with the entire planet.

Quintessence

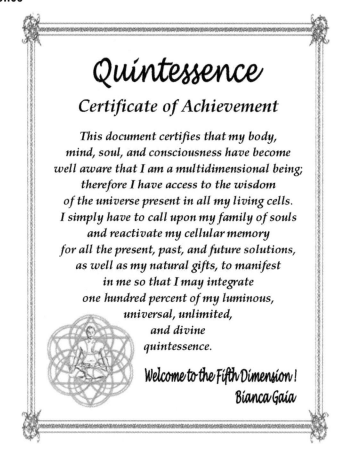

Quintessence

Certificate of Achievement

This document certifies that my body, mind, soul, and consciousness have become well aware that I am a multidimensional being; therefore I have access to the wisdom of the universe present in all my living cells. I simply have to call upon my family of souls and reactivate my cellular memory for all the present, past, and future solutions, as well as my natural gifts, to manifest in me so that I may integrate one hundred percent of my luminous, universal, unlimited, and divine quintessence.

Welcome to the Fifth Dimension!

Bianca Gaia

Certificate of Achievement

This document certifies that my body, mind, soul, and consciousness have become well aware that I am a multidimensional being; therefore I have access to the wisdom of the universe present in all my living cells. I simply have to call upon my family of souls and reactivate my cellular memory for all the present, past, and future solutions, as well as my natural gifts, to manifest in me so that I may integrate one hundred percent of my luminous, universal, unlimited, and divine quintessence.

Welcome to the Fifth Dimension!

—*Bianca Gaia*

Recap Tables
The Multidimensional Being

DIMENSION OF BEING	PART OF THE BRAIN, ENERGY FIELD, SPHERE OF EXPERIENCE	SOUL FAMILY, RULING CHAKRA	INCARNATION CONTRACT
First Dimension **Body** **State of Body** (Physical health)	**Reptilian Brain** Cerebellum and brain stem First field: physical/ etheric body **Metabolism**	Builders △ **Root and Chakras**	Those who lead the way, break free from the past, and help build the new world
Second Dimension **Heart** **State of Soul** (Emotions)	**Mammalian Brain** Limbic system Second field: emotional/astral body **Sentiments**	Artisans ◇ **Solar Plexus and Heart Chakras**	Those who celebrate life investing themselves with passion in things they believe in: charities, causes, artistic creation, etc.
Third Dimension **Brain** **State of Spirit** (Intellect)	(Intellect) Cerebral cortex Third field: mental body **Thoughts**	**Visionaries** ▽ **Throat and Third-eye Chakras**	Those who help humanity's evolution through knowledge, communications, and scientific discoveries
Fourth Dimension **Consciousness** **State of Consciousness** (Spirituality)	**Consciousness** Pituitary gland Fourth field: causal/ interconnecting body **Chakras 1 to 7**	Facilitators ☐ **Crown Chakra**	Those who bring in the light and help raise human consciousness through healing, teaching, coaching, and spiritual guidance
Fifth Dimension **Quintessence** **State of Grace** (Plenitude)	**Higher Self** Epiphysis/pineal gland Fifth field: celestial/ supracausal body **Chakras 8 to 13**	Sages ✸ **All Chakras**	Those who radiate love, joy, and light no matter where they are or what they are doing; they are simply showing us how to be who we truly are.

The Human Experience = Divine Quintessence

DEFENSE MECHANISM, CONTROL DRAMA, WAY TO ACQUIRE ENERGY	WHAT IS THIS PERSON TRYING TO TEACH ME— AS A SOUL GIFT?	ARCHANGEL, HARMONIZER, HEALTHY FOOD, THERAPEUTIC HEALING	ASCENSION, PHASE, ENERGY PERCENTAGE
Perpetrator Intimidator Anger: imposes, controls, threatens, attacks	I am being invited to ask myself whether I affirm myself and take my place. Do I have the courage to express my opinions and claim what I need?	Uriel Red and orange; earth **Protein, root vegetables** Massage, osteopathy, kinesiology, yoga; percussion; "oh"	Instinct Grounding process and incarnation 40%
Victim "Poor Me" Sadness: complains, despairs, begs, implores	I am being invited to the sensitive and vulnerable child inside of me. Do I have the courage to ask for help and support or simply to be comforted when I need it?	Gabriel Yellow and green; water **Carbohydrates, leafy vegetables** Art therapy, music, humor psychotherapy; wind instruments; "ee"	Inspiration Creativity and feeling 30%
Indifferent Aloof State of Shock/ Denial: feels paralyzed, escapes reality, stays out of reach	I am being invited to create appropriate distance and to be less demanding of myself. Do I sometimes allow myself to say "no" to others?	Raphael Blue and indigo; air **Lipids, flowering vegetables** Wellness through awareness, hypnosis, respiratory reeducation, walks in nature; stringed instruments; "oo" as in "who"	Intuition Evolution and adaptation 20%
Savior Interrogator Blackmail/Guilt: makes himself indispensable, unable to say "no," forgets to take care of himself	I am being invited to find my own solutons and to recognize my strengths and my inner power. Do I allow myself to let the dormant hero in me emerge?	Michael Violet; fire **Dairy products, eggs, fruits** Energy healing, hydrotherapy, relaxation, acupuncture; singing; "ah"	Illumination Reconnection 10%
Witness Centered Acceptance/ Detachment: remains centered, allows herself to let go, lives in the now	I am being invited to recognize that all the wise people in my life are the reflection of my own inner light, which also aspires to shine like a thousand suns.	Metatron, **Ascended Masters** White and gold; ether **Raw food, sprouts** Holistic medicine, meditation, prayer; silence	Integration Ascension Total: 100%

BIBLIOGRAPHY

Braden, Gregg. *Awakening to Zero Point: The Collective Initiation.* Questa, NM: Sacred Spaces Ancient Wisdom, 1995.

Brennan, Barbara, and Jos. A. Smith. *Hands of Light.* New York: Bantam, 1987.

Coelho, Paulo. *The Alchemist.* New York: HarperCollins, 1998.

Katie, Byron. *Loving What Is: Four Questions That Can Change Your Life.* New York: Three Rivers, 2003.

Kübler-Ross, Elisabeth. *On Death and Dying.* London: Tavistock, 1973.

Losier, Michael J. *Law of Attraction: The Science of Attracting More of What You Want and Less of What You Don't.* New York: Hachette, 2007.

Melchizedek, Drunvalo. *The Ancient Secret of the Flower of Life, Vols. 1 and 2.* Flagstaff, AZ: Light Technology, 1990.

Monbourquette, Jean. *À Chacun Sa Mission.* Montreal: Novalis, 1999.

Monbourquette, Jean. *How to Forgive: A Step-by-Step Guide.* Cincinnati: Saint Anthony Messenger, 2000.

Peacock, Fletcher. *Water the Flowers Not the Weeds.* Concord, CA: Open Heart, 2000.

Redfield, James. *The Celestine Prophecy.* New York: Bantam, 1993.

Redfield, James, and Carol Adrienne. *The Celestine Prophecy: An Experiential Guide.* New York: Warner, 1995.

Redfield, James. *The Tenth Insight: Holding the Vision.* New York: Warner, 1996.

Simon, David, and Deepak Chopra. *Freedom from Addiction.* Deerfield Beach, FL: Health Communications, 2007.

Tolle, Eckhart. *The Power of Now: A Guide to Spiritual Enlightenment.* Novato, CA: New World Library, 2004.

Twyman, James. *Emissary of Light.* Fairfield, CT: Aslan, 1997.

Walsch, Neale Donald. *Conversations with God, Book 1.* Charlottesville, VA: Hampton Roads, 1996.

Whitworth, Eugene E. *Nine Faces of Christ: Quest of the True Initiate.* Camarillo, CA: DeVorss, 1993.

Williamson, Marianne. *A Return to Love: Reflections on the Principles of "A Course in Miracles."* New York: HarperCollins, 1992.

INDEX

Page references in *italics* indicate charts and illustrations

A

Index

third energy field. *See* mental dimension (or field)
third eye
  bioenergetic correspondences, *129*, 131
  brain location of, 95
  entry gate of the pranic channel, 276
  and the multidimensional being, *318*
thoughts
  choosing them with care, 101–102
  as creative, Bianca Gaia on, 124
  and destructive pain, 241–242
  others as mirror, 242–244
  self-destructive, 227
throat chakra, *129*, 131, 318

U

unity, recreating, exercise for, 134–135
Uriel, archangel, 78, 79, *266*, 319

V

veiling of the chakras, 45
vibration
  for access to multidimensional being, 5
  and the soul families, *78*
  your vibratory level, 260
Victim, the
  Charles-Antoine as, 278–280
  as control drama, 160–162, 182
  and the game of mirrors reinvented, *245*
  health care for, 268
  how to act when faced with, 247
  living fully, 184–185

and the multidimensional being, *319*
the Perpetrator/Victim dance, 219–220
and the pyramid of duality, *232*
uniting all the aspects of the self, *266*
vs. Artisans, 234
what they offer you, 248
violet Ray, 4, 275–277
virtues of the soul families, *69*
Visionary soul family
  description of, *61*, 63–64
  and Émile, 281–282
  health care for, 269
  and life choices, *69*, 70–71
  the multidimensional being, *318*
  and the pyramid of duality, *232*
  reconnecting and rebalancing, *78*, 80–81
  spiritual gifts of, *286*, 288
  and transmuting primal reactions, *238*
  uniting all the aspects of the self, *266*
  vowel sound of, 271
  vs. Indifferents, 233–234
visualization exercise, 100
Vitale, Joe, 136–138

W

Watson, Lyall, 5–6
"Will I die from it?", 114, 181, 193, 226
Williamson, Marianne, 72, 299
Witness, the
  and the game of mirrors reinvented, *246*

ABOUT THE AUTHOR

In her teachings as well as in her book Welcome to the Fifth Dimension, *Diane LeBlanc, better known as Bianca Gaia, highlights the most important aspects to consider in the life of every human being in order to feel better, establish proper balance, and live happily every day.*

A personal coach and channel, for several years Diane has hosted a number of seminars, conferences, and workshops on personal growth as well as spirituality, therapeutic creativity, and global health. Since 2004, Diane's popular French-language Web site has been visited monthly by over eight thousand people from more than twenty-five different countries.

To learn more about her various activities, visit www.biancagaia.com.